AF361335

A Curriculum of Control

A Curriculum of Control

Compliant Classrooms and the Students They Fail

Nicole Mittenfelner Carl

SUNY PRESS

EU GPSR Authorised Representative:
Logos Europe, 9 rue Nicolas Poussin, 17000, La Rochelle, France
contact@logoseurope.eu
Excelsior Editions is an imprint of State University of New York Press
For information, contact State University of New York Press, Albany, NY
www.sunypress.edu

Library of Congress Cataloging-in-Publication Data
Name: Carl, Nicole Mittenfelner, author.
Title: A curriculum of control : Compliant classrooms and the students they fail / Nicole Mittenfelner Carl, author.
Description: Albany : State University of New York Press, [2026] | Includes bibliographical references and index.
Identifiers: ISBN 9798855805086 (hardback) | ISBN 9798855805109 (epub) | ISBN 9798855806854 (PDF)
Further information is available at the Library of Congress.

For my middle school students and the students at Baker. You taught me more than you will ever know.

Contents

Preface

A Curriculum of Control: Compliant Classrooms and the Students They Fail brings to light the often-ignored daily lives of elementary and middle school students at Baker School, a K–8 urban, public school in Philadelphia, Pennsylvania. Based on two years of ethnographic fieldwork and my prior experiences teaching middle school and coaching teachers in similar Philadelphia schools, *A Curriculum of Control* depicts students' daily schooling routines; messages students receive from the school, teachers, and the community; and how students navigate this complex and often challenging environment. Few monographs position students as the primary actors, and by doing so, this text compels readers to reckon with students' experiences at Baker School and how these compare to the vision and goals of public education. The text focuses on a core group of students in grades 4 and 8 — Nyeisha, Jayalya, Rashanna, Bianca, and Renee — and their teachers and families to demonstrate how students subtly and overtly resist this oppressive schooling environment.

This book does not seek to degrade Baker School and the individuals who work there. Baker School is a real school with dedicated and caring professionals who come to work everyday, and those people became my colleagues. I taught for several years at a school similar to Baker, and this is one of the main reasons I chose Baker as my research site. I understood the joys and challenges of teaching at an underserved school in a low-income community, and the biggest joy was always my students. I can empathize with the burnout and stressful working conditions that are described in this book. Parents were both frustrated with and appreciative of me, many of my students appreciated me but others were frustrated with me, and a couple of students threatened to kill me. The students are why I came to work every day, and why I was up late at night creating lesson plans, calling parents, and thinking about how to do things better. My students, all students, deserve better schooling experiences. This book operates from the premise that students are more perceptive than many adults give them credit for, and a goal of this book is to illuminate those perspectives.

When I was a new teacher, I did not fully understand the structural forces shaping teaching and learning. It was not until I had the time and space in graduate school for the second time that these aspects became clearer to me. In my current job as a director of a teacher education program, I work with graduate students to prepare them for the realities of teaching in underserved schools and the ways that systems of racism and oppression shape these schools. At the same time, I impress on the teachers I work with about the power and importance of their work to make a direct difference in the lives of children and that this begins by listening to their students. Thus, this book focuses on the lived realities of schooling for elementary and middle school students while highlighting how structural forces shape those realities.

This book is written for academic and practitioner audiences. By centering student perspectives, *A Curriculum of Control: Compliant Classrooms and the Students They Fail* offers a new angle and depth of understanding of how a school reproduces social inequality by controlling student behavior and preparing students for low-paying jobs that require compliance. The text contributes to the theoretical frameworks of cultural capital (e.g., Bourdieu, 1986; Lareau, 2011; Yosso, 2005) and habitus (Bourgois & Schonberg, 2007, 2009) as it discusses how students cultivate a *habitus of fierceness* in the school and the local community. This habitus of fierceness refers to the ways students demonstrate that they are fierce so that they are not bullied at school or in the community and presents implications for scholars and practitioners interested in culturally responsive ways to respond to student behavior (Hammond, 2015; Khalifa, 2018). The study contributes to education scholarship and practice about parent engagement narratives and ways that schools simultaneously parentified and infantilized students at Baker and schools like it. *A Curriculum of Control* also contributes to scholarship and practice by supporting teachers to teach in anti-oppressive ways (e.g., Kumashiro, 2015) that consider how student resistance can present opportunities for possibility instead of punishment.

By highlighting the consequences of compliance-driven classrooms, *A Curriculum of Control: Compliant Classrooms and the Students They Fail* urges teachers, teacher educators, and school leaders to consider whether they are sustaining or dismantling oppressive structures. The book promotes a shift toward culturally responsive pedagogy that embraces student resistance as a catalyst for meaningful learning and systemic change. The text also presents inquiries for districts and states to consider funding formulas in relation to students' experiences and issues of equity. Finally, the book can contribute to conversations at schools, districts, states, and universities about the topics of diversity, equity, and inclusion by presenting opportunities for readers to question the purpose of schooling in places like Baker School and examine their assumptions and biases about urban schools and the people who learn and work in them.

A Curriculum of Control contributes to debates about the opportunities public schooling does and does not provide for low-income students of color. While much is written about the achievement gap, most empirical studies focus exclusively on quantitative data or on the perceptions of teachers and administrators. Adopting a student-centered focus helps reframe understanding of schooling and equity and presents questions for new and veteran practitioners as well as academics to think about schooling structures and possibilities from the student perspective. Additional implications include ways to value and incorporate student voice in schools, lessons about how policy is experienced by students and teachers, opportunities to rethink parent engagement narratives, and ways that schools simultaneously parentified and infantilized students at Baker and schools like it. In addition, the text offers insights for school leaders seeking to change a culture of control in their schools. Finally, this book centers the candid lived experiences of elementary and middle school students at Baker School;

listening to and learning from these experiences is important for all educators in Philadelphia and other parts of the country. This research shows how the curriculum of control begins in elementary schools and that the impacts of these experiences have profound implications for students' future opportunities.

Overview of Chapters

Chapter 1: Hidden Curricula and the Myth of Opportunity

This chapter situates concepts such as the myth of meritocracy and individualism in relation to ideas about control, resistance, and possibility in urban schools. In particular, the concepts of hidden curricula and social reproduction (e.g., Apple, 2018; Bowles & Gintis, 1976; Lareau, 2011; McFadden, 2023) are connected to schools and their impacts on students and families. The chapter critiques the White Western individualistic notion that educational "failure" is the result of students and families lacking the drive and motivation to improve their lives. These framing concepts demonstrate how schools in the United States socialize children for lines of work based on hidden and tacit curricula, which instead of producing a meritocratic society continues to reproduce the status quo of economic inequality (e.g., Anyon, 1980; Gorski, 2018). The chapter sets the stage for how Bourdieu's forms of capital, habitus, and symbolic violence occur in schools and their surrounding communities. It concludes by bringing in the theories of critical and liberatory pedagogy (Giroux, 2001; McLaren, 2015; Tosolt, 2020) and student resistance (Toshalis, 2015) as ways individuals, in particular students and teachers, can work against systems of oppression. The chapter briefly overviews the research methods and situates the author's positionality as a researcher, practitioner, and scholar in relation to Baker School, detailing how Baker is one example of the phenomena described in this book and specifying how the findings have been witnessed by the author as a researcher, teacher, teacher mentor, parent, and teacher educator. Philadelphia and the local schooling context are also introduced.

Chapter 2: The Curriculum of Control

Chapter 2 illuminates the framing concepts of hidden curricula of work and social reproduction presented in chapter 1 and details the chaotic nature of Baker School and the resulting ways that schooling becomes about controlling student behavior instead of learning. Teachers at Baker are praised for "controlling" their classes, which means that students are in their seats and the classroom is quiet and orderly. Students, likewise, are praised for how well they follow directions. Thus, chapter 2 details how the school operates according to a curriculum of control and includes narrative fieldnotes from classrooms, hallways, the lunchroom, and recess. Despite this curriculum of control, Baker School is still largely described by students, teachers, leaders, and parents as chaotic. In turn, teachers and administrators reinforce efforts to control children's behavior so that the curriculum of control is reinforced and, as discussed in the next chapter, teachers and students engage in a struggle for power and autonomy.

Chapter 3: Relational Dynamics, Power Struggles, and Resistance

Chapter 3 details how the curriculum of control complicates and strains relationships between teachers and students. Despite the semi-professional status of the teaching profession because of teachers' lack of autonomy over their work (e.g., Ingersoll & Collins, 2018; Wronowski, 2021), significant responsibility and blame are attributed to teachers for student behavior and achievement outcomes, and thus teachers at Baker attempt to control the behavior of their students. Not surprisingly, students resist these attempts, and this resistance culminates in power struggles between teachers and students. One of the ways that students and teachers respond to the simultaneously chaotic and controlling environment is by demonstrating a *habitus of fierceness*. Habitus encompasses one's embodied preferences and includes the ways in which individuals internalize the rules that structure their social world. This chapter details the rules surrounding a habitus of fierceness and how students demonstrate this fierceness so that they are not bullied. One eighth grade student describes this habitus by stating why she fights with other students, "Well in this school, I just had to show people that I'm not really scared." The habitus of fierceness is also one way that students fend for themselves, examined in the next chapter that builds on the discussion of how students are simultaneously parentified and infantilized.

Chapter 4: Parentification and Infantilization of Students

Chapter 4 begins by overviewing four common parent narratives at the school, including (1) they do not work and are supported by government assistance, (2) they are in jail, (3) they are on drugs and/or mentally ill, or (4) they work several jobs and barely make ends meet. The chapter introduces readers to two different parents who exhibit combinations of the preceding narratives, and it focuses on Ms. Carol as an example of a counternarrative. After illustrating how the school does and does not engage parents, the chapter focuses on a family who has three kids in the school and how the oldest child, fourth grader Nyeisha, is both parentified and infantilized at Baker School. The school environment infantilized children by demanding unquestioned compliance while simultaneously acknowledging that students like Nyeisha were "raising themselves," as teachers called it, and responsible for younger siblings. Teachers and administrators recognize the struggles that Nyeisha and other students experience; however, they continue to blame students and parents for frustrations that are often beyond anyone's control. The chapter concludes by setting the stage for the *deficit default* surrounding the school that is introduced in the next chapter.

Chapter 5: Implications of Internalizing the "Deficit Default"

Chapter 5 shows how a deficit default, which is the negative way that students, teachers, parents, and administrators viewed each other, themselves, and the school, becomes internalized by students, teachers, and their families. A common narrative was that students attended Baker as a "last resort." If there was another option, students would take it. Students with more involved parents often transferred to charter schools, and many students in the middle grades attended Baker because they were kicked out of their charter school for behavior infractions. Teachers reinforce this narrative and discuss how they try to help certain students transfer to a "better" school. The habitus of fierceness is one way that students push back against the deficit default, but students are often disciplined for fighting or talking back to teachers, meaning the resistance and the negative perceptions about themselves and the school persist. The chapter concludes by raising questions about individual accountability and sets the stage for the systemic questions raised in the next chapter.

Chapter 6: The Realities of Systemic Failure

Chapter 6 details the invisibility of macrostructural forces such as poverty, health care, and tax systems and how these structures directly impact students, teachers, and families connected to Baker School. Furthermore, students are aware of the poor state of the school and make comments about how "dirty" the school is or how certain teachers are not "qualified" to teach certain subjects. Students' recognition of broader issues such as teacher turnover reinforces how students internalize negative ideas about their school, themselves, and their community and highlights how a lack of resources and systemwide failures impact students. This chapter connects to theories of social reproduction introduced in chapter 1 and uses interview and observational data to demonstrate the lived realities of underfunded and understaffed schools, like Baker, and the impact on everyone who attends and works at the school.

Chapter 7: Struggling for Humanity

Chapter 7 shows how systemic failure and the deficit default combine to enact symbolic violence on students at Baker School. Symbolic violence occurs when an individual's position in society is considered natural and systemic failures are ignored (Bourdieu, 2001). Instead, students at schools like Baker are expected to "work harder" or "care more about school" (Theoharis, 2009, 2020). Using ethnographic fieldnotes and interviews, this chapter focuses in depth on two students, fourth grader Nyeisha and eighth grader Rashanna, and demonstrates how both students demonstrate resilience through a habitus of fierceness amid structural, symbolic, and physical violence they experience in and out of Baker School. Despite how resilient the students are, the chapter forces readers to reckon with the limited options and possibilities for students who attend Baker School and presents direct evidence of an opportunity as opposed to an achievement gap.

Conclusion

This chapter offers recommendations for theory, practice, and future research based on the study findings. The chapter describes the various ways educators, scholars, and policymakers can positively humanize students' experiences rather than blame students for problems that are out of their control. In addition, implications for ways that inner-city schools can be improved are offered. One implication discussed is democratizing the schooling process so that students, their parents, and the community bring their insights and ideas into the solutions that educators and policymakers consider. Other implications include suggestions for ways to train and support teachers who can make a powerful difference in students' lives. The book concludes by suggesting that readers think about the multiple resources students have, including their habitus of fierceness, from an asset instead of a deficit orientation as a way to make schooling less about control and more about possibility.

Appendix: Research Methodology and Design

The appendix details the methodological approach, based on two years of participant observation fieldwork at Baker School and in the local neighborhood. Sampling, data collection, and analysis methods as well as validity and ethical considerations are described.

Acknowledgments

To all the teachers, mentors, and coaches who have guided me from preschool through graduate school and beyond: thank you for your care, guidance, and encouragement.

To my students — whether from my time teaching middle school, working as a camp counselor, or now supporting graduate students — you consistently challenge and inspire me, and I'm grateful for all I've learned from you.

I also want to thank my family, especially the many educators among you. To my mother, grandmother, brother, uncle, and great-aunt — thank you for your dedication to teaching and learning.

Finally, my deepest thanks go to my husband, Jason, and children, Max and Evey, for your unwavering support.

Chapter 1

Hidden Curricula
and the Myth of Opportunity

By centering student perspectives, *A Curriculum of Control* offers a new angle and depth of understanding about middle school students' experiences of schooling when a school reproduces social inequality by controlling student behavior and unintentionally limiting students' opportunities. Educational issues tend to be conceptualized from the perspectives of teachers or school leaders. This book focuses on students' experiences and describes how students attending underserved schools tend to be at a cumulative disadvantage when their values, beliefs, resources, and understandings do not align with those considered dominant when practices of control for students begin as early as elementary school. This introductory chapter sets the stage for key concepts that are central to contextualizing the experiences described throughout the book, including the myth of educational opportunity and underlying factors that contribute to educational inequalities. In addition, this chapter overviews theoretical concepts such as cultural capital, habitus, symbolic violence, and hidden curricula and details how these operate in schools. I then describe how socialization processes help reinscribe a hidden curriculum in schools that reproduces structural inequality. The chapter overviews the important role of teachers and teaching and discusses how teachers and students can resist oppressive institutional structures. It also sets the stage with relevant information about the educational landscape in Philadelphia to contextualize how students and teachers are impacted by state and local policies. The chapter concludes with an overview of the methodological approach to the research.

The Myth of Opportunity

In the United States, public education is central to our country's belief in a meritocracy, a system in which individuals are rewarded for their hard work and achievement. Education that is free and open to all fuels the belief that if one goes to school and works hard they can change their social status and work their way out of poverty. There are many individuals who have seemingly achieved this myth. However, these examples obscure the inequity of education in the United States. Consider, for example, how K–12 public education is funded. Public schools are funded based on property taxes, and families who live in expensive homes and pay more taxes attend better funded public schools. Thus, children's future success and economic opportunities largely depend on where they live. A premise guiding this book is that the concept and reality of meritocracy is primarily symbolic rather than a reflection of societal functioning (e.g., Fuhrer, 2023; Ladson-Billings, 2006; Milner, 2013; McCrory Calarco et al., 2022). The neoliberal claim that individuals succeed based on their merit and hard work is part of how those in power use the idea of a meritocracy and individualism to justify their dominant positions. Yet, in the United States, a neoliberal, capitalist nation, the socioeconomic system is set up so that only *the people who already have* the financial, social, residential, and educational resources they need can improve their lives (e.g., Bowles & Gintis, 1976; Brathwaite, 2017; Chasin, 2022; Contreras, 2012).

The myth of meritocracy is important to schooling in the way that it allows the "reproductive" nature of schools to persist unquestioned (see, e.g., Anyon, 1980; Apple, 2018; Backer & Cairns, 2021; Bourdieu, 1986; Bowles & Gintis, 1976; Giroux, 1983). Broadly, a social reproduction argument denotes that schools reinforce (and thus reproduce) structural inequalities. *Structural inequality* refers to how systems in society are informed by policies and laws, how some people benefit from these laws and policies and other people do not. When laws are structured such that they work against certain groups of people, structural inequalities are created. Education is just one example of structural inequality. Research has consistently found that students in low-income neighborhoods receive inferior public education to students in wealthy neighborhoods (e.g., Barshay, 2020; García & Weiss, 2017; Simon, 2021). In the United States, the inferior education that students in low-income neighborhoods receive is not often acknowledged, and instead society blames individuals and groups that do not succeed in this presumed meritocracy. Instead of recognizing the symbolic nature of educational meritocracy, educational failure is often blamed on the cultural deficiencies of students, families, or communities (Duncan-Andrade & Morrell, 2008; Sharma, 2022; Torrance, 2017) or attributed to personal shortcomings (Bowles & Gintis, 1976; Williams et al., 2020).

Explanations for Educational "Failure"

The ways that educational "failure" results in blaming certain groups of students for not working hard enough is related to the strong belief in individualism in the United States, in which individuals tend to be criticized for lacking the personal drive and motivation to improve their lives. An example of this is the dominant and enduring language of the "achievement gap" rather than the other phrases such as "resource," "access," or "opportunity gap" that critique the prevailing deficit orientations, which tend to blame individuals rather than institutions or systems and do not recognize the positive assets of students, families, and communities (Milner, 2008). Furthermore, deficit orientations are often perpetuated by cultural hegemony in which dominant understandings of the world appear to be "common sense" (e.g., Kincheloe, 2008; Marsh & Walker, 2022). These dominant, hegemonic ways of seeing the world often culminate in a culture of power (Delpit, 1995). The culture of power inequitably elevates certain groups of people by codifying specific values, beliefs, and ways of being (Barton & Yang, 2000; Mandviwala et al., 2022).

The Culture of Power

The culture of power functions according to arbitrary norms, established by those with power, which are perceived as natural and which become normative and enforced by institutions. The culture of power is enacted in schools and classrooms through codes, rules, linguistic forms, communicative strategies, and ways of presenting the self that reflect the broader culture of power in the society (Delpit, 1995, 2018). The naturalization of these habits, systems, values, and beliefs is directly related to understandings of capital and habitus.

Forms of Capital

Capital consists of all the resources that allow individuals to profit and can be economic (financial and material), cultural (qualifications and goods), social (connections and networks), and symbolic (misrecognized as "natural" competence) (Bourdieu, 1986, 2000). Because the acquisition of cultural capital is often more disguised than economic capital, it can often be symbolic and unrecognized as an advantage. Thus, symbolic capital represents other forms of capital that are often taken for granted or misrecognized as intelligence, talent, or some other personal competence (Bourdieu, 1986).

An example that Bourdieu (1989) describes is how the cultural capital of a diploma functions as symbolic capital. Because a diploma is universally recognized as a legitimate symbol of achievement, the other forms of capital necessary to get the diploma are not acknowledged, including the economic and social capital. Another example of symbolic capital is when "noble" qualities are attributed to wealthy individuals who donate time or money because the economic capital necessary for such individuals to be able to do this is not recognized (Bourdieu & Wacquant, 2013; Wacquant, 2008). Thinking of attributes as natural often leads people to misrecognize the resources (capital) necessary to participate in the culture of power.

Habitus

Habitus is defined as how individuals act and make sense of the world; it encompasses one's embodied preferences and includes the ways in which individuals internalize the rules that structure their social world (Bourdieu, 1977,

1989, 2017). Habitus, like cultural and symbolic capital, is often perceived as "natural" or "earned." This means that dominant forms of habitus and cultural capital are a part of cultural hegemony and perpetuate the culture of power in which certain values, behaviors, and interactions are valued and others are punished.

Social Reproduction

The favoring of certain values and actions over others is primarily invisible and unconscious, and this is precisely what makes cultural capital and habitus such powerful contributors to social reproduction. It appears as if individuals are rewarded because of their natural abilities instead of their advantages (Bourdieu, 1984, 1986, 2001). The forms of capital and habitus that individuals develop through socialization processes from infancy to adolescence lead to both cognitive and noncognitive skills and habits that ultimately influence employment and economic opportunities (e.g., Farkas, 2003; Gertler et al., 2021). Furthermore, the cultural capital of the dominant group[1] is manifest in schools in ways that reinforce hegemony, reinscribe deficit orientations, and that ultimately further sediment inequity (Bourdieu, 1998; Lareau, 2011; Mills, 2021; Mills & Gale, 2007).

Unfortunately, schools in underserved communities tend to not prepare students in development of the cognitive and behavioral skills needed for middle-class occupations (Farkas, 2003, 2018). This means that by privileging certain forms of capital over others, whether consciously or unconsciously, schools contribute to reproducing social inequality. Having and maintaining more capital and resources is also known as cumulative advantage, which is colloquially referred to as "the rich getting richer" (DiPrete & Eirich, 2006). Therefore, people who mirror the dominant group continue to acquire more resources, while those who don't are at a cumulative disadvantage for acquiring such resources.

Because of the capital that students do or do not have, students from racial and lower-social-class backgrounds are often at an additional disadvantage when they are silently blamed for not being determined enough to improve their life chances. The way that capital is legitimized and perceived as individuals' natural abilities contributes to the reproduction of social inequalities and has significant implications for students. For example, it is often codified in the culture of power (Delpit, 1995) or in what others (e.g., Kuriloff & Carl, 2015) refer to as the "hidden curriculum" of power. The ways that schools reproduce rather than change the status quo has significant implications for the current and future opportunities of students attending schools in communities with high rates of poverty (see also Calarco, 2018; Carter, 2005; Ferguson, 2000; Morris, 2016; Nolan, 2011).

Socialization and the Hidden Curriculum

The term *hidden curriculum*, coined by Jackson (1968), means that schools operate not only with stated purposes and goals, but also in the beliefs and values transmitted tacitly through day-to-day social interactions and routines (Bernhardt, 2022; Giroux, 1981). The hidden curriculum has come to include the subtle messages of schooling that, according to many (e.g., Anyon, 1980, 2013; Bourdieu & Passeron, 1977; Bowles & Gintis, 1976; Reay, 2017, 2020, 2022), continue to reproduce the hegemonic status quo.

An example of this hidden (or not so hidden) curriculum in perpetuating class structures is how schools reflect the broader economic conditions available to students. Students from minoritized backgrounds tend to be concentrated in chaotic schools that emphasize rule-following. At the same time, these underserved schools automatically reflect a sense that there are minimal possibilities for students, which therefore limits the opportunities that will eventually be available to them (Bowles & Gintis, 1976). In contrast, schools in affluent areas tend to offer more opportunities for student participation and creative instruction (Anyon, 1980; Bowles & Gintis, 1976; McFadden, 2023).

Other examples of this include the ways that pedagogical practices are connected to socioeconomic status, and children from poor and working-class schools are prepared for jobs that require rule-following and procedural processes (Anyon, 1980) or function as carceral sites that surveil and punish Black and Brown students (e.g., Sojoyner, 2018). This book considers the role of elementary schooling in initiating the process of control in public education.

Whether or not the curriculum is hidden, it is still experienced. This impacts students, their experiences, and their opportunities. Because of the entrenched belief in the myth of educational meritocracy, students in underserved environments are often blamed for individual deficiencies. Moreover, the forcing of expectations and standards on students who are not prepared to meet them is often misrecognized (Duncan-Andrade & Morrell, 2008; Sharma, 2022; Torrance, 2017). In addition to the hidden curriculum that is invisibly present in schools, the overt curriculum and its socializing effects affect both students and teachers. When schools in underserved communities adopt practices that do not promote student creativity and teacher agency, they contribute to reproducing, instead of changing, the status quo (Carl, 2014).

The "Banking Concept" of Education

Hidden and overt curricula are often represented in a school's pedagogical approach. An example of this is reflected in how the "banking concept" of education — in which teachers are distillers of information that students passively receive — keeps people passive and therefore in subjugation (Freire, 2000, Lopez Kershen et al., 2018). The banking method of schooling perpetuates myths that preserve the status quo — myths that promote hegemony and become normalized by adults, the schools, and the students within them. These myths include the beliefs that people live in a free and equal society and that anyone who is motivated and hard-working can become an entrepreneur. Too many schools, especially in underserved communities, operate with a banking approach or a *transmission model* of education.

Community Devaluation

While teachers typically do not consciously endorse such hidden curricula, even unintentional actions, especially by those with power over students, have powerful consequences. Teachers working in underserved or low-income communities (even teachers who may have previously lived in the school's neighborhood) often have misconceptions about the local community. When teachers do not recognize the abilities and intelligence of their students (their "funds of knowledge"), students can experience constraints and disadvantages (González et al., 2005; Kennedy & Soutullo, 2018). The next section describes the potential consequences that can result when schools, and the individuals in them, do not challenge the hidden curricula and continue to deliver messages about certain groups that are perpetuated within such curricula.

Symbolic Violence

The ways in which schools legitimize certain capital and habitus over others is a form of *symbolic violence*. This violence does not involve physical or bodily harm, and in the same way that symbolic capital is invisibly transmitted, symbolic violence is largely invisible; it is a form of cultural domination in which the symbols and practices of the dominant group are imposed on all of society. For example, because schools tend to reproduce the values, tastes, and ideals of the dominant culture, symbolic violence is acted upon students because their own habitus and capital are degraded. Bourdieu (2001, p. 102) describes symbolic violence as "a gentle violence, imperceptible and invisible even to its victims, exerted for the most part through the purely symbolic channels of communication and cognition (more precisely, misrecognition), recognition, or even feeling."

Symbolic violence tends to be unconscious, occurring in daily interactions, and it causes individuals to believe that inequity is natural and justified, and to blame themselves for their status in society (Bourdieu, 2001; Bourgois & Schonberg, 2009). One example is the way in which schools often assume that all students should exhibit middle-class cultural capital. Students who do not have these expected forms of cultural capital can experience symbolic violence. Some students are marginalized because the school legitimizes certain cultures and sidelines others. Students with a different cultural background, no matter how rich, can experience racial and class "othering" that causes emotional pain and trauma (Horvat & Antonio, 1999).

How Teachers Unknowingly Participate

Socialization processes primarily occur in the family and the school, and the relationship between the school and the family also plays an important role in the reproduction of social inequality. Schools tend to privilege middle- and upper-class parenting styles, and schools also tend to favor specific values and attitudes that reflect middle- and upper-class social and cultural capital (Lareau, 2011; Lareau & Shumar, 1996; Reay, 1998). Teachers expect to teach students who are similar to themselves, and teachers' individual teaching habitus is formed by the many years they spent as students, in which they determined what are and are not appropriate behaviors for teachers, students, and parents (Zevenbergen, 2006).

There are consequences when the habitus and symbolic capital of teachers differ from those of their students. Some students may cultivate a "hustler" or an "outlaw" habitus as a mechanism for surviving in schools when their forms of capital differ from the institutionally valued and mainstream forms of habitus and symbolic capital (Bourgois & Schonberg, 2009; Wacquant, 1998). Students from middle-class backgrounds see their habitus represented by the values that the school consciously (and unconsciously) legitimizes (Mills, 2008). However, students of color and lower socioeconomic status often do not see their values represented at school. Instead, their habitus is not valued and/or is devalued, and additional constraints are placed on these students.

The Impact of Social Class and Race

Research finds that students defined as low-income perform less than one standard deviation lower or approximately three years behind peers not identified as low-income (Hanushek et al., 2020).[2] Potentially contributing to these outcomes is the disconnect between teachers who tend to be middle class teaching students living in poverty (Keibler, 2019). A majority of teachers in the United States have postbaccalaureate degrees, whereas many of the families of their students do not have the same levels of formal education (NCES, 2021). This disconnect can have negative consequences especially since teachers can be considered highly qualified without any training in how to support students living in poverty (Bertrand, 2017). At Baker School the students experienced both the impacts of race and social class as 100% of the students were classified as economically disadvantaged, and 98% of them identified as Black.

Students' race clearly matters a great deal and informs the ways that they are treated by teachers and school leaders. There is evidence to suggest that there are educational benefits in the early grades when students, both Black and White, are taught by a teacher sharing their race (Dee, 2004; Gershenson et al., 2022). Teachers' perceptions about students from different racial backgrounds have also been shown to impact students' opportunities, particularly for students from lower socioeconomic backgrounds (Goldhaber et al., 2019).

From an opportunity gap framework, in many schools, students of color are not exposed to college preparatory classes (Tyson, 2013; Wright et al., 2017). From a cultural capital framework, social class tends to dominate the discourse about the types of capital that students have and how this affects their opportunities. However, it is important that teachers recognize that students often bring to school cultural capital that can differ from mainstream forms of cultural capital (Howard, 2003; Redding, 2019). Race matters, and the success of racially diverse students in the United States necessitates that teachers acknowledge and address their perceptions of racially diverse students. When teachers have deficit perceptions of students from different racial, socioeconomic, and cultural backgrounds, many unintended consequences can result.

Schools are sites where individual and familial values and cultures intersect daily. Navigating between these intersections, or different worlds, can be difficult for some students. The symbolic violence and preference for certain values and habits at schools can make traversing these worlds even more difficult. Explicitly teaching students about the unequal power dynamics that can be manifested in school or society can help students to feel (and be) less marginalized and discriminated against. This kind of explicit teaching can help teachers and students uncover the symbolic violence and hidden curricula in schools, and it points to the powerful potential of teachers.

The Transformative Potential of Teachers

Teachers profoundly shape students' experiences, and they can help resist continuing the culture of power and change the status quo. One explicit way to do this is to directly teach students about the "rules of the game." This involves acknowledging and incorporating the different funds of knowledge (González et al., 2005; Moll, 2000) that all students bring to school as well as explicitly educating students about the power that is involved in these differences. Broadly speaking, these practices may be considered culturally relevant pedagogy in which teachers' actions affirm that all students, regardless of race, ethnicity, gender, sexual orientation, or social class, can succeed (Ladson-Billings, 1994).

These transformative practices can also be conceptualized as critical pedagogy, in which teachers welcome and embrace the cultural differences of their students and deemphasize their role as conveyors of knowledge with students as the receivers (Cortina & Winter, 2021; Freire, 1998; Johnson, 1995). These practices entail that teachers are not only aware of the capital that schools tend to privilege but also work to combat these power asymmetries (Giroux, 1983, 2001; Nieto, 2008).

Teaching marginalized students the rules of the game helps teachers to be part of the change that needs to occur rather than promoting the status quo (e.g., Mills, 2008). Understanding the powerful role of cultural capital and habitus becomes especially important for teachers because cultural capital is what sets the rules of society (Bourdieu, 1986). In practice, this may involve teachers acknowledging first that they are a part of the "culture of power" and then giving students the tools of this culture, such as being able to speak in what is considered standard English (Delpit, 1995). To be clear, according to Delpit and others (e.g., Alim, 2004; Cummins, 2009) this is not taking a deficit view of students; they are advocating for letting students in on the cultural tools that will help them be successful.

Habitus contributes to the reproduction of social inequities (Bourgois & Schonberg, 2007) and constitutes an understanding "for the game" (Bourdieu & Wacquant, 1992). In the game of schooling, certain students may not have the "tools" to be as successful as other students. These tools can lead to cognitive and noncognitive skills that can translate into future economic opportunities (Farkas, 2003). Thus, educating students on the rules of the game is important, but teachers should also elevate students' consciousness so that they understand how powerful these rules are and how to manipulate them. Because habitus is not fixed and can change when in different environments (Bourdieu, 1990), teachers can help students develop the tools that are valued by schools and the broader society *without making them feel inferior*. Schools are sites of power and reproduction as well as dialogue and liberation (Giroux, 1983, 1985, 2001; Green, 2020; Kincheloe, 2008). To educate critically, educators need to understand the complex, historical, and individual ways that students understand the world (Darder et al., 2023; Giroux, 1985).

In addition to educating students on the "rules of the game," transformative education involves understanding and incorporating students' habitus. For example, this may mean recognizing the power of a hustler habitus (Wacquant, 1998) or an outlaw habitus (Bourgois & Schonberg, 2009) and how these sensibilities can be harnessed in schools so that these students do not experience symbolic violence of being "othered" (Borrero, 2012; Horvat & Antonio, 1999). Although leveling the playing field for students from minoritized backgrounds can be difficult (Bourdieu, 1986; Mills, 2008), there is great potential for schools and teachers, through critical teaching practices, to act as positive socializing agents and help increase students' current and future opportunities (e.g., Cruz et al., 2020; Nieto, 2008).

There are also ways in which students can resist the hidden curriculum and social reproduction (see, e.g., Giroux, 1983; Willis, 1977), and teachers can critically approach teaching (see, e.g., Darder et al., 2023; Freire, 1998, 2000; Giroux, 2001; Kincheloe, 2008; McLaren, 2003) in ways that educate students on the rules of the game and promote critical consciousness (Duncan-Andrade & Morrell, 2008; Freire, 2000). As children develop into adolescents, they often want to exert autonomy in their actions and decisions (Nakkula & Toshalis, 2020). There are ways that teachers (and schools) can create schooling experiences that acknowledge student autonomy and agency and invite students to experiment and take ownership for their learning.

Philadelphia and Baker School

Income and wealth disparities in the United States have increased since the 1970s (see, e.g., Hanushek & Lindseth, 2009; Hoffmann et al., 2020; Reardon, 2011, 2018), and the goal of funding compensatory public education to help reduce these disparities has not been achieved (Hanushek & Lindseth, 2009). While there is not a consensus in the literature, recent research (Jackson, 2020; Jackson & Mackevicius, 2024; Miller, 2018) has found that increased school spending improves student achievement outcomes. Although the United States has increased public education spending over the past four decades, great disparities exist in the amounts spent on students depending on the city (or zip code) in which they live. For example, the per-pupil spending for Philadelphia when this research was conducted was approximately half what the per-pupil expenditure was in neighboring Lower Merion School District. During 2021–2022, Philadelphia spent $10,796 per pupil, the state average was $13,688, and neighboring Lower Merion School District spent $26,362 per pupil (Graham, 2022). School funding matters in producing achievement gap–closing effects on academic achievement and life outcomes (Jackson et al., 2016).

Pennsylvania's school funding formula, which was based on state, local, and federal funds, had been considered one of the most regressive in the country (Mezzacappa, 2015) and was ranked 45th for its K–12 funding formula in 2022 (School Funding in PA, n.d.). In February 2023, the Pennsylvania Supreme Court ruled that the state's education funding system was unconstitutional and left it up to lawmakers to determine solutions (Fitzpatrick, 2023). The majority of state and local funding comes from property taxes, which burdens poorer areas. Philadelphia is the only city in Pennsylvania that is unable to raise its taxes for schools, which makes it entirely reliant on elected officials to raise money for schools (Wolfman-Arent & Mezzacappa, 2017).

Philadelphia is the sixth most populous city in the United States according to the 2020 census, and 2021 census data noted that city residents are 39% Black, 33% White, 7% Asian, 16% Hispanic, 4% multiracial, and 1% Other (Loeb, 2022). While on paper Philadelphia appears to be a diverse city, its residents tend to live in neighborhoods that are racially segregated. Philadelphia is one of the most racially segregated cities in the country (Mezzacappa, 2022), and recent research suggests that Philadelphia public schools are roughly as segregated as they were 30 years ago (D'Onofrio & Contreras, 2024). This racial segregation was reflected at Baker School as it is in many other schools in the city. At the time data were collected, the student body of Baker was 98% Black and a majority of the teachers, staff, and leaders were also Black. The number of students at Baker School categorized as "economically disadvantaged" was

100%. In addition to racial segregation, Philadelphians tend to be segregated by class.

Philadelphia has higher concentrations of residents living in concentrated poverty than comparison cities, and most of these residents living in concentrated poverty are non-White (Philadelphia City Council, 2019). In particular, Blacks and Hispanics of all income levels are more likely to live in Philadelphia neighborhoods with high poverty rates (Pew, 2017). At the time data were collected, the poverty rate in Philadelphia was approximately 25% overall and 37% for children under 18. Recent data still lists Philadelphia as having the highest poverty rate of the nation's 10 largest cities, but this rate has come down slightly to 22.3% for the city, but 34% of children and 28% of Black Philadelphians live in poverty (Loeb, 2022). What is important to note is that the students attending Baker School, as noted in the preface, are mostly Black and poor, they have been historically underserved by public schooling in Philadelphia, and they are attending a school that is both racially and economically segregated.

In addition to this racial and economic segregation at Baker School, the schooling landscape in Philadelphia, including the prevalence of charter schools, also impacts racial segregation of schools (Mezzacappa, 2022). Philadelphia has many schooling options, including elite independent schools, private parochial schools, public district schools, and public charter schools. Some charter schools in Philadelphia have admissions criteria and can remove students for behavioral infractions. Many students in the middle grades at Baker had been kicked out of surrounding charter schools. In 2022, students of color made up 82% of Philadelphia's public school population, and White students comprised 14% despite White residents totaling approximately 34% of the population (D'Onofrio & Contreras, 2024). Thus, more affluent students, who tend to be White, do not attend Philadelphia's public schools. The more resourced or connected students may attend private schools or charter schools, which further contributes to higher concentrations of students who may have less social and economic capital in schools like Baker.

Baker School is a public school in Philadelphia in a low-income neighborhood. Like many schools in the Northeast, it is racially segregated. Baker School serves students in grades kindergarten through eighth in Philadelphia. At the time of the research, there were more than 500 students in the school and approximately 30 teachers. About 80% of the staff was Black, as was the principal, and most of the school leadership.

Opportunity Gap

This text interrupts positivist discussions of student performance data at schools like Baker that detail "achievement gaps" rather than "resource," "access," or "opportunity" gaps (e.g., Milner, 2012). The lack of resources, years of disinvestment, structural oppression, and testing systems that prioritize White cultural knowledge culminate in the culture of power previously described that unfairly and unevenly elevates certain groups of people. This book contextualizes and illuminates the experiences of students who attend underserved schools like Baker School in high-poverty neighborhoods and demonstrates firsthand how the opportunity gap plays out every day for students like Nyeisha, a fourth grader, and Jayalya, an eighth grader, reinforcing the ways that schooling continues to operate as a hidden curriculum of control and social reproduction. *A Curriculum of Control: Compliant Classrooms and the Students They Fail* illuminates scenes of students' daily experiences and lives at the intersection of ethnography and education; it portrays the layers of complexity, pain, and triumph in student resistance, resilience, and brilliance at Baker School.

This text discusses educational inequity from an opportunity-gap framework in which students' opportunities are influenced by school and community resources and broader social inequalities (Carter & Welner, 2013; Milner, 2021; Pendakur, 2023). Examples of factors that influence the opportunity gap include a deficit of high-quality teachers, poor housing and health care, unsafe schools and neighborhoods, as well as a lack of up-to-date textbooks, tutors, and test-prep programs (Carter, 2013). Students who do well on tests have usually benefited from very different economic and social realities (Au, 2016; Carter & Welner, 2013; Reardon & Kalogrides, 2019). By shifting attention to "deficiencies in the foundational components of societies, schools, and communities that produce significant differences in education" (Carter, 2013, p. 3) instead of on students, this book critically examines students' schooling experiences within one school. The role of schools in social reproduction directly challenges notions of meritocracy. However, schools, as a primary socializing agent, can and do impact students. Despite the prevailing meritocratic argument and critiques of it, little is known about students' experiences and opportunities in underserved schools (Quaglia et al., 2010). Even less is known within frameworks that index these students' holistic lived experiences in ways that do not simply deficitize them and instead view them from a resource orientation and funds of knowledge perspective (González et al., 2005).

Methodological Overview

Aside from a limited number of youth participatory action research (YPAR) studies, students' voices and perspectives have not been thoroughly reflected in academic literature (Bautista et al., 2013; Voight & Velez, 2018; Zion et al., 2021), and this has had significant consequences for scholars, practitioners, and especially students. A powerful lesson from YPAR studies is that students have thoughtful opinions and ideas about schooling and ways to improve it. Although I did not employ YPAR methodologies, I focused on learning from and with students and generating data based on their experiences and perspectives. Students are experts of their experiences, and they have important thoughts, opinions, and perspectives that can inform theory and practice. More information about the study's methods can be found in the appendix.

My research found that students internalized negative perceptions about themselves, their school, and their community. These deficit orientations created a culture of symbolic violence in which students were expected to be (and then blamed if they were not) intrinsically motivated in a school dominated by disorder, disparaging language, and disruption.

What makes this ethnographic monograph stand out is the unique focus on elementary and middle school students' experiences. With students as the primary actors and lenses in this book, the student experience of schooling comes to light and offers critiques of how such schools are structured as well as ways that they can be improved. Drawing on two years of ethnographic fieldwork and over a decade of teaching and coaching teachers in schools like Baker, *A Curriculum of Control* foregrounds students' experiences through detailed fieldnotes and ethnographic interviews structured as student narratives.

Summary

This chapter begins by discussing how framing student outcomes as an "achievement" gap as opposed to an "opportunity" gap misplaces blame on students, schools, and families instead of recognizing the systemic and structural forces that result in inequitable schooling opportunities. The chapter overviews theoretical terms used throughout the text, including cultural capital, habitus, social reproduction, and symbolic violence to show how students attending underserved schools tend to be at a cumulative disadvantage when their values, beliefs, resources, and understandings do not align with those considered dominant. It demonstrates how socialization processes help reinforce a hidden curriculum in schools that continues to reproduce structural inequity. In addition to this reproduction, significant negative consequences can result for students when their backgrounds are not valued. Teachers, as primary socializing agents, can help foster transformative, rather than oppressive, experiences for students by engaging in pedagogies that engage families and communities while resisting the deficit thinking that results from symbolic violence that blames students for individual deficiencies rather than acknowledging the structural inequities that have shaped their opportunities. In the next chapter, I specifically detail how the hidden curriculum plays out at Baker School and the ways that students, teachers, and families often unconsciously reinforce this hidden curriculum of control.

Chapter 2

The Curriculum of Control

Baker School was often described as "chaotic." Although there were less chaotic days, which were considered "good days," most teachers, staff, students, and parents believed that Baker was "out of control." In response to this, a majority of the adults (teachers, staff, parents, and administrators) and students contended that students "needed" to be controlled.

Based on these assumptions about what students at Baker "needed," a hidden curriculum of implicit and explicit control developed at the school and affected students, teachers, parents, and administrators. The primary concern of adults at Baker School became controlling student behavior. As a result, this environment of unrest and disorder shaped the relational dynamics between students and adults, and a deep power struggle developed as both groups vied for control and autonomy.

While teachers attempted to control students, teachers also struggled for autonomy as professionals. At the same time, the hidden curriculum of control contributed to students' internalization of control narratives. Students ended up adapting to this environment by demonstrating a *habitus of fierceness* and *micro-resistance strategies*, which are described in more detail in this chapter.

Implicit Policing:
Socialization Processes of Control

For the most part, the processes of control at Baker were less explicit than those of schools with a "no excuses" approach to discipline (e.g., Whitman, 2008) or in schools with technical "paramilitary" (Devine, 1996) and "penal" discipline approaches (Nolan, 2011). As a K–8 school, Baker did not have metal detectors. There was one school police officer at the school about three or four days a week. Instead of hypersurveillance and policing, the control processes were more implicit.

From the moment that students began school at Baker, they were considered in "need of controlling," and the duration of students' schooling experiences was founded on this premise. The notion that children need to be suppressed and controlled is rooted in the deficit ideology some adults have about students. Teachers, school leaders, staff members, and parents made paternalistic assumptions that students in urban schools needed rigid discipline policies and traditional academic approaches because progressive education was "ill-suited" for "inner city schools" (e.g., Golann, 2018; Hyde, 2023; Stahl, 2018; Whitman, 2008).

Creating Compliant Classrooms

Because of narratives that Baker School was chaotic and that students needed controlling, schooling and teaching practices at Baker focused on behavioral management instead of learning processes. The following fieldnote from a social studies class exemplifies a typical day in this class and in many classes at the school. As the fieldnote shows, the arrangement of the desks (see figures 2.1–2.4), student interactions (and lack thereof), transitions in the hallway, messages conveyed to students through rules and posters (see figure 2.2), and the approach to instruction illustrate how behavior, as opposed to learning, is the priority of the class.

> I open the double doors to the middle school wing on the third floor. A glass panel is missing from one of the doors, and there are several ceiling tiles missing above them. Three boys are standing in the stairwell, two of them are holding their arms like a gun and are pretending to shoot each other from behind the doors. I walk into Mr. Barnes's room. Mr. Barnes is a White, first-year teacher. He is currently teaching an eighth-grade social studies class, and there are 14 students in the room when I walk in. They are working on the "Do Now," which consists of two questions. A "Do Now" is a common name for a warm-up exercise that students are expected to do as soon as they arrive to a class; Do Nows typically consist of a brief exercise to focus students' attention. The two Do Now questions are projected on the screen in the front of the room.
>
> The lights are off in the room, and there are papers and food wrappers on the floor. The desks are arranged in rows with desks facing the front board, and most of the rows consist of scattered desks. Several students have their heads down on their desks, and other students are talking to each other. I sit at an empty desk at the end of the second row. I ask the student in front of me, Rashanna, if anyone is sitting here before I sit down.
>
> Haliegh puts her middle finger up to the student behind her; she looks back and notices that I saw her and says, "Sorry" to me. The back "wall" of the classroom is a room divider and is shared with another middle school classroom. There are bulletin boards on this divider with seventh- and eighth-grade student work. The divider between the classes is very thin, and you can hear chairs dragging across the floor and students yelling and running in the other room. (See figure 2.1 for an overview of the classroom layout.)

Figure 2.1. Mr. Barnes's Social Studies Classroom Layout.

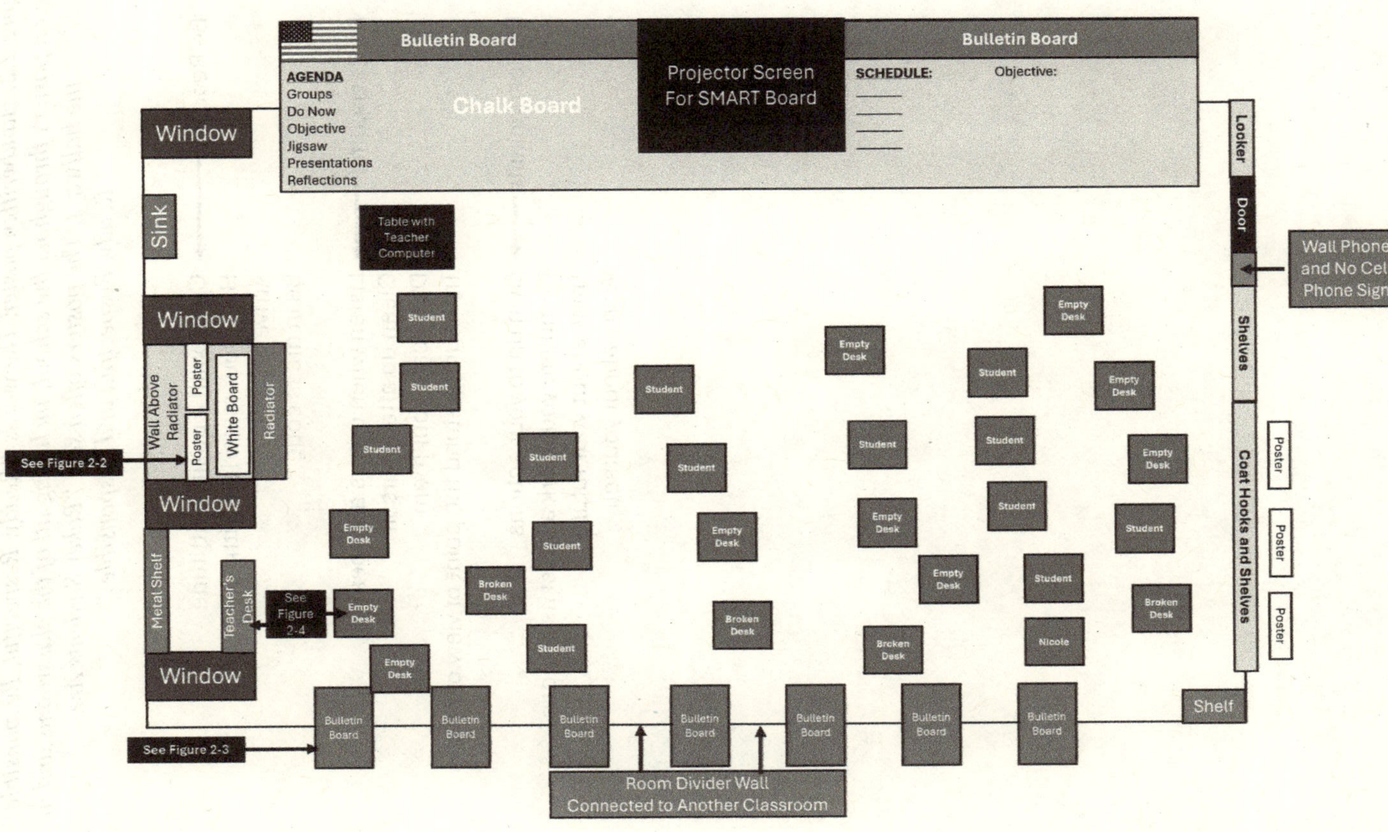

Figure 2.2. Handwritten poster. The words "Ready, Respectful, Responsible" are on posters throughout the school, including all of the classrooms and in the hallways. The posters often say, "Baker Students Are Ready, Respectful, and Responsible."

Be Ready ⟶ Come with a positive attitude
Have your materials with you
Arrive on time
Be in dress code

Be Respectful ⟶ Listen when others are speaking
Clean up after yourself
Don't eat in our room
Try to understand the point of view of others

Be Responsible ⟶ Own up to your actions
Complete your work as best as you can
Think about your future
Worry about yourself

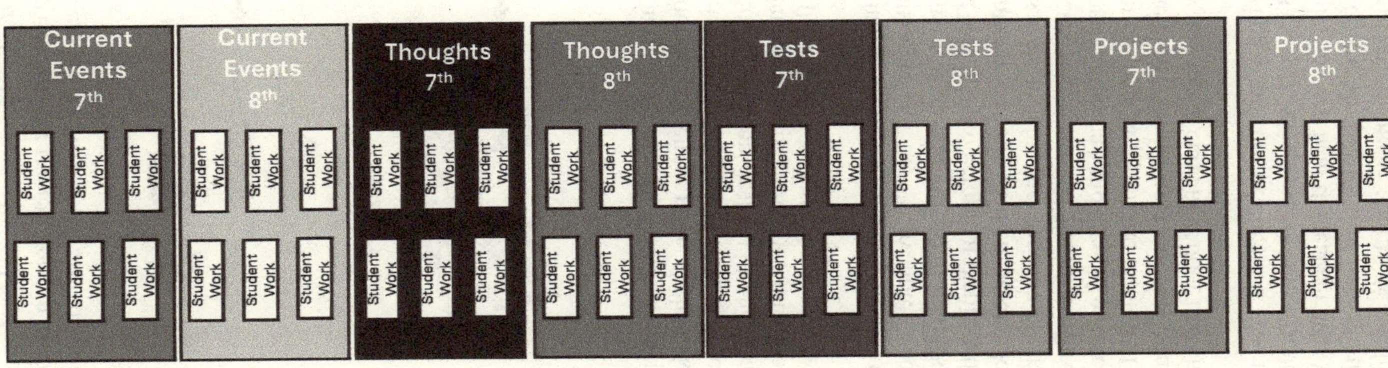

Figure 2.3. Bulletin boards along the back wall. The bulletin boards are covered in colored butcher paper and lined with a border. The butcher paper is ripped in places, and the border is missing and ripped in places as well. The white rectangles represent student assignments.

Figure 2.4. Pictures of the desks. There are several broken student desks in the classroom. This typically entails that the top portion of the desk, as shown figure 2.4, is no longer secured to the bottom and falls off frequently.

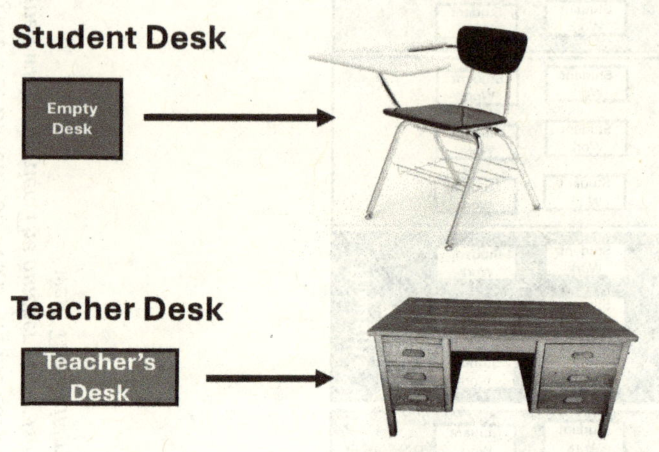

Most students sit at their desks with their coats on and their backpacks on the floor beside them or under their desks. A few students hang up their backpacks in the designated coat rack area, and a few students sit at their desks with their backpacks on and never take them off. A minute or two after I sit down, there is screaming in the hallway, and one female student walks in late.

After about 15 minutes are spent on the Do Now, the class moves on to what students call the "copy notes" portion of class. These notes consist of several PowerPoint slides of large bullet points of text. There is a projector that displays the bullet points that the students are to copy in their notebooks. Three more female students walk in late, one after the other. One of these students, Ameena, walks around the room three times while eating chips from a small bag and then takes a seat, takes out a soda bottle from her bag, and starts to drink it. There are now 19 students in the class. We can hear students running and yelling in the hallway and in the class next door that shares the room divider wall.

During the "copy notes" portion of the class, it is now relatively quiet in Mr. Barnes's classroom, but it is still very loud next door. Occasionally, you can hear the teacher, Mr. Webster, asking students to sit down. Mr. Barnes walks around the room while students are copying the notes, and he is writing some kind of notes in a journal that is sized like a large trade paper novel. About five students are copying down the notes. The rest of the students have their heads down, are playing on their phone, or are eating.

The objective of the eighth-grade social studies lesson, which has not been discussed, is written on the board. It states, "SWBAT [students will be able to] identify dissent." I am curious if students know what dissent means, as it has not been discussed. About 30 minutes into the class period, it sounds like the class next door is finally getting started, and I can hear the teacher speaking to the class.

After students have finished copying the notes, Mr. Barnes asks them to make an inference about their notes. They are supposed to write 3–5 sentences about this inference and then turn the assignment in. Mr. Barnes walks around and checks on a few students' work, and he says, "Excellent work" to one student.

During the time for students to write 3–5 sentences, a majority of students are on their phones, have their heads down, or are talking to other students. Amir and Haakim, who sit on opposite sides of the room from each other, are yelling insults back and forth. They get up and start play fighting, meaning that they are both laughing and pretending to throw punches at each other. They sit back down after Mr. Barnes asks them several times. After about five minutes of the inference assignment, the students are now allowed to answer the questions in groups. Mr. Barnes tells them again that they will turn this assignment in.

Ameena is eating another bag of chips, and other students are asking her for a chip. Jalayla is also eating chips, but she is hiding them in her backpack. Haliegh sees this and asks her for a chip. Jalayla refuses, and Haliegh says to Jalayla, "Don't be so light-skinned."[1] A few students ask Mr. Barnes to put the "notes" back on the projector. Students seem a bit unclear as to what they are supposed to be doing, and approximately two students are working on the assignment. Haakim and Amir start arguing again, and they are now chasing each other around the room. They are both laughing, but it appears as if they are going to start actually fighting.

The rest of the class is commenting on what Amir and Haakim are doing, and Mr. Barnes is following the boys around the room and asking them to sit down. Amir starts to get very angry and begins screaming at Haakim, and the two students begin to fight.

Almost immediately, Khalil breaks up the fight and separates the students just as it is almost time to change classes. Khalil walks Amir out of the classroom and appears to be trying to calm him down. The rest of the students get packed up and head out into the hallway to go to their next class.

As the students are getting packed up, Mr. Barnes tells me, "You might want to sit at my desk. The next class, seventh grade, coming in is really big." I move over to his desk. There is utter chaos as the students transition. Ms. Forbes, the Community Liaison, is upstairs blowing a whistle and yelling, "Get to class!" The seventh-grade students are slowly trickling into the room.

During the class change, there was a fight. From what I can gather from the students' conversations as they enter Mr. Barnes's room, a "big fat eighth grader" was fighting a "small seventh grader." It takes a long time for the students to get settled.

After about 10 minutes, students start doing the Do Now. One male student comes up to me and asks, "Are you Mr. Barnes's girlfriend?" I tell him that I am not, and he follows up with another question, "Do you work here?" I state that I do not. Another male student asks loudly, "Who is this young lady?" I state, "I am a researcher."

Kiandra states, "That is Ms. Nicole!" She comes over and gives me a hug. The class is pretty full about 10 minutes after class started. There are currently 23 students.

It is hard to count exactly because of my viewpoint at Mr. Barnes's desk and the lights are off. I have learned that he rarely turns them on so that it is easier to see what is on the projector screen. He also thinks it calms the students. Another male student walks in late. The class is talking to each other quietly. Mr. Barnes pauses and says that he is waiting for them to get quiet. There is screaming and hollering going on in the classroom next door.

Mr. Barnes says, "This is the 50th day of school and I am not getting a lot of respect. I am going to wait." He waits silently for a few minutes. "Class, it has been since early October that we did not get through a lesson." Mr. Barnes is still waiting for the students to be quiet. Some students are very frustrated and yell out, "Shut up y'all."

The students get quiet after a few minutes and continue working on the Do Now. It is very loud next door. I hear Mr. Webster yelling at his class. A few students get up and walk out of Mr. Barnes's room. Mr. Barnes walks over to me and says, "It is a really hard job, but it is also really rewarding to see how far the classes have come. Students cut class. There is a fight almost every day, as you saw. I can't believe it was worse last year."

He then continues walking around the room looking at students' work and jotting notes in his book. Mr. Webster is hollering next door; he says, "I am up at 5 AM every day planning lessons." A student yells out, "I am up at 8." Mr. Webster continues, "I come here every day despite being disrespected to help you make more money and improve your lives to help you live anywhere you want to live and so that you can have a better quality of life."

As students are working on the Do Now, Mr. Barnes says to me, "This class has come a long way. Normally it would take them a long time to get quiet."

"Do you like working here?" I ask. He responds, "I like working with my colleagues. And I like to see how far the students have come. This class, we used to not be able to do anything. It was utter chaos."

The students are supposed to learn about Columbus's atrocities, but they don't make it to the lesson because it took so long to come into the class and get started on the Do Now.

The class gets packed up and lines up to go to lunch. I walk downstairs to the lunchroom with them. The students are supposed to walk in two straight, quiet lines, one line for girls and one for boys, as it was at the school where I taught. There are not two lines, it is more like one large group, and the students are not quiet. We reach the lunchroom, and Mr. Barnes turns to me, "Are you going to come up with me?" I say, "No. I am going to hang out with the students during lunch." Mr. Barnes looks surprised, "OK. I'll see you later." (Fieldnotes, December 1, 2015)

Learning *Means Being Compliant*

All of the activities in Mr. Barnes's class were structured to control behavior, including the arrangement of the desks in rows (as opposed to groups), the instructional activities that primarily consisted of copying notes and the warm-up "Do Now," which took the entire 45-minute class period in the seventh-grade class, as well as the halfhearted insistence that students be silent and walk in straight lines to lunch.

Learning in this class, as well as many others throughout the school, was synonymous with being compliant. When Mr. Barnes discusses that the class has come so far, he is talking about students demonstrating compliance not learning. The classes consisted of uninspired learning activities that aligned with the notion that students at Baker "needed" structure and control because, as Mr. Barnes states, it was worse last year. Students do not fully buy into the rigid environment. For example, students' actions, such as their disregard for the "no eating in class" policy and Haliegh putting her middle finger up to another student, reflected the students' attempts to resist the controlling culture.

Although many students resisted these structures, students also expressed frustration when other students deliberately disregarded the rules or if a class was considered out of control. For example, the students in the seventh-grade class hollered at each other to be quiet. Both students and teachers appeared to internalize messages that schooling was about controlling behavior. For example, when students were asked about their day, they often responded by stating whether they got in trouble or "did work." Teachers spoke in the same terms, "She didn't do any work today" or "He did his work."

Work, for example, consisted of copying the notes in Mr. Barnes's class or completing a worksheet in another class. Schooling at Baker consisted of very little discussion or active engagement with concepts and learning. Instead, adults and students discussed school in terms of how compliant students were or were not. Student progress is measured by whether students are seated and able to get to the "copy notes" portion of a class rather than by student learning. At its "best," learning was reduced to the behavior of completing an assignment, along the lines of performing rote actions, and instruction resembled the transmission model of education discussed in chapter 1 (see Cochran-Smith & Lytle, 2009; Freire, 2000; Koretz, 2017; McLaren, 2015; Ravitch, 2011). This transmission and behaviorist model of education also directly translates to ways that the pedagogy of Baker School is preparing students for future work that involves following rules and procedures with little explanation or creativity and contributes to social reproduction and relegating students at schools like Baker to low-paying jobs (Anyon, 1980). In this regard, compliance was the standard of success at Baker.

Consequences of Compliance

Denise, a counseling intern from a local university who worked with Baker's school counselor, Ms. Johnson, discussed how the school needed more resources in general as well as specific training for staff. She specifically mentioned training for the teachers who worked in an emotional support classroom for students who were classified as having "emotional issues." Without prior discussion of control, Denise described how in this specific class, which had a much smaller student-to-teacher ratio, focused on controlling student behavior.

> Denise: I was there [in the Emotional Support class] an hour if not more every week because Ms. Johnson [the counselor] did a class there. Basically what I was told was that it was a special class for kids with emotional issues. I think it was referred to as Emotional Support. There was a little girl in there who asked, because I would ask a bunch of questions, and basically this one

little girl was just emotional.

They said pretty much all the kids had ODD [oppositional defiant disorder] or were diagnosed with ODD. It started off with seven kids with one head teacher and maybe three support teachers, and then [the number] got up by the time I left, because another school's teacher for that classroom in another school just left one day and never came back. So those kids had to be filtered to another school. It ended up being like eleven or twelve kids in that classroom, and that transition is hard for any child. So then it's like transitioning all these kids with similar issues in one classroom. And they had, they brought in, one more support teacher. There was one, two, three, four, five teachers in there and maybe twelve kids, and it was just, I mean it was chaos all the time.

Nicole: Really?

Denise: It was sad because a lot of them just needed individual attention. You did have a fair amount of teachers, but . . . I feel like more time was spent in that classroom on controlling the child's behavior, which is obviously important, rather than teaching. I feel like it was always "put on a movie because you are quiet" or I saw some things I didn't really like as far as restraints being used or things like that.

I know they had, after I left on Wednesdays, they had someone come in. I think he was from [the university] to do some type of cooking class with them, and they seemed to really like that. A lot of times I think Ms. Johnson would say they didn't get to go outside today, and, I'm like, those kids probably need playtime more than anyone, so they should be going outside. But they would spend so much time on getting them under control. Then it was difficult because a lot of the kids fed off each other, so they'd be more behavioral when one was more behavioral and that was part of the attention-seeking. That classroom literally was always chaotic and I know . . .

Nicole: They were young kids right?

Denise: They were, like I want to say, third grade and younger; like third through first or something like that, first through third. I know one of the kids who was very behavioral and always hard to deal with. I just sat down with him to do a worksheet. At first, of course, as most kids do, he was asking me for all the answers, and I wouldn't give them to him. But if I took the time to sit down with them and work with them, he got it.

But I also understand with thirteen kids you can't give everyone specific attention. Some of those issues . . . go to training, but [there are] also larger systemic issues that are at play within the school as far as their resources. I remember telling some of my professors, I was like, "This obviously isn't a critique for you, but a lot of the literature we read or a lot of just the things we are exposed to in schools do not prepare you for schools like Baker."

You have kids who aren't able to focus on academic work and you chuck it up to them being bad or not, I don't want to say, not being smart. But . . . They have so many outside factors going on that they need support for that they are not getting support for. How [do] you deal with that? I know with some of the students I talk to they were worrying about probation, they had parents in prison, they have been shot at, and things like that. They wouldn't have necessarily gotten support for . . . in school. Ms. Johnson is one person for all those kids, even if they did want to talk to her. And you don't really read too much about . . . [how] kids have all they worry about. We have kids who are trying to work already and are taking care of their siblings and all that stuff. They are trying to navigate and it's just going to be hard for anyone to be able to do. (Interview, July 25, 2016)

Denise and Mr. Barnes both described being unprepared for the type of problems they encountered at Baker. It is important to keep in mind that 75% (3 out of 4) of the middle school teachers at Baker are first year teachers, including Mr. Barnes, and many novice teachers struggle with what educators call classroom management, which refers to establishing norms, procedures, and routines in a classroom so that it is run smoothly and orderly. Novice teachers in urban schools that I have observed, taught, or coached are working hard to establish "control" while veteran teachers are working hard to maintain it. Denise explicitly discusses the pedagogical methods of controlling behavior (i.e., showing a movie), as well as deliberately keeping children inside because of the focus associated with controlling behavior. Despite the attempts at control, Denise still described the Emotional Support class as "always chaotic." Similarly, parents and students described the school as "bad" and "out of control." As Denise mentioned, students experience many outside factors that impact their feelings of safety and security. The systemic issues and lack of resources that impact schooling at Baker are discussed in more depth in chapter 6.

Denise explained how when she worked one-on-one with students, they did well. Students were aware of teachers' expectations. Depending on the teacher, students acted differently in different spaces. In one class, students sat in their seats and talked quietly. In other classes, middle school students refused to attend and instead they played "manhunt" (a combination of tag and hide-and-seek) in the hallways. When this happened, someone announced over the loudspeaker that broadcasted to the entire school: "The eighth-grade students in the hallway need to report to room 504 immediately."

Students made decisions about whether to attend class or complete assignments based on (1) if they liked their teacher and/or (2) if they believed that the work was worth completing. Despite the attempts to control students, students resisted, and in turn, teachers believed there was very little rule-following or enforcement at Baker. Like a vicious cycle, this exacerbated the problem and reinforced teachers' beliefs about the need to control students.

Mr. Barnes did not articulate being aware of attempting to control student behavior in the same way that Denise clearly described how instructional decisions were intended to promote compliance. However, a majority of Mr. Barnes's instructional activities were designed to limit chaos and disruption, which had the unintended impact of being unengaging. Mr. Barnes asserted that lack of accountability was the biggest problem in the school. What he described appeared to be ways that students resist what I am describing as a culture of control:

> There doesn't seem to be any [accountability] to the students, and I've heard these remarks so many times by the students themselves that they can get away with whatever they want and they're aware of that. There really aren't any consequences for their actions, so as teachers we are told if we are dealing with behavior, or academics, or what have you, the correct solution is to write up a pink slip and call home. And there are probably I would say 20 students who I've done that for on almost a weekly basis, and nothing happens. And you have students who remark on it. Who, for instance, I had a student who was just yelling and beating this other student yesterday and I asked, "Why are you doing that? What are you getting out of that? Why are you doing this?" And his response was "because I can."
>
> And like it's hard to come back from that because [pause] it seems from the top — from on high there is really nothing that will be done. We don't really suspend students, there's in-house here, aside from that, the consequences are pretty limited. We can't hold students after school for detention. (Interview, February 1, 2016)

Mr. Barnes articulated the frustration many teachers experienced because they did not believe that they were being supported in disciplining students. The attempts to control behavior at the classroom level (e.g., calling home and writing behavioral referrals to the office (pink slips) in addition to the other classroom structures described previously) did not have the desired effect. So, the entire school continued to be generally perceived as chaotic.

Although what I described as a "hidden curriculum" in chapter 1 may be visible to many people after these examples, remember that it is not the expressed or stated curriculum of the school or the district and thus functions as "hidden." As can be seen in the previous data excerpts, adults believe that they have no support from school leaders and believe they have no other choice but to control or subdue students in any possible way. Thus, an implicit curriculum of control emerges at Baker School, and one consequence of this is the deficit ideology about "inner-city" students. Furthermore, Baker School reproduces social inequalities by preparing low-income students for menial jobs or prison (Anyon, 1980; Bourgois, 2003; Bowles & Gintis, 1976; Edelman, 2012; Heitzeg, 2023; MacLeod, 2018). In the preface of the second edition of *In Search of Respect*, Bourgois writes, "The most vulnerable inner-city residents are the children of children. They are chewed up and spit out by the American Dream, only to find themselves years later at extraordinary financial and human cost to the prison industrial system" (2003, xxiii). Many of the students at Baker School potentially fall into this category, and some, as Rashanna discusses in chapter 4, are acutely aware of this possibility.

The teachers at Baker, many of whom were middle-class Black women, adopted a philosophy that they "had to yell." One faculty member, a veteran, Black, female teacher told me and another veteran teacher, "I might say 'please, be quiet' ten times, but the students won't listen to me until I scream, 'Shut up!'" The other teacher chimed in, "It is what they know. It is what they are used to" (Fieldnotes, December 11, 2015).

I heard many teachers, staff members, and fellow parents express this philosophy. Some adults adopted a mindset that there was nothing left to do but yell. However, this mindset came from highly negative assumptions about students and their families and home lives that many adults did not fully understand (see Gorski, 2023; Valencia, 2019). The mentality that students at this school had to be yelled at carried over in all environments of the school, even in the lunchroom, which is a place where students would ideally be able to have fun with their peers.

Controlling Chaos in All Spaces

From my experiences as a teacher, student, and researcher in numerous schools throughout the United States, I have never been to a lunchroom that is silent. Students are generally expected to remain seated while they are eating, but it is also expected that lunch is a time when students will socialize and talk to their peers. At Baker, the lunchroom was always a place of contention and chaos, even for the youngest students.

The seventh- and eighth-grade lunchroom was considered a place no one, including the students, wanted to be. After a visit to the seventh- and eighth-grade lunchroom, the secretary, a middle-aged Black woman, saw me leaving the cafeteria and asked me, "What were you doing in the jungle?" I did not respond because I did not know what she was talking about, and she asked me again, "What were you doing in the jungle?" I finally realized she was talking about the lunchroom after she walked away when I did not respond to her (Fieldnotes, December 1, 2015).

Students adopted a similar mentality that the lunchroom was a dangerous place. Kiandra, a seventh grader I knew from the after-school program, ran up to me in the cafeteria and exclaimed, "Ms. Nicooooole!" She walked up to me, gave me a hug, and asked, "What are you doing here?" I responded that I was hanging out to see what lunch was like. Kiandra then warned me, "Be careful. You might get beat up in here," and she ran off chasing Fahiym, a seventh-grade boy who also attended the after-school program. Kiandra ran back over to me, and I asked her what they did in the lunchroom. She responded, "Run around. Duh. We are kids." I smiled and laughed quietly and then asked if they go outside. She states, "Sometimes. Right now we are in trouble and can't go outside for recess" (Fieldnotes, December 1, 2015).

As Kiandra described, the seventh- and eighth-grade students were frequently "denied" recess after lunch. I came late to lunch one day and was surprised to find the seventh and eighth graders playing in the schoolyard. I remarked to the security officer, "I thought recess was canceled for the rest of the year." He responded, "It was supposed to be." I said, "I'm glad they are outside. Recess is a good thing." The security officer responded in a judgmental tone, "Well, they won't have recess in high school."

During recess, the adults (the disciplinarian, the lunchroom staff, the school police officer, and Mr. Kelly) stood against the wall closest to the auditorium and talked to each other. They occasionally hollered at students to come away from the fence where students often talked to older teens walking past the schoolyard. When students were not allowed to go outside, the adults stood in front of the doors to the cafeteria to try to prevent students from leaving. However, the students typically found a way into the schoolyard.

A Counternarrative to Compliance

Kiandra astutely pointed out that she and her peers ran around because they were kids. At Baker, it appeared as though the students were not allowed to be kids. Instead, their behavior needed to be controlled in all spaces of the school. In many public schools, including all of the 16 Philadelphia public and charter K–8 schools I spent considerable time in as a teacher or teacher coach, elementary and middle school students were expected to walk in two straight lines, one line for girls and one for boys. The younger students were supposed to "hip and lip" at some schools, including Baker. This meant students were to put one hand on their hip and one on their lip to remember to keep their mouth closed. Students at these underserved, urban, public schools are powerfully controlled in all spaces and grades.

In contrast, in the many resourced suburban schools and elite independent schools I researched or spent time in, students were allowed — and expected — to run around. This kind of physical freedom was seen as something they needed for their successful learning. I remembered the stark comparison seeing first-grade students at an independent school rush past me on their way toward the dining hall. No adults scolded them, but instead, a dean commented, "They should be running. It is good for them." The hidden curriculum of control and implicit policing at Baker implied that students in "these types of schools" (i.e., underserved, urban, public schools) should not be able to run or have recess.

Why is it that some children, who tend to be White and affluent, do not need to "hip and lip" and can run and play, while other children, who tend to be Black and poor, must be controlled in all spaces of school? Some scholars (e.g., Anyon, 1980; Apple, 2018; Noguera & Syeed, 2020) argue that this curriculum is by design to socialize poor children for low-paying jobs that require following directives, and that wealthy children are prepared for creative jobs that require independent thinking. In addition, structural and institutional racism impacts the experiences and outcomes for many students of color. Although primarily racially homogeneous in terms of staff and students, I believe that institutional racial stress undergirded the culture at Baker School. This included the often invisible, relational processes that resulted in "emotional overload or shock to an individual's coping system before, during, and after racial interactions" (Stevenson, 2014, p. 28).

Racial stress has not been studied as frequently in racially homogeneous settings, yet it is ever present (Stevenson, personal communication, December 15, 2017). The racialized stress I am describing is not really the racial stress experienced by individuals who are reacting to certain control mechanisms. I am describing *institutionalized* racial stress. Baker has Black leadership, Black students, and a majority of Black teachers and staff. However, the education system is designed for and by White people who have a long history of believing that Black, Brown, and poor students lack an internal locus of control and are likely to be unwieldy. Unfortunately, the adults as well as the students at Baker School internalized those beliefs, which contributed to the hidden curriculum of control. These racist ideas have deep historical roots in long-held conceptions of Black people as less than human and in need of corporal punishment and subjugation, which dates back to slavery and even before (David et al., 2019; Hinton & Cook, 2021; Jardina & Piston, 2021).

Yelling as a Control Measure

Just like at the urban public school where I taught for five years, lunch was often the place where fights occurred, and students got in trouble. Teachers at Baker did not have lunchroom duty; thus, students were in the lunchroom with nonteaching staff members who may not have known students well. Controlling the students was often even more difficult for these staff members, and at Baker they attempted to establish control by yelling. The kindergarten lunch, for example, consisted of Mr. Kelly, a tall, Black man, yelling at the students to sit down and be quiet.

> I stopped by the kindergarten lunchroom because I promised a few students in the schoolyard that I would say hello to them during lunch. Earlier that morning I also met a man, Mr. Kelly, who told me that he runs a structured recess program at the school during lunch, and I was excited to see what this program looked like, as I thought it might have been good to have something like this when I was teaching.
>
> Ultimately, I did not see structured recess. The lunchroom included a very noisy hum of kindergarten and first-grade students talking and running around. Students were repeatedly yelled at by Mr. Kelly to sit down and be quiet. There were about five other adults in the lunchroom, which was also the gym, who handed out the lunches to the students one at a time, and the line for lunch wrapped halfway around the gym.
>
> The lunches are prepacked meals that are heated under a lamp, as no food is prepared at the school. While I was helping a couple of kindergarten girls, Taylor and Malaya, who brought their lunch, open up their lunches and clean up a mess after juice spilled, I noticed some commotion in the back of the lunchroom. I learned a few minutes later from a university student volunteer that several students had accidents in the bathroom because they were not allowed to leave class to go to the bathroom because they are afraid the students would run the halls. "The kindergarteners are running the halls?" I asked. The volunteer says, "Yeah. That is what they think will happen." The students sit at tables separated by class and sex, meaning that the female students and male students for each class sit at different tables.
>
> The university student volunteer had been coming to the school since last year, and, without asking her anything, she told me that "Mr. Kelly has to be really mean, because last year it was utter chaos during the kindergarten and first-grade lunch." I speak to Taylor and Malaya for a few more minutes, and then I tell them that I need to head upstairs to see another

> classroom. They hug me and ask me to stay and play with them.
> I tell them that I will come to the playground with them tomor-
> row for recess. (Fieldnotes, October 6, 2015)

The university volunteer sums up the control mentality when she described that Mr. Kelly had to be mean and that students had to be controlled or else there would be "utter chaos." However, despite the attempts at controlling students and yelling, the lunchroom and the school was still universally described as "chaotic." During subsequent visits to the kindergarten and first-grade lunch, elementary students stated that Mr. Kelly yelled at them and made them "stand on the wall." Students who were "on the wall" were not allowed to play during recess, and they had to stand against the wall until their teachers picked them up. Isa, one of the first graders mentioned in the following fieldnote, articulated an example of how good behavior becomes synonymous with compliance, even in nonacademic spaces like the lunchroom.

> During the kindergarten and first-grade lunch, a group of first-
> grade girls called me over to their table. I squatted down at the
> end of their table. A girl got up and walked over to me. She said,
> "Hi. I'm Isa and sometimes I am bad in school, but I am going
> to take a deep breath and try to have a good day so that I can
> get an OK face." Students in the younger grades are sent home
> with behavior charts daily, and a smiley face is good, a frown
> face is not good. An OK face is neither a smile nor a frown and
> entails OK behavior.
>
> Nicole: Hi Isa.
>
> [Mr. Kelly walks by and yells, "Sit down!"]
>
> Liana: I'm Liana. L-I-A-N-A.
>
> Nicole: Hi Liana.
>
> Liana: I'm scared of Mr. Kelly.
>
> Nicole: Why?
>
> Liana: He makes you get on the wall.
>
> [Mr. Kelly walks right by our table.]
>
> Liana: Hi, Mr. Kelly!
>
> [Liana smiles at me and gives me a look while raising her

eyebrows, kind of like "see, he's scary." After she says this. Mr.
Kelly does not say anything to her.]

Nicole: What is the wall?

Liana: It is boring. You have to stay on the wall until your
teacher comes.
[I jot a quick note in my book.]

Liana: What are you doing?

Nicole: Research, so I am taking notes.

Liana: Does that mean that you are mean?

Nicole: No.

Liana: OK. Good.

[Mr. Kelly yells, "Sit down!"]

Liana: See? He says, "Sit down!"

Alexis: I'm scared of him too.

Nina: Me too.

Liana: My little brother is in my mom's belly. He name is "No
No."

[The first-grade girls want me to write down all of their names.
They are Chelsea, Isa, Alexis, Liana, Nina, and Noel.]

Nicole: Nice to meet you, Chelsea, Isa, Alexis, Liana, Nina, and
Noel. (Fieldnotes, December 8, 2015)

In addition to Liana's description of the control by fear and yelling atmosphere
in the lunchroom, Isa's statement about being "bad in school" and hoping to
get an "OK face" was further evidence of the hidden curriculum of control.
Teachers communicated with parents about student behavior rather than student
learning as evidenced in the behavior chart with the smile and frown faces that
Isa describes. Isa also internalizes these messages as, for instance, when she
first meets me she tells me that sometimes she is bad in school. Schooling for
Isa and the other students at Baker revolves around how well they behave.

A Different Stance on Yelling

Although a great many adults yell at students to get them to listen, some do not. Mr. Barnes was a first-year, White teacher who studied education as his undergraduate major. In the excerpt that follows, Mr. Barnes and I were talking in a stairwell because the gym teacher was teaching in Mr. Barnes's classroom, there was a meeting going on in the faculty breakroom, and it was loud everywhere else we tried to talk. Two students from Mr. Barnes's homeroom, who frequently tried to avoid being in class, stumbled upon us.

> Nicole: I want to continue something that really stood out to me that I've just been thinking a lot about, and this — I wonder where it comes from, I don't know if it's for you personally, or something you were taught at [School Name], or — but the idea that you're like, "I'm not going to yell at my students." Can you talk a little more about that?

> Mr. Barnes: I just don't see what it accomplishes. And I think as a kid you always kind of saw that the kids who got screamed at the most, screamed the most, you know. So it always seems like a perpetuating thing. I think it comes out of decent human decency if you're kind to people, you have a good shot that they'll be kind back to you. So I always say, "Please do this, please do that, sir, ma'am," and stuff like that. Even if I don't get shown respect, which I am disrespected on a daily basis, I think it has helped, no matter how minuscule. I think showing them that they are people and they deserve respect, just like I'm a person and I deserve respect, that all people deserve that basic human courtesy. I think that's a powerful thing, and I think yelling at someone violates so much of that. And that's like the thing like I first hear in the corporate world, you know, I feel like my boss is screaming at this guy and I can't imagine it. Like, you are adults! Like, I wouldn't even treat my thirteen-year-olds that way in such a condescending manner. Yeah, I'm not going to yell at you, you know. And it is like one of the more shameful things in life where it's like beginning this year when I was so depressed and so stressed, I did yell once. But just once, but it's like it's probably going to weigh on me to my dying day that I yelled, you know, and it was just like this sensory overload, and I can't — like I can't make an excuse for it but it was just like I felt like I was drowning and I just like had to yell to stop it. And it didn't. It made me feel crummy and terrible.

> Nicole: So do you think students pick up on it? Do they notice, like do you think that they appreciate it . . . ?

Mr. Barnes: Yeah. The other day one of my students said I was one of the nicest teachers in school, which I don't even think is true. But I think he picked up on the fact that I was asking someone to please sit in their seat, there was a kid who was running around, and I think they saw that most teachers would yell at them; whereas I say, "Please have a seat. Can you please do it?" And like, I get that it's a double-edged sword, because at one point you totally come off as a pushover. Like this Mr. Barnes isn't going to be, like, hard on us you know, and I think that's what they're used to. So I'm kind of setting myself up for failure in the discipline part of it because I think some of the best managed classrooms in this school have that really scolding kind of discipline that makes students feel lousy. It's effective, but I don't think it's good for the end product, you know. I don't think it helps the kids in the long run because then they're only becoming responsive to threats, and yelling, and all kinds of stuff like that. Speaking of . . .

[Bianca and Jalayla walk up to us.]

Nicole: Hi! What are y'all up to?

Bianca: Looking for Deshawn and helping in the office, but the office is full right now and they don't need us. What are you guys doing?

Jalayla: They're doing an interview, you can't tell?

Mr. Barnes: We're doing an interview.

Bianca: Oh, you all recording?

[Nicole and Mr. Barnes nod affirmatively.]

Bianca: Hi recorder.

Mr. Barnes: Do you guys remember that time I yelled at you?

Bianca: What time you yelled at me?

Mr. Barnes: Like when I actually raised my voice in the class, you remember that?

Bianca: No.

Mr. Barnes: You don't remember that?

Bianca: No.

Mr. Barnes: [Turning to Jalayla] Do you remember it?

Jalayla: I don't know. The last time . . .

Mr. Barnes: It was their class.

Jalayla: The last time you yelled at us is a long time ago.

Mr. Barnes: Yeah, that's the time I'm talking about. In October.

Nicole: Do other teachers yell at you?

Bianca: Mr. Webster sometimes. Ms. Jenkins because we be bad.

Mr. Barnes: Why do you think they yell at you?

Bianca: Because people be running around the class and stuff.

Mr. Barnes: How does that make you feel when you get yelled at? Like not just like, "Could you please sit down?" Like when someone raises their voice, say, to you like, "Bianca, blah blah blah."

Bianca: I gonna get mad back because — like if somebody yell at me, I'm not going to just let you yell at me because if you don't like to be yelled at, so why are you yelling at me?

Mr. Barnes: So it all makes you feel like disrespected?

Bianca: Um huh.

Mr. Barnes: OK. So what's the best way to get you to do something?

Bianca: So behave and do what you've got to do.

Mr. Barnes: No, I'm saying OK; let's say you're out of your seat you are across the classroom. What's the best way to get you in your seat doing your work?

Jalayla: To ask nicely.

Bianca: To ask nicely and — like if they don't listen just like just write them up.

Jalayla: Or just — I don't know.

Bianca: All right, you did well, just ask nicely.

Mr. Barnes: OK. Well, thank you, this concludes our interview.
(Group Interview, February 3, 2016)

Not surprisingly, students would rather not be yelled at. Thus, neither Mr. Barnes nor the students appreciated the "control as yelling" atmosphere. However, this atmosphere was dominant at Baker School.

Mr. Barnes, like a majority of other first-year teachers, struggled during his first year of teaching at Baker School. He was dedicated to his students, and he never missed a day of school until May, when he left to teach in a suburban district. Mr. Barnes had an especially hard year, and he was physically assaulted by students five times. In March, a serious assault occurred when Melvan, a seventh-grade student, slammed Mr. Barnes up against the locker inside the classroom multiple times because Mr. Barnes had confiscated Melvan's cell phone at the beginning of the class period. The school had a "no cell phone" policy. As you can see in figure 2.1, there was a sign in Mr. Barnes's classroom, as well as other classrooms, that had a picture of a crossed-out cell phone and the words "No Cell Phone Zone."

Mr. Barnes no longer felt safe at the school, and he also later felt like the school and district were punishing him for reporting the assault. Mr. Barnes prided himself on not yelling at his students, and many students believed Mr. Barnes cared about them because he "tried to teach" them. However, although Mr. Barnes did not yell at students, he was still a part of the hidden curriculum of policing and controlling behavior that, in this case, by policing student behavior and taking Melvan's phone, ultimately led to pressing charges and formal policing — even though that is not what Mr. Barnes wanted.

When Mr. Barnes decided whether he would press charges against Melvan, he spoke to many teachers at multiple schools in the district, and all of them had previously been assaulted and pressed charges against students. The American Psychological Association considers violence toward teachers "a silent national crisis" (American Psychological Association, 2016). This research occurred before the pandemic, during which one third of surveyed teachers (from March 2020 to June 2021) reported experiencing at least one incident of verbal or threatening violence from students during the pandemic and over 50% are considering quitting because of school climate and safety concerns (McMahon et al., 2022). Research suggests that teachers perceive school interventions to violent incidents to be inadequate (Moon et al., 2021), which can in turn contribute to more teachers leaving the profession (Walker, 2022). As past and recent research indicates, violence against teachers has long been an issue, and the pandemic has only made the issue more prominent and potentially worse.

The narrative of needing to control students is reinforced when teachers, like Mr. Barnes, who refused to yell at students, are physically assaulted. Mr. Barnes, like other novice teachers educated with progressive approaches to education, resisted the controlling nature of the school, but he attempted to teach without any structure, which further added to the control narrative and chaos at the school. Subsequently, the relationships between students and teachers at Baker were based on tension, stress, and a struggle for power, which I discuss in the next chapter.

Summary

At Baker School, a hidden curriculum of control emerged in which learning was forfeited for behavioral control. The culture of control at the school manifested by adults attempting to foster compliance in all spaces at the school was connected to assumptions that students at Baker "needed" controlling. The consequences of compliance and control are that it does not adequately serve students or teachers. Despite the attempts at control and compliance, Baker School continued to be described as chaotic. Both students and teachers contribute to this sense of chaos — with students "misbehaving" and teachers yelling. Good teachers were considered strict disciplinarians, and some of these teachers blamed the parents for the lack of discipline in the home, which is discussed more in chapter 4. However, this conclusion is superficial considering that the students at Baker were impacted by many forces beyond their control. A deficit narrative about Baker School and the children attending it developing as a result is discussed in more detail in chapter 5. An immediate consequence of culture and curriculum of control and compliance is the challenging relationships that emerge in this environment, and this is discussed explicitly in the next chapter.

Chapter 3

Relational Dynamics, Power Struggles, and Resistance

Students are controlled at schools like Baker, but so are the teachers. During this study, teachers' professional autonomy was becoming increasingly limited as schooling focused primarily on test preparation. There were several reasons for this limited autonomy, but the most important to teachers was the fact that the teaching profession had been widely regarded as a "semi-profession" for many years (Agopian, 2022; Ingersoll, 1999; Ingersoll & Collins, 2018), and teachers' perceptions of the de-professionalization of their work stemming from more scripted accountability measures increases teacher turnover and demoralization (Wronowski, 2021). This chapter begins by detailing the semi-professional status of teachers and how this comes into conflict with the relational dynamics at the school and the ways that students resist the culture of control described in the previous chapter.

Teachers' Semi-Professional Status

There are a variety of explanations for teachers' semi-professional status. For one thing, teaching has historically been, and still is, an occupation dominated by women. For another, there is a widely held and derogatory assumption that "anyone can teach." Third, because teaching is influenced by laypersons, including noneducator school board members, it often produces subpar working conditions and compensation, especially in urban districts. The professional status of teachers has been further limited by policies such as the No Child Left Behind, Race to the Top, and Every Student Succeeds Acts and similar standards and accountability reforms that require high-stakes testing, value-added teacher evaluations, fast-track teacher licensure and preparation programs, and scripted curricula that decrease the amount of autonomy that teachers have over their work (see, e.g., Agopian, 2022; Carl, 2014; Guerriero & Deligiannidi, 2017; Mathis & Welner, 2015; Milner, 2013; Wronowski, 2021).

Teachers at Baker frequently discussed how they were told to implement a different curriculum, program, or test-taking strategy at every professional development session. Ms. Smith made several comments similar to this one: "Well, class, we were going to have a science lesson, but we have to work on textual evidence with this handout by the end of the day." When I respond to

Ms. Smith that I can relate to that experience from my time as a teacher, Ms. Smith asks:

> Ms. Smith: Where did you teach?
>
> Nicole: [School Name].
>
> Ms. Smith: Oh, OK. Because if you taught somewhere else, I would wonder if you knew what you were talking about. But you get it and understand the students that are at our school. Writing with them takes a long time. It is also the time. We have people coming everyday checking to make sure that we are on track. We have so much to do and so much monitoring. (Fieldnotes, November 30, 2015)

Some teachers, including Mr. Barnes, were involved in external activist organizations. Teachers in these organizations often stated that participation helped to enhance their professional autonomy. However, these organizations have had limited appeal because of their perceived political nature (Quinn & Carl, 2015). Although some teachers have attempted to expand their influence through involvement in external organizations, what is important to note here is that teachers are still being controlled, monitored, and assigned lesser status.

Relational Dynamics

At Baker, teachers were trying to control student behavior, and this resulted in a struggle for ultimate power. The relationship between students and teachers, which is considered one of the most important aspects of schooling and student achievement (e.g., Kuriloff et al., 2017; Raider-Roth, 2005; Sethi & Scales, 2020; Stevenson, 2014; Walker & Graham, 2021), was seriously strained and in many cases broken. Instead, relationships between students and teachers often turned into battles for control.

These power struggles created an environment in which students and teachers were positioned (and then positioned themselves) in opposition to each other. One example is that teachers and staff looked for anything to make the controlling of student behavior easier. For example, some teachers and other staff at Baker had the mentality that the fewer students that came to school, the "easier" the day would be, meaning there would likely be fewer disruptions or behavior issues to contend with. They would be "relieved" when students were ousted, either temporarily (suspensions or absences) or permanently (expulsion). This created a system that automatically sought punitive opportunities and measures.

Children as a Burden

For example, when Nyeisha, whom Ms. Smith considered a "problem" student, was absent or had been removed to another room, Ms. Smith once commented to me, "Nicole, I'm so sad you missed our lesson on synonyms and antonyms. Nyeisha was not here, and we were able to get so much done." Ms. Smith and other teachers believed that their struggle to control behavior would be easier when students like Nyeisha were absent. Mr. James, the director of the after-school program, articulated a similar mentality in the following fieldnote:

> It was about 5:30 p.m., and I was getting ready to leave. I stopped by the after-school programming room to say goodbye to James, the director of the after-school operations at Baker. James asked me, "How was cooking class today?" [I responded,] "We had a nice time. I was with the red team today, and we made a good quinoa dish. However, there were few students participating, and a lot of students were running around the gym." James said, "Yeah, I know. We kind of just let them run around in there if they are not into it." I responded, "I have noticed in general that there seem to be fewer and fewer students attending cooking club." He responded, "Good. Especially on a day like today." (Fieldnotes, November 30, 2015)

Mr. James and other staff members frequently made similar comments expressing relief when students were not there, when engagement went down, and when they could "get rid of" their "troublemakers." If Mr. James saw me before the formal school day was over, he often asked, "How many fourth graders are here today?" He would then get visibly pleased when I said there were several absent or a specific student was absent.

It is important to note that most teachers would like smaller classes because they believe that they can be more effective when they have fewer children to teach. However, at Baker, the hidden curriculum of control enforced a primary focus on suppression rather than interaction. Thus, when "problem" children were absent or when a large number of students were not at school, adults believed that it was easier on those days to control behavior and teach. Even in spaces where academics was not the central focus, including in the after-school program, controlling behavior was paramount and "problem kids" were considered impediments. Part of teachers' desire to do this may have been related to their own conceptions of what made a "good" or "bad" teacher.

Faulty Teacher Assessments

Indeed, the hidden curriculum of control was reinforced by preconceived notions about who was a "good" or "bad" teacher and why. At Baker and schools like it, including the school I taught at for five years, teachers were celebrated or denigrated because of their ability to "control their class." Parents, students, staff, and administrators spoke in the same terms: *Good teachers control their classes and bad teachers do not.* Danielle, a grandparent and occasional volunteer, believed that controlling your class meant not taking "any stuff" from children. Describing a teacher who was threatened by a student the previous school year after the student was caught watching porn on the teacher's phone, Danielle stated:

> He [the student] told him, "You better not get me in trouble." It was like, I think if the boy had pushed him or something like this, the man, he really would not have been able to defend himself because it would look like . . . with him being the adult. But this boy actually threaten[ed] him. I would say you can't come back in my classroom ever. I'm going to call the police because you're threatening me now. You know how things are in the streets? They might try to bring somebody up here or some of the other boys might jump him in the classroom. He's just here to trying to teach. I really felt bad for him. (Interview, June 21, 2016)

The teacher Danielle is referring to, and all of the other middle school teachers that year, did not come back to Baker the next year. The rest of the staff had mixed reactions to these teachers. Some made comments, such as "It is crazy up there [the middle school wing]," "Those kids are out of control," "The teachers really tried, but they couldn't control their classes." Students also adopted this language of dominance. For example, if a student was asked why he or she was cutting class, a common response was, "I don't want to go to her class. She don't do nothing, and she can't control her class."

However, rather than blaming the teacher for "not controlling" his or her class or the student for cutting class, we should think about the *relationships* between the teachers and students as a way to reframe the issue (see Toshalis, 2015). At Baker, the relationships between teachers and students as well as the relationships between students and the school were deeply strained. As a result of the hidden curriculum of control and policing, students and teachers understood each other and interacted within a continual power struggle. Cutting class was one way that students demonstrated resistance, or what I call *micro-resistance strategies.*

Micro-Resistance Strategies

It has long been held that compulsory schooling and dominant schooling strategies often result in students resisting constraints put on them in the form of behavioral norms and imposed curricula (Waller, 1932). Resistance can be interpreted as a reaction to oppressive systems regardless of how unproductive that resistance may ultimately be (e.g., Ogbu, 1978; Willis, 1977). Ogbu's (2003) framing of such resistance assumed that Black students unconsciously decided to disengage because they did not want to "act White." Subsequent research refuted Ogbu's claim and stated that all students, regardless of race, were achievement oriented (Tyson et al., 2005) and are instead burdened by structural, institutional, and interpersonal racism (Tyson & Lewis, 2021). The danger in Ogbu's theory is that it reinforces myths of equality of opportunity that do not actually exist for a majority of students in underserved schools and communities.

Thinking about student behavior, or in this case what is generally considered student misbehavior, as a form of resistance to punitive or disaffirming external forces can help educators consider the various reasons why students act a certain way (Toshalis, 2015). Considering resistance as important information about students can be a way to engage instead of punish, police, or control them (Toshalis, 2015). Micro-resistance strategies can be viewed as ways that students respond to their environment. If educators attempt to understand students' experiences, they can help students redirect their efforts.

Students' primary way of resisting, especially in the middle grades at Baker School, was cutting class. The middle school students frequently cut class, came late to class, and spent considerable amounts of time hiding and/or playing games in the hallway. As discussed in the previous chapter, students began to skip class as early as kindergarten. Even many students who were considered by teachers as "good" did everything possible to avoid class. Their responses varied from "we're not learning nothing," "he don't be teaching us," "he picks on me," or "it is boring in there."

I spent countless hours in the classroom, and instruction frequently consisted of copying "notes" verbatim as they were written on the PowerPoint or board in middle school history classes or in answering questions on a generic worksheet in a fourth-grade class. Instruction times were often few and far between in the middle school classes. Teachers had a hard time getting through a lesson because of fighting, arguing, or other disruptions. Throughout the fieldnotes and interviews presented in this chapter and the previous chapter, there are many other examples of behavioral infractions that highlight ways students attempted to resist a culture of dominance and control.

Another micro-resistance strategy that students employed was when they responded with the phrase "I don't care." For example, Nyeisha was often yelled at for being late or not having her homework complete the very minute that she walked into Ms. Smith's class. Nyeisha tended to respond by yelling back: "I don't care! Stop messing with me." Then Ms. Smith immediately became angry at her for talking back to a teacher, and Nyeisha's day is already off to a rocky start. Students in other grades often responded to teachers or other staff by stating, "I don't care." These comments, which occur often from multiple students in all grades, are interpreted as students lacking motivation and discipline. Of course, taking the time to interpret the motivations and reasons behind students' micro-resistances, which may be because they do not feel safe or respected, can help educators to include instead of exclude students. This responsibility should not solely belong to teachers, who are often unfairly blamed and struggling, without support, and who themselves are controlled in a system that confers dominance on certain kinds of teaching. To engage, rather than exclude, students involves systematically reenvisioning and resourcing urban public schools to help address the multiple issues facing the schools and communities.

Challenging Dominance

Thus far, I have discussed micro-resistance strategies that students use to challenge dominant structures. In this next section, I explore how students challenge dominant structures and control mechanisms by using violence, overt aggression, or other forms of resistance. From the explicit and implicit curriculum, students at Baker learned that they were in "need" of being controlled and that there were limited opportunities for them to succeed — both in and out of the classroom.

Students, especially seventh- and eighth-grade students, were beginning to mistrust school and the opportunities it claimed to provide for them. They still internalized messages of success that involved "staying in school" (Jalayla), "not letting other kids bring them down" (Bianca), and "doing my work" (Renee). But the middle school students were also aware of the limited opportunities that were the reality for their parents. For example, Jalayla, Bianca, Rashanna, and Renee's fathers (along with many fathers of children in the school) were in jail along with some of their siblings.

In an environment dominated by narratives of control, who needs to be controlled, and chaos, students developed certain sensibilities in order to survive and thrive. The sensibilities are related to Bourdieu's concept of *habitus*, individuals' habits of heart and mind that influence how they react and respond to and in situations. Habitus is developed throughout a person's life, but the adolescent and childhood years have the most formative influence (Bourdieu, 1977, 1984, 1989).[1] Habitus involves the ways that individuals unconsciously learn how to act in situations that are influenced by their perceived opportunities (Bourdieu & Passeron, 1977). From the implicit policing practices and the attempts to control them, which often do not succeed in the ways adults would like, students at Baker were cultivating a *habitus of fierceness*.

Habitus of Fierceness

This habitus of fierceness is a mechanism for surviving in schools when students' learned experiences and reactions differ from the institutionally valued and mainstream forms of habitus and symbolic capital (see Bourgois & Schonberg, 2009; Wacquant, 1998). Furthermore, this habitus of fierceness, which includes students' micro-resistance strategies, functions as a form of coping (see Stevenson, 2014). For example, students often demonstrate this habitus when the behaviors the school attempts to inculcate do not align with their own inclinations. It is important to remember that habitus functions at a "preconscious level," and habitus is often "misrecognized as natural attributes" (Bourgois & Schonberg, 2009, p. 42). Thus, thinking of the habitus of fierceness that students exhibit as a coping mechanism is one way to avoid thinking of this behavior as a deficit.

Physical Aggression

At Baker, students performed a habitus of fierceness in multiple ways. For example, some students, like Talik, were overtly physically aggressive and violent. He frequently fought with peers, punched walls, and threw and broke objects. At the beginning of January, Mr. Barnes asked students to reflect on their goals. The following fieldnote includes Talik's goals for 2016.

> I was talking to Talik, and I asked if he could tell me about his goals. I read them, and I asked if it was OK if I wrote them down. He said, "Sure." They read: "Talik's 2016 goals. My 1st goal is to make it thru 2016 alive. The 2nd goal is to graduate 8th grade. Last but not least I want to make my family happy by dropping all negative feelings."
>
> These were written neatly on a piece of white computer paper, and they were written in different colors and decorated with a few intricate designs. Talik is tall and skinny and his hair is in cornrows. I asked him about his first goal.
> Talik: The news says lot of people be dying.
> Nicole: Are you scared?
> Talik: A little. I have a temper, but I get good grades.
> (Fieldnotes, January 5, 2016)

Talik's mother, Rachele, worked with Talik to help him "control his behavior." This was the goal after the report card conferences, which I observed with Talik and his mother and teachers. Talik acknowledged that his "temper" could have serious repercussions, and his mother was trying to support him to stay on track. Talik's teachers also appeared to be invested in him and were working with his mother to help him get into a better high school that had more arts programs. According to his mother, he was heavily influenced by his peers, as most children his age are.

However, at the end of the school year, the teachers seemed to have given up on Talik, and I saw him get into more frequent fights. He told me, reluctantly but with a smile, that he was the one who punched the window in Mr. Webster's room and that he broke the glass on the hallway door. When I asked him why, he said, "Because they made me mad." Reflecting on Talik's behavior toward the end of the school year, Talik's teacher, Mr. Barnes, stated:

> I am 99% certain that he is on drugs. Yeah, because of how erratic his behavior was, how just explosive he could be at times and then totally sedated at others. So unless he is severely bipolar which, again, could be possible, but it was also not consistent throughout the year either, particularly as we got to the end. He would just stand up and walk around in a daze, just like something seemed so wrong and it kind of came out of nowhere.
>
> It wasn't just him messing around. There was something was seriously wrong with this guy. Again, we didn't have anyone to refer to, so on the pink slips I would just be like symptomatic of marijuana use and stuff like that. I was trying to report it as best as I could and nothing came. I don't know what the school policy is if you suspect someone is on drugs, but I didn't ever see anything. I didn't even see any confrontation happen. I don't know if that's because my pink slips ever got read or not. (Interview, August 1, 2016)

Being Tough

While Talik's situation was complex, at the root of his behavior, and the behavior of many students at Baker, was that they did not want to show weakness or fear. Students' habitus is formed by a variety of factors related to their perceived opportunities in different environments. While the "laws" of schools are different from the "streets," protection behaviors learned in the community carry over into the school (Coates, 2015). Thinking of Talik as "bad" or "violent" misrecognized the multiple factors, including systemic racism as well as daily life in Talik's neighborhood, that informed why Talik believed that he could not show weakness. A habitus of fierceness can be thought of as similar to Anderson's (1999) "code of the street" in that individuals are attempting to prevent future violence and protect themselves. However, a habitus of fierceness does not sort students and families into two categories of "decent" and "street" (Anderson, 1999).

Other students were not frequently physically aggressive, but they still took on identities based on not appearing scared. Jalayla, for example, said that she does not have to fight anymore; people knew she was "not scared." She communicated that she felt strongly that she had proven herself to her peers. In this regard, Jalayla accomplished a habitus of fierceness because she did not need to fight anymore. Every seventh- and eighth-grade student I spoke with, which was approximately 75% of the students, had been in at least one physical fight in school. A common response was "If someone puts their hands on me, I put my hands on them." Logically, they knew they should tell a teacher. But teachers, for a variety of reasons, did not always respond, at least in a way that was satisfactory to students. In the following transcript, Jalayla described how she got into an argument with a younger student who had been picking on her younger brother. Jalayla said that she was just screaming at the girl and could not calm down.

> Jalayla: The girl in sixth grade, she was hitting my little brother. My little brother came and got me and told me. I was walking around the school looking for her. When her teacher told me she was in the classroom, I went in there and I started yelling and screaming at her.
>
> Nicole: Do you think that there could have been any other response?
>
> Jalayla: Probably could have just told her teachers, but that was the one that hadn't did nothing.
>
> Nicole: How come?
>
> Jalayla: Sometimes the teachers don't say nothing. So, I just took it upon myself to say something to her myself.
>
> Nicole: I'm curious, how many times have you told a teacher and nothing happens?
>
> Jalayla: A few times.
>
> Nicole: Can you maybe give me an example?
>
> Jalayla: For instance, a boy can hit you and I go tell the teacher, "He hit me." The teacher blame it all on me and say, "Well, if you wasn't in this place and you was over there where you are suppose to be, then none of that would had happened."
> (Interview, June 10, 2016)

I saw the situation Jalayla described many times at Baker, so it was not surprising that students adopted a mentality of addressing problems themselves.

To many students and parents that I encountered at Baker, fighting could also be necessary: "If someone hits you, you hit them back." Renee discussed when one might need to fight and talked about how students had a logic behind what they did.

> Renee: [Talking about another school]. No. Nope. We don't smoke in the bathroom, we might fight, but we don't fight-fight, like they [at the local high school] do. They be having riots, they be jumping people there. We don't jump people here and do all of that stupid stuff.

> Nicole: I remember hearing about them jumping that new boy.

> Renee: What new boy? Oh! No, not that new boy. Well, yeah. I heard that he got jumped. That was outside of school, that was some other people. They never jumped inside of school. I know they tried to, but they usually don't though because it's not right to jump people.

> Nicole: Right. So when is it OK to fight?

> Renee: It's not. If you have to fight, you have to fight. That's it. It's not OK to fight all of the time.

> Nicole: Are there some rules that everybody just knows? I'm not meaning rules-rules, but people know that in this situation, you needed to fight. How do people know that?

> Renee: Are you feeling threatened? If somebody keep messing with you, keep messing with you, just keep picking with you, keep pushing you to the point and you feel threatened, you have to. They keep hitting you and stuff, you've got to hit them back. You can't just let somebody keep messing with you, keep messing with you, keep messing with you, 'cuz it's going to be irritating.

> Nicole: Mm-hmm [affirmative].

> Renee: Yeah that's irritating. Mess with you, mess with you, and mess with you.

> Nicole: Mm-hmm [affirmative]. Fighting is kind of a way of standing up for yourself?

Renee: Yeah.

Nicole: Have you been in a fight?

Renee: Yeah [smiles]. A couple of times, but yeah.

Nicole: What happened?

Renee: Somebody kept saying stuff to me, and I got irritated. I've got issues, anger issues, so I just kept getting mad. The person kept saying stuff so I got up and that person got up. She got in my face and I pushed her out of my face, then she hit me, then we started fighting. Then I blacked out.

Nicole: You blacked out?

Renee: Yeah.

Nicole: Did you go to the hospital?

Renee: No. I blacked out when we was fighting. After we stopped fighting, I was all right [sniffs].

Nicole: What does that mean, you blacked out? You don't remember anything?

Renee: I don't remember what happened during the fight. She punched me then I hit her, then that's it. They said I scratched her and stuff and pulled her hair, and I don't remember that.

Nicole: When was this?

Renee: This was last year.

Nicole: What did your grandmom say?

Renee: She didn't say nothing. I told my mom and she was like, "Well, you had to fight, you had to fight."

Nicole: Mm-hmm [affirmative]. Did your grandmom know you got into a fight? No?

Renee: Nuh-uh [negative].

Nicole: What would she have said?

> Renee: "Why are you always fighting?" and all of this other stuff.
>
> Nicole: So your grandmom doesn't want you fighting?
>
> Renee: No.
>
> Nicole: How come?
>
> Renee: I don't know. I think she doesn't want me to go to jail and stuff. Get into trouble and messing up going to high school and stuff.
>
> Nicole: Is that why you don't fight anymore?
>
> Renee: Yeah, and people don't mess with me so I don't fight.
>
> Nicole: You felt like, after you fought, people realized that "OK, I'm not going to pick on Renee anymore?"
>
> Renee: I don't know. They probably did.
>
> Nicole: Mm-hmm [affirmative].
>
> Renee: But they don't mess with me. (Interview, May 13, 2016)

Renee offered a counternarrative to the one-dimensional view of fighting as universally "bad" and reinforced how broadly associating fighting as negative did not consider the survival logics that students cultivated and that reflected their habitus of fierceness.

Many students, like Renee, described needing to have a reputation as someone who "can't be messed with." In communities that experience high levels of poverty and violence, combined with limited economic opportunity, strategic violence toward others can generate respect and prevent future conflicts (Bourgois, 2003; Brotherton & Barrios, 2004). Jalayla, an eighth-grade student, describes how the school changed her: "I really felt myself changing once I hit fourth grade. I would get into fights with teachers, throwing chairs, fighting, cursing, all that stuff. Every time the teachers used to tell my parents, then my parents they seemed shocked because they never thought I would be that type of girl." When I asked why, Jalayla stated:

> Jalayla: Well in this school, I just had to show people. [Pause]. I don't know. I just had to show people that I'm not really scared. Just because I'm short that don't mean I'm not going to say anything or do anything.
>
> Nicole: How do you show people you're not scared?

> Jalayla: By sticking up for yourself, like fighting back. I'm not going to let nobody child bully me because I'm shorter than y'all or anything like that.
>
> Nicole: What happens if you don't stand up for yourself?
>
> Jalayla: They just going to keep picking with you because you not doing anything back, not saying anything. (Interview, June 10, 2016)

In their environment, there was a real possibility that students at Baker could be picked on and harmed if they were perceived as weak. Thus, while such behaviors were typically considered negative by schools, teachers, and others, students were clear that they were adapting to their environments and "doing what needed to be done" to protect themselves. Other important considerations included that students did not feel safe or protected at school; in the absence of protection, students protected themselves. In addition, the students at Baker School knew the "rules" associated with demonstrating a habitus of fierceness, which included standing up for oneself or one's family, not "starting stuff," and "doing what you need to do." Students also knew when the benefit outweighed the cost (if it was worth fighting), to protect themselves. Finally, students knew what the limits were, which may include jumping someone for no reason.

The mindset of not showing fear by acting / being tough was reflected not only by students but by teachers and administrators. For example, the principal at the school where I taught for many years would often get into screaming arguments with parents, and other teachers had to hold her back on numerous occasions when she took off her earrings and charged a parent. Teachers at Baker would also comment directly to students that they were not afraid of them. Ms. Smith, a fourth-grade teacher at Baker, "got in students' faces" daily and made comments, including, "Hit me. Hit me and see what happens. I don't play with these children." Fear and intimidation became an important concept/process at Baker, and no one wanted to appear afraid.

The teachers that students respected were the ones they believed were not afraid of them. Jalayla, Bianca, Renee, and Rashanna described their favorite teachers to me.

> Jalayla: It's like this. It's not a racist thing. Usually White teachers, the first thing they say, "I'm going to press charges on you if you hit me, if you do this stuff like that." A Black teacher will be like . . .
>
> Renee: I'm hitting you back.
>
> Jalayla: Yeah.
>
> Rashanna: Like, Ms. Ferguson and Ms. Glenn, they'll pull out a broom on you in a minute.

All: Yeah.

Jalayla: Ms. Glenn will pull out a broom on you.

Nicole: Really?

Rashanna: Yeah, she'll pull out a broom on you.

Nicole: A Black teacher would hit you back and a White teacher would not. But could a White teacher hit you back? Or would . . .

Jalayla: The cool ones would, like some of them. Some of the teachers would.

Rashanna: Mr. Webster might.

Renee: Yeah, because he's from the hood.

Rashanna: They hit Mr. Webster with the ball and he popped it with the scissors in front of they face and threw it back at them.

Jalayla: Mr. Crowley he will sit there, he'll write you up, he'll press charges.

Rashanna: Yeah, because he definitely threatened to press charges on me if my dad didn't come to get me that day. I heard him, he was trying to be sneaky, but he was super loud that day. He talking about if you don't do nothing about it then I'm going to press charges right now. I'm calling the cops. (Group Interview, June 15, 2016)

Rashanna, Renee, Jalayla, and Bianca described Ms. Glenn and Ms. Ferguson in ways that clearly showed that the students believed these teachers cared about them. In this schooling context, it is clear that these teachers were also developing a habitus of fierceness — just as I did as a teacher in order to survive and thrive in a particularly fraught and tense environment. Students would say about me, "Don't mess with Ms. Mittenfelner. She is just as crazy as we are." At the heart of that comment was a belief, at least I like to think, that students knew that I cared about them. I approached them within an asset-oriented framework that guided me to engage these kinds of issues and behaviors firmly and directly rather than simply scolding, deriding, or punishing them for some of their less-desirable (but nonthreatening) actions.

Other staff members, however, like Ms. Forbes, the Community Liaison, behaved aggressively toward students but did not garner student respect because of *how* she did so. Ms. Forbes, a Black woman in her 50s, often ran around the school with a whistle hollering (often with rage in her tone and manner) at students to go to class. She did not have a reciprocal relationship with students and used her power to antagonize them. Her behavior was instead interpreted as disrespectful, even though it appeared that Ms. Forbes was trying to mimic what she believed to be student behavior. For example, Ms. Carol and her grandsons discussed a time when Ms. Forbes antagonized a student.

> Andrew: Ms. Forbes, she can get smart. She antagonizes students.
>
> Ms. Carol: One of the kids, I think her name was Jayden.
>
> Nicole: I know her. She's in eighth grade, right?
>
> Ms. Carol: Yes.
>
> Nicole: Yes.
>
> Ms. Carol: She was coming up the hall, and she said something disrespectful to Ms. Forbes. [Cat meowing in the background.] That's Jayden, you be the bigger person, you be the adult. Whatever. Forbes took something from her. She said you better give it back. Forbes says, "I'm not giving you back nothing." So Ms. Forbes called the [name of case worker organization] people; the people came down. As Jayden was walking, she's walking behind the girl, stand up Jalil. [Ms. Carol is yelling and demonstrating what Ms. Forbes was doing.] "Ha, ha, What you going to do? Ha, ha ha ha! What you going to do? What you going to do?"
>
> Nicole: Ms. Forbes was doing that?
>
> Ms. Carol: Yes. That's antagonizing all right.
>
> Nicole: Oh my goodness.
>
> Ms. Carol: Yeah, that's abuse. The case worker came down with Ms. [pause] not Ms. Hill, Ms. Hill's boss. I think her name is Margaret.
>
> Andrew: The Africa lady?
>
> Ms. Carol: No, not Ms. Lee. She's their boss, I can't think of her name. Anyway, she comes in, she walks rather fast, tall, short hair, I can't think of her name. Anyway, when Forbes came back, she said she's [Jayden's] so disrespectful. I said,

"Forbes, you made a mistake." I said, "You antagonized that child, and you did it in front of the case worker supervisor." She looked at me, I said, "You followed her from the auditorium out the door to the steps. You were wrong." She looked at me, and Ms. Ameile said, in the kitchen, she said, "Oh Ms. Carol, I'm surprised you said anything." Because she was wrong. Forbes looked at me, and she went upstairs. I'm thinking she might have went to the [name of the social outreach organization]'s room. When she came downstairs she was rather nervous, I could tell by her body language, because she was wrong.

Nicole: Yeah.

Jalil: Was this from last year?

Ms. Carol: No. This was two weeks ago. I was telling the kids how she is, and she did. If someone had asked me, you did it. You were wrong. (Group interview, April 28, 2016)

As Ms. Carol describes in the preceding story, Ms. Forbes did not comprehend that she did not understand students' experiences and behavior. In a way, she tried to mimic a habitus of fierceness but was not able to achieve the respect she wanted because students want adults to care about and respect them, not to intimidate and mock them.

Summary

In a culture of control and chaos combined with limited teacher autonomy, teachers and students engage in power struggles for control in this schooling environment that places teachers and students in opposition to one another. Teachers blame students and are often relieved when certain students are absent and the struggle for control is lessened. Students, through micro-resistance strategies such as declaring they do not care or cutting class, push back against the culture of control at Baker School and navigate this environment by demonstrating a habitus of fierceness. The habitus that students cultivate demonstrates resilient and adaptive problem-solving, which are necessary skills for their environment in and out of school. In this regard, both teachers and students are operating in survival mode at Baker School. To think about this habitus from a resource instead of a deficit orientation involves understanding students' experiences and trying to learn from, instead of controlling, their behavior. However, this habitus can also be misinterpreted and reinforce the chaotic narrative that students at Baker "need" to be controlled. Students' experiences outside of school and the multiple contextual factors that impact their schooling experience are discussed in more detail in the next chapter as students are simultaneously parentified and infantilized in the curriculum of control.

Chapter 4

Parentification and Infantilization of Students

The perpetual disinvestment of urban schools and neighborhoods contributes to the distrust parents and the local community feel about the school and the way that staff engage with parents. Many teachers and staff members accuse parents of being uninvolved, and, as this chapter describes, students become "parentified" as they take on roles considered to be more typical of adults, and at the same time students are infantilized in the curriculum of control that attempts to control student behavior. This chapter begins by describing common narratives about parents whose children attend urban underserved schools and presents examples and counterexamples of these narratives. The chapter then demonstrates how students are simultaneously parentified and infantilized through the curriculum of control at Baker School.

The Disengagement of Parents and Guardians

Parents are central stakeholders in education. Yet, urban public school systems tend to not view them as such. While teachers and staff members often describe parents as "uninvolved" and "not engaged," many schools and districts have failed to engage them (Allen & White-Smith, 2018; Auerbach, 2002, 2007, 2012; Posey-Maddox & Haley-Lock, 2020). Despite trying for decades to increase parental involvement, public school systems continue to try to engage parents, many of whom are living in poverty, in the same ways that they engage middle-class parents (Lareau, 2019; Lareau & Horvat, 1999; Lareau & Shumar, 1996). Although these strategies of engagement do not work (and never have), schools and districts continue the same actions and are surprised when they get the same results.

Because the behaviors of these parents do not conform to middle-class parenting values, parents in these environments tend to be perceived as "not caring," "uninvolved," and "lazy." This rhetoric is a classic example of a deficit orientation (see, e.g., Kennedy & Soutullo, 2018; Valencia, 2010), and describing parents in these terms overlooks the continuing failure of multiple systems that has contributed to the lack of economic and educational opportunities (see Anyon, 1997, 2005). The education system was not "successful" for many parents whose children attend Baker, and yet educators and policymakers are consistently asking parents to trust and believe in this system. Danielle, a grandparent who has three grandchildren and two great-nieces attending Baker and whose five children and their father went to Baker, explains why parents do not come to the school.

> Danielle: I'm not sure if the parents have just stopped caring because the system has failed so much, maybe for them, in certain instance[s] or whatever, but it's really hard to pinpoint why. I guess if we could figure out why, we wouldn't have that problem. We could get them here — back to school night. As a parent, I would want to come, I want to be there, I want to see who's who and get that one-on-one with the teacher so you can know who the teacher is so you can have that relationship . . . Sometimes what's going on at home you can't really, you may not have money to get there and that might be the case. The parents might not have the funds to get to school and they might have a lot of children at different schools, so they might have gone to another school. I think sometimes that what's going on in the household with the parents, the parents may be young. That doesn't mean that things should be going on, but sometimes things are going on in the household. They may not have much. Their mom may have different boyfriends coming in and out. Just maybe what a lot of people call ghetto, that person [gets to] where they just don't care. It's a lot different. How can I put it? They just may not care, "I'm not going over to the school because I don't feel like it. It's too hot." They just have any kind of excuse not to do it, and they just won't do it. I have no idea why and I'm trying to think of someone that I may know or may have seen. I think maybe the parents need help. If you help the parents, then you'll be able to help the children; and the parents will be able to see that it's not as bad as you think. Even if it is, there's someone out there that may be able to help you, that you can talk to. You have to start somewhere.
>
> Nicole: So what would that help look like? I think that's an interesting suggestion, and I've actually heard it from a couple other parents that I've talked to. What would that help look like?
>
> Danielle: Maybe sending a letter out or a questionnaire and ask the parents, "What would help you to help your child?" or "What would help you? It's not just about the children, we want to help you. If you need help or if you know of someone that needs the help. What would they need help with?" I think it would come better from the parents' point of view. Maybe

if you had a checkoff list or something, so that way, they may not want to actually write something down, so maybe put a checkoff list, like help with higher education. Maybe if they had something over here where the parents could get help maybe with their household. Maybe like an area that would bring the parents in to here and not just at the different community places that does that type of help. That might be a good thing. They could get in here.

Nicole: Yeah.

Danielle: Because it's supposed to be a community connected school now.

Nicole: It is, but I don't see a lot of that.

Danielle: Right, so maybe we have to get more community things going on here at the school, where the community is.

Nicole: Right. (Interview, June 21, 2016)

Danielle acknowledges the way the "system has failed" parents, and she is confused and frustrated by what she perceives to be parents not caring. Danielle suggests that the school reach out to parents to solicit information about the kind of help they would be interested in for themselves and their children. Danielle had been a part of the Parent Association when her children attended the school. She had recently been asked to help create a new association, as there was not one currently. She explained that when she was a leader in the Parent Association, she often had to "bribe" parents with food or other items to get them to come to the school. However, she noted that the school was more involved with the community than it was now, even though the school states that community engagement is one of its top priorities. Parents, like Danielle, believe that these priorities are in name only as there is very little involvement with the local community.

Although Danielle's family had been "successful" by middle-class educational standards, with a daughter finishing her doctorate in another major city, Danielle and her family still lived in the neighborhood. She described the local community as getting "better and worse." She said:

It's getting better and worse at the same time. We are trying to improve the neighborhood. They have the delis that are open and people just hang around. It's not really good. They just hang out there all day and go into the store. People do things that are illegal, but we still try to keep a positiveness with the children even though they have to deal with that themselves and they're

> just children and they really shouldn't have to. That's the way
> society is. If you don't get any help from everyone, if everyone
> doesn't pitch in and help and do their part, it makes it harder for
> the people that are trying to help and improve. We'll get there.
> It may take a little longer but we will get there. (Interview, June
> 21, 2016)

Danielle's hopefulness and what she describes as a "positiveness" is in contrast with the four common and essentialized narratives that adults, including other parents, have about parents whose children attend Baker.

Parent Narratives

There are four common narratives of parents at the school, including (1) they do not work and are supported by government assistance, (2) they are in jail, (3) they are on drugs and/or mentally ill, or (4) they work several jobs and barely make ends meet. I met parents and families that fit these narratives to some extent, but I also met parents and families who offer counternarratives, and I discuss one counternarrative example later in this chapter.

Ms. Redmond

Ms. Redmond was a mother of eight and currently had three children in the school. She frequently talked about how she was trying to get them into another school. Ms. Redmond aligned with the narrative of parents who did not work, and teachers and other staff frequently mentioned this. For example, Ms. Smith would often make comments similar to other teachers: "I'm glad she is here, but you know she is here every day so you know she is not working." Thus, teachers had a negative impression of Ms. Redmond and other parents — even when they were engaged in the school. Ms. Redmond was at Baker School almost every day, and she was in frequent contact with her children's teachers. Her interactions with Ms. Smith that I observed centered on making sure her son was completing his assignments, doing well on exams, and was following Ms. Smith's directives. I heard her strategize with Ms. Smith many times about how she could try to apply to get her son into a different school. Ms. Redmond wanted the best for her children, and was an engaged parent; however, teachers assumed that she was only at the school because she did not have a job and they disparaged her for that.

Parents, it seemed, could not win. They were almost universally blamed by teachers. It is also important to note that Baker did not have the additional resources that might be necessary to better engage parents. The school was not functioning, was in disrepair, and did not have adequate staff, such as a full-time nurse. This situation with parents was emblematic of the larger systemic disinvestment of urban public schools like Baker in which they were not given the resources and investment to be successful (Anyon, 2005; Ladson-Billings, 2017; Noguera, 2019; Silva-Laya et al., 2020; Snyder, 2020).

Ms. Crawford

Nyeisha's mother, Ms. Crawford, was a parent struggling with mental illness. The school had reached out to help support her, but these efforts were largely superficial. The interactions with Ms. Crawford were tinged with a combination of judgment and frustration. The belief that parents do not work was shared by staff and fellow parents. Ms. Carol, a grandparent and regular volunteer at Baker, talked about the Crawford family in the following fieldnote.

> Ms. Carol and another woman from an outside agency are arguing about whether it is or is not neglect if your children are late to school every day. Ms. Carol believes it is. After the other woman left, Ms. Carol says to me, "I think that is neglect. Your child is late to school every single day. Then you pick your child up early every single day. They are missing a lot of instruction, and I think that is neglect." Ms. Crawford is at the school this morning and has been in a lot of meetings. She walks out of the office and into the counselor's office. After seeing her, Ms. Carol says to me, "You know Nyeisha, she is the oldest, and she is raising all those other babies." I ask, "Who supports them?" Ms. Carol responds, "You do. Welfare." She pauses and says, "We do." Ms. Carol continues, "I almost cried, Nicole, when I found out that she [Ms. Crawford] was going to have another baby. One day at the beginning of the school year, she [Ms. Crawford] comes in here and says to me that she is so overwhelmed that she wants to go home and kill herself. This is when I learn that she is pregnant with her seventh. I told her, "You wait right here." I went into the office and I got the counselor, Ms. Johnson, and I told her what Ms. Crawford said, and Ms. Johnson [the counselor] came out here and took her into her office. I never would have forgiven myself if something happened. (Fieldnotes, December 1, 2015)

During Nyeisha's report card conference with Ms. Smith, Ms. Crawford, Nyeisha's mother, and I sat at a group of desks in Ms. Smith's classroom. Ms. Smith began the conference by saying, "Nyeisha is going to be retained if she doesn't start doing her work." Ms. Crawford turned to me and asked, "What is retained?" I said, "It means Nyeisha would repeat the fourth grade again." Ms.

Smith jumped in, "It means left back." Ms. Crawford got upset, "Well, Ny Ny [Nyeisha's nickname], I told you your teacher likes you or else she wouldn't leave you back. I want more for you, Ny Ny. I didn't graduate eighth grade, but I got farther than you are now."

Nyeisha's mother often tried to convince herself and Nyeisha that Ms. Smith liked Nyeisha. She wanted Ms. Smith to help nurture and parent Nyeisha, but Ms. Smith decidedly stated, "That is not my job." Ms. Smith is a middle-aged Black woman who used to live in the neighborhood; her siblings went to Baker. She seemed to genuinely care about students' prospects. But Ms. Smith was often frustrated. For example, two of Nyeisha's younger siblings, Nadira, in second grade, and Niles, a kindergartener, were also in Ms. Smith's room running around during the conference. Ms. Smith got so annoyed with them that she sent them to another teacher's room.

At the end of the conference, I was curious about what our game plan would be moving forward, and I asked, "Do we have a plan?" Ms. Smith responded, "Nyeisha is going to get it together. Right?" Nyeisha smiled sheepishly. Ms. Crawford then asked me, "You are checking in on her right, Ms. Nicole? How is she doing in the after-school program?" Before I could respond, Ms. Smith stated, "You know I have been talking with Mr. James, and he said she is acting up in the after-school and that she might get kicked out. I have been talking with the people in the [behavior support program], and Nyeisha might get sent to an alternative school."

Ms. Crawford then stated, "I am just so tired. I am so tired." Ms. Smith then asked, "What about Nyeisha's father? Is he around? Can I get his number?" Ms. Crawford stated, "Yes. Call her father. I can't do all this by myself. Ny Ny, give your teacher your dad's number." Ms. Smith then stated, "I've asked for it. Nyeisha says she doesn't know it." Ms. Crawford responded, "She knows it. Give it to her. Nadira and Niles, let's go get your report cards."

Ms. Crawford was 29 years old. She had six children and was expecting her seventh in July. She self-described as bipolar and often admitted that she was overwhelmed and needed help. Ms. Crawford fit two of the four basic parent narratives: she did not work, and she received government assistance because she was dealing with mental illness. It is also important to note that I saw Ms. Crawford at the school quite frequently; although she admitted being frustrated and not knowing what to do, Ms. Crawford was trying.

There were parents at Baker who did not fit neatly into the common narratives. Ms. Carol, a grandparent, was one of these individuals.

Ms. Carol: A Counternarrative

At Baker, with more than 500 students, there was one consistent parent (grandparent) volunteer, Ms. Carol. Ms. Carol and I became good friends, and I visited her house several times. We had an immediate connection because her sister was a former colleague of mine when I was taught in Philadelphia. Ms.

Carol sat at a desk in the front hallway every day from approximately 8:00 a.m. to 2:00 p.m. Her primary responsibility during the morning was filling out late slips and giving students a late note to take with them to class. She was often very busy, especially between 8:45 and 9:45 a.m. After that, she asked visitors to sign in on the visitor log and then to report to the office.

Ms. Carol had three adult children. Her son had one daughter in college, and her youngest daughter's son, Jalil, attended Baker. Ms. Carol had another adopted son, Marshall, who had just graduated high school. She was a foster mother to Marcus, Tyree, and Andrew, who all attended Baker. Tyree and Andrew were brothers, and they came to live with her when Andrew was 10 months and Tyree was 2 years old. Marcus had been with Ms. Carol since he was 3. She was fostering Marshall for several years as well before she adopted him.

The boys (Jalil, Marcus, Tyree, and Andrew) referred to Ms. Carol as "grandmom," and that was how she described her relationship to them at Baker. It was only after a year of getting to know each other that she told me she was technically Marcus, Tyree, and Andrew's foster mother. Tyree and Andrew saw their biological mother occasionally, and Marcus saw his mother more frequently. When Marcus won the African American History Contest at Baker, Ms. Carol made sure to text his mother pictures of the event. Ms. Carol was very dedicated to her grandchildren and the rest of the children at Baker. She was universally loved. I spent considerable time sitting with her at her desk in the front hallway. As students walked by, she would greet them by name, and many students stopped to give Ms. Carol a hug.

Ms. Carol said that she was at the school every day to check on her "babies." She had been hoping to send all four of her grandchildren to a different school next year. Ms. Carol shares a similar mentality to Ms. Smith about getting the "good" children out of Baker School. When I asked why, she stated, "I don't want them going here. The school offers nothing for these children." She had been trying to get them into a new school since her boys started at Baker. So far, she had been unsuccessful in her efforts.

Previously, all her grandchildren attended a nearby elementary school that Ms. Carol described as "much more like a family" and with a "principal who did not tolerate any nonsense." When that school closed, the boys started attending Baker. Ms. Carol was the primary consistent parent-grandparent volunteer in the school, and she offered an important counternarrative to the other parent narratives. Ms. Carol was also an important positive figure in the daily life of Baker School.

Parentification and Infantilization of Students

Part of the narrative of unengaged parents involves the fact that students at Baker take care of themselves and are in turn parentified. The teachers at Baker believed that this parentification began in third grade. Definitions of parentification include role reversal in which children take care of their parents, when children act more like a peer to their parents, or when children take on parental roles for their siblings (see Borchet et al., 2018; Burton, 2007; Chase, 1999; Hooper et al., 2015; Nuttall et al., 2019). The greatest challenge of parentification or "adultification" for students is that despite seeing their parents as peers and/or taking on increased responsibilities at home, such youth are expected to behave subordinately toward adults in school (Thompson & Maris, 2014). This is especially problematic when Black boys are seen as violent or threatening (Ferguson, 2000; Thompson & Maris, 2014).

Students Taking on Parental Roles

Teachers at Baker School often noted that once students were in third grade, their parents tended to show up to the school less frequently. Looking at sign-in sheets for parent events such as back to school night and report card conferences and comparing these across grades, teachers noticed a decline in parental attendance beginning in third grade. This is the grade when students began walking to and from school by themselves. Many students at Baker, like fourth grader[1] Nyeisha, began to take on additional parental responsibilities, including taking care of younger siblings. On the way to school, fourth grader Nyeisha and two of her younger siblings, Nadira in second grade and Niles in kindergarten, walked several blocks by themselves to school. According to Nyeisha and her siblings, it was a "good day" when they had money to stop by the corner store on the way to school to pick up lunch, which consisted of a couple of twenty-five-cent chip bags, a soda, and a Little Debbie cake or Honey Bun.

All students were provided a free lunch at school, but these were not universally liked, and many students also brought their lunches in a black plastic bag from the corner store. The school lunches were referred to as "schoolies" or "freebies." These were prepacked lunches that were delivered to the school in large boxes and warmed before serving, as no food was prepared on the premises. Nyeisha, Nadira, and Niles's teachers frequently complained to the counselor and other school leaders that the Crawford (their last name) children smelled of urine and were late to school every day. Thus, despite being parentified in some ways, such as walking to school and caring for younger siblings, the Crawford children also seemed to need more support, which Ms. Crawford frequently made clear when she spoke to school personnel.

Students Labeled

I spent considerable time in Nyeisha's classroom. As soon as Nyeisha opened the door to her classroom, she was greeted with remarks and questions from her teacher in front of the rest of the class, including, "Why are you late?" or

"Late again?" As noted in the previous section, Nyeisha's mother was 29 years old and pregnant with her seventh child. Nyeisha was responsible for caring for her four younger siblings, and as a result, Nyeisha was often late to school because of these responsibilities. The family had been in and out of homeless shelters and agencies. Ms. Crawford, Nyeisha's mother, explained: "You know. My children and me, we are kind of growing up together. And when we are in a program for [homeless] mothers and children, we do good. Then as soon as we are out on our own again, things start to fall apart. It is so hard for me to get my bipolar medicine, and I really be about to lose my shit on these kids" (Fieldnotes, January 27, 2016).

Nyeisha, aged 10, had a lot of pressure to get herself and her siblings to school. Then, once she got to school, she was "in trouble" most of the day. Nyeisha's experience illustrates how so many factors make schooling complex at Baker. All the adults Nyeisha was frequently in contact with, primarily her teachers and her mother, were frustrated and overwhelmed. For example, Ms. Smith, Nyeisha's teacher, once said: "I am fed up with Nyeisha. She needs a parent. I did not sign up for this. This is not my job. But, you know, I can't teach here. You know how hard it is. Day after day, I am told to implement a new thing to prepare for the test. I don't ever have time to teach" (Fieldnotes, December 8, 2015). Adults like Ms. Smith and the counselor knew that many students like Nyeisha had little parental support at home and that they were helping to take care of younger siblings. However, at school, they infantilized Nyeisha and students like her in a school environment that expected absolute control. For example, Ms. Smith often screamed at Nyeisha for coming late to school and attempted to control her behavior (and the behavior of the other students) by commanding students to walk in a straight line with their hands behind their backs. Students are expected to sit in their seats without talking or fidgeting. Nyeishia, like many fourth-grade students, my children included, often had trouble sitting still. In addition, Ms. Smith got repeatedly frustrated when Nyeisha did not do what Ms. Smith demanded. Ms. Smith often expressed these requests in shaming and disparaging ways that erased the heroic nature of Nyeisha's daily life caring for her younger siblings.

The Need for "Discipline"?

Mr. Dixon, a tall, middle-aged Black man and the school disciplinarian, acknowledged that students were raising themselves and taking on parenting roles for younger siblings. He also asserted that students need structure and discipline at home.

> Mr. Dixon: These moms wants to give they children everything
> they didn't have, but the students also need a foot in they ass.
> The students don't listen to their parents because there are no

consequences. Students are essentially raising themselves and raising their little brothers and sisters. They don't always have the time or understanding to see that school matters. They lack motivation.

Nicole: Why is that?

Mr. Dixon: Because they don't see motivation or success. They are working hard in the day-to-day. The students also don't listen to they parents.

Nicole: Why do you think that is?

Mr. Dixon: They see their parents doing drugs and other things, and they lose respect for their parents . . . You know, and you and I have talked about this before, students need structure, and at home, they don't have that. You know, I am just trying to help as many as I can. (Fieldnotes, March 9, 2016)

Mr. Dixon also recognized the ways that students were often parentified as he described how many were raising themselves. However, he believed that students needed to be controlled or disciplined more, as he referenced in the fieldnote above as well as in the following fieldnote, which is an example of the infantilization that students experience at school.

Mr. Dixon and I are speaking in the schoolyard during recess. "Everyone is really hype today because Jada is going to fight someone," he states. "Jada and her boyfriend are the new Ike and Tina. They fight all the time. Jada's aunt is here. She is a teacher at a fancy school, but Jada doesn't listen to her. Jada doesn't listen to anyone." I met Jada's aunt earlier during the day, and she was called down during our conversation to come to the office to talk to Jada. Mr. Dixon continues, "You know some students, like Ameena, they really only listen to me. Rashanna only listens to me." Mr. Dixon calls over to Edward and tells him to chill because he looks like he might be about to get in a fight. Then says to me, "Too many of these mom[s] spoil they kids. Edward is an example." A student throws the basketball at another student in the head. The student who threw the basketball is Vance. Mr. Dixon explains, "Vance, he is another one, his mom lets him do whatever he wants. I tried to 21 him [kick him out of the school]. He tried to burn the school down on the first day. He wasn't even registered to go to school here yet. He went into [the] bathroom and then smoke started coming out. His mom just sent him to school and told him to register himself. I couldn't 21 him because his mom said he was trying to hurt himself and not anyone else. They put him in crisis and then said he did cyber school. He has been back for a couple of months now. His mom. Come on. How you send your kid to school to register himself? He listens to me, but I'm not afraid to put my paws on him. More of these kids need a foot in they ass.

Ameena walks by us and screams to another student, "What the fuck are you thinking?" Mr. Dixon and I hear her. Mr. Dixon asks Ameena, "What is on your head?" Mr. Dixon is referring to her hijab. Ameena touches her head and smiles, "Oh. I'm sorry." Ameena walks over to us, and we discuss high school for a few minutes. I ask Ameena, "Where are you going to school?" She responds with the name of the local neighborhood high school, which is considered a terrible place by all students and adults, and then laughs. "No psych. I'm going to [name of another neighborhood high school]." Mr. Dixon tells her, "You'd have to join a gang if you go to [the local high school]." Ameena retorts, "No. I wouldn't. I'm not going there." Ameena walks away and rejoins a group of her friends. Mr. Dixon says, "She has so much potential. She is a natural leader." I ask, "What is going on with her?" Mr. Dixon states, "No structure, no consequences, no structure. Her dad drives a cab and always says he has to work. Her mom is some diplomat in Ghana or something. I've never seen her. I keep telling the dad that he needs to do something about her or else she is going to get in big trouble." (Fieldnotes, March 30, 2016)

Ameena's father worked long hours as a cab driver, and according to Mr. Dixon and other teachers, her mother was not involved. Thus, Ameena was parentified in many respects. Yet, Mr. Dixon feared that because of this, Ameena would end up in trouble because she needed more parental involvement, which to him involved providing structure and consequences.

A common belief that teachers discussed was that students acted "bad" because they were "not afraid of their parents," for instance, Mr. Dixon mentioned to me multiple times that the students needed consequences. On another occasion, he said, "These kids need a boot in they ass. My son does not act this way because he knows I will put a boot in his ass." Ms. Smith expressed a similar version of this: "The parents need to do something." She demonstrated hitting someone as she said this. She continued, "These kids aren't afraid of their parents because the parents don't do anything." Ms. Martin, a 40-year-old Black teacher from Jamaica, chimed in, "I was always afraid of my parents." Ms. Smith adds, "Me too. If I acted the way these kids act, my mom would beat my ass." Ms. Martin agrees (Fieldnotes, September 21, 2015).

What many teachers either did not know or forgot was that these students were often fending for themselves. Thus, when students acted like adults and took on parental roles, it made sense that they did not need to fear adults in the ways that Mr. Dixon, Ms. Martin, Ms. Smith, and other staff think they should. In this regard, teachers and school leaders essentially blamed students for situations that they could not control.

From my conversations with students, they also agree that many students do not listen to their parents. For example, Rashanna explained to me that students who take care of themselves do not need to listen to or depend on their parents. She stated, "Yeah, most of the kids don't listen to their parents." "Why not?" I ask. We continue our conversation.

> Rashanna: Because they [kids] do what they want. Destin and them, Destin's dad doesn't really tell him what to do, because Destin makes his money, pays his own phone bill. Destin does what he wants.
>
> Nicole: Really?
>
> Rashanna: The way he makes his money, I can tell what his future is going to be. Behind something that looks like that door, that gate right there. [Rashanna points to a large metal gate on the inside of the library door.]
>
> Nicole: Does he not see that that might be the future he has?
>
> Rashanna: Yeah. Him and his brothers sees it and his friends, but in their mind, they're not going to end up there.
>
> Nicole: Why do they think that?
>
> Rashanna: Because in their words, they have two feet and they're going to use 'em.
>
> Nicole: To run?
>
> Rashanna: Yeah, but you can't run forever.
>
> Nicole: Do you think most of the boys in this school have that mentality or just some?
>
> Rashanna: All of them.
>
> Nicole: All of them? What about the girls?

Rashanna: Some of the girls. Some of the girls just follow the
boys. (Interview, May 3, 2016)

Rashanna described how middle school students, like Destin, took care of themselves financially. She referenced that Destin would likely "end up in jail," but that he and his peers did not think it would happen to them. Rashanna referred to one of the consequences of parentification in which students like Destin joined the illegal economy as a means of surviving, which required fending for themselves.

Melvan, a seventh grader, was another student who fended for himself and appeared to not listen to his parents. He was also one of the students who assaulted Mr. Barnes. Melvan has been at Baker since fourth grade. Melvan's mother, Ms. Green, started attending school every day in November and December because of frequent phone calls from his teachers and the disciplinarian, Mr. Dixon. Ms. Green admitted that she did not know what to do about her son. She went to all of Melvan's classes with him. His teachers stated that there was no change in Melvan's behavior with his mother there. According to Mr. Barnes, Melvan seemed to think it was funny that his mother was there. Melvan and his mother got into an argument on the second floor outside Ms. Smith and Ms. Martin's classrooms. They were screaming at each other, and the principal, Ms. Washington, was called to intervene. When Ms. Washington arrived, Melvan hit his mother and then ran out of the school building. When she was retelling this story, Ms. Smith shook her head and said: "He hit his mother in front of the principal! Our parents are so young" (Fieldnotes, December 17, 2015).

The school disciplinarian, Mr. Dixon, thought that students "need[ed] more structure and consequences." He believed that Melvan, who was sent to an alternative disciplinary school, was an example of what happens when parents are busy and/or absent and students do not have consequences. Mr. Dixon, who was getting ready to go to Melvan's disciplinary hearing, explained why Melvan did not listen to his mother: "Melvan has no real consequences, and he has seen his mom doing things, and he lost respect for her. So many of these kids are really just raising themselves" (Fieldnotes, March 9, 2016). Mr. Dixon believed that parents needed to be more involved and provide more structure. However, he also knew that many students did not have that structure and were taking care of themselves and their siblings. Thus, while students were simultaneously infantilized and parentified, the adult staff at Baker, who acknowledged how students were parentified, still expected students to conform to rigid behavioral requirements. When students resisted the culture of control, the reason, according to school staff, was because they did not have structure and consequences at home. The next section discusses how the culture of control and the essentialized parent narratives contribute to the ways students are infantilized and parentified.

Projecting Frustration

Ms. Smith's actions demonstrate a curriculum of control at Baker School and how this curriculum contributes to the parentification and infantilization of students. Ms. Smith was a middle-aged Black woman with dreadlocks who had been teaching for 14 years. She taught at Baker for several years, and prior to teaching at Baker, she taught at two charter schools. Ms. Smith was both respected and feared. She said:

> Ms. Washington [the principal] told me to use classroom management the other day because Nyeisha was in the hallway. I start screaming at her. This is the second time we have had it out. You are not going to talk to me any kind of way. I am an adult. I was going to address her again today, but I have to cover because too many people are out. I don't think she is going to want to talk to me. Ms. Washington told me, "You are too aggressive." I yelled at her in the lunchroom the first time in front of my class. My kids were saying that I cursed Ms. Washington out and I didn't, but I got in her face. She hasn't brought that up to me again. She just says, "You are too aggressive for me, Ms. Smith." (Fieldnotes, March 16, 2016)

Ms. Smith had an established presence in the school. Faculty in the school looked to her for advice and guidance and listened to her opinions. I asked the counselor, Ms. Johnson, if Ms. Smith is respected and she said, "Yes. She controls her class[2] and controls everything actually. She is respected, and as a staff, we all respect everyone. However, some teachers don't agree with her methods. Baker is about survival. The environment is hard. There are four teachers like Ms. Smith. I'm not perfect. I yelled 'Shut the hell up!' yesterday at the students" (Fieldnotes, June 14, 2016). In addition to reinforcing how teachers were valued and celebrated if they could "control their class," Ms. Johnson declared that "Baker is about survival." Ms. Smith, like all teachers at Baker, was struggling and attempting to survive. Ms. Smith, who was originally from the local neighborhood, demonstrated a habitus of fierceness, as evidenced in how she engaged with students and the principal. However, Ms. Smith had considerably more power at Baker than the students, and this habitus, while still very much a coping mechanism (e.g., Stevenson, 2014), had direct and indirect consequences on students.

Ms. Smith prided herself on having her class under control, and she did not tolerate misbehavior. The following fieldnote illustrates common interactions between Ms. Smith and her students. The fieldnote begins with Ms. Smith using fear to have the class engage in a close reading of a text.

> Ms. Smith asks the whole class, "As I read, you are supposed to?" The students respond in unison, "Track." Track means that

students are to follow along and point to the words with their finger while Ms. Smith is reading. Ms. Smith comments, "You are not tracking, Lashaya. You told me yesterday that you mess with me on purpose, but I can mess with you more." Lashaya smiles and then starts tracking. After Ms. Smith finished reading, she says to me, "Nyeisha was good yesterday. It was her first day of after-school. Christopher is gone. He moved and started at a new school. Thank God. Kristen moved too." She then turns back to the class and asks about words from the text, "What is distraction?" Many students answer. She asks, "What is embarrassed?" Ireena states, "When you feel silly and ashamed." Ms. Smith says now to the students, "OK. Use context clues. Is this story in the past or present?" A student answers, "The past." Ms. Smith asks, "How do you know?" The student states, "The picture of the car looks old." Ms. Smith responds, "Good. And what about the price of a car. Can you buy a new car for two hundred dollars now? They said you could buy a new car for a couple hundred dollars." A couple of students say you can, but that it would not be a new car.

Ms. Smith then tells the students, "Let's make an inference. What did the family use Thunder [the name of the horse] for? They didn't want the horse to feel like it has been replaced by the car." Ms. Smith is asking inference questions related to details. She called on five or six students, and no one knew the answers. At 9:59 a.m. Nyeisha walks in. She waves at me, and I wave and smile at her. A student from another class is sitting in her desk. Nyeisha is upset, and Ms. Smith asks the student to move and points to another desk. This student is from another class and is taking a break in Ms. Smith's room. Ms. Smith returns to the rest of the class and asks, "Why is the car important?" No one knows, and she is getting frustrated. She states, "Sit up. No leaning. Kids. This isn't my life. You don't get it. You have to get it together. We talk about this all the time. When you get older you need a career, because there won't be a lot of jobs. We talk about this all the time. Come on." Marshall sneezes, and she says to him, "Cover your mouth. That is so basic." This is the fifth time she has asked him to cover his mouth since I arrived. Ms. Smith asks the class again, "What are you being asked to do? Will you look at the question? Come on. I have had it. I have to work very hard. You do nothing. Just sit there." Ms. Smith asks again, "What is the inference?" The class finally gets the answer. Marquise says, "I said that." Ms. Smith yells, "What are you going to do. You didn't say that. How are you going to tell me what you said?" Ms. Smith gets right in front of his face, and she speaks to him in a severe tone as she says this. She goes over to the phone and calls for Marquise's social worker. She says, "I'm tired of him arguing with me. He needs to leave." After she hangs up the phone, she says to the class, "OK. Plan your writing." The students are writing an answer making an inference about the passage they just read. It is called a constructed response question, which is a type of open-ended question that the students will have on the PSSA [Pennsylvania System of School Assessment]. Marquise's worker comes to the door, and Ms. Smith says, "I'm tired of it. He is always talking back to me. I'm tired of it." Marquise leaves the class with his worker. Ms. Smith turns to the rest of the students and tells several to "sit up." As Nyeisha is settled in her desk, I say, "Good morning, Nyeisha." She tells me, "I was good yesterday." I say, "That is what Ms. Smith told me this morning. I am so glad to hear that you had a good day." Nyeisha continues, "My mom told me that I should be good every day." Ms. Smith tells the whole class, "OK students. Sharpen your pencils." Students line up near Ms. Smith's desk to sharpen their pencils. Ms. Smith says, "Back up. Back up. You need to be here." She motions to the end of her desk. Ms. Smith sharpens the pencils and passes them back to the students.

Ms. Smith talks to Lashaya privately and then Lashaya moves to a new seat to sit by herself. She asks Rashed, "Are you tired?" Rashed says, "Yes. I stayed up late." Ms. Smith says, "I'm going to have to talk to granddad." Ms. Smith says quietly to me, "Rashed came from [another school]. He was so on point when he first got here. His writing is excellent. Now he is starting to slip up. I am going to talk to his granddad. Rashed is sweet. The girls like him. He is cute." She continues to talk to me while the students are working independently, "I just don't know what to do about the lack of achievement . . . You know Stefon. He is so smart. His mom is worried he is going to end up like his dad who was in jail for eight years. He is so smart. I am having him go to the fifth grade for reading. There are so many jailhouse lawyers. They don't have common sense."

Sammy gets up to throw something away. When he sits down, Ms. Smith whispers to me, "Sammy's dad is White. He talks Black. It is kind of funny. He really cares and is involved. I am not sure where the mom is. Nyeisha's mom was here yesterday. She is a waste, and it is so sad." (Fieldnotes, February 10, 2016)

The near-complete lack of trust in students to behave or "act right" is cemented into the school culture and is an example of how they are infantilized at school. Ms. Smith was able to teach more than other teachers because she was feared; however, she lacked confidence in her students primarily because she considered their parents "a waste." Ms. Smith's frustration with students when they did not comply or follow directions was projected onto the parents. Ms. Smith acknowledged that her students might not have positive experiences or certain structures at home, and she considered this to be the parent's fault. However, at school, Ms. Smith continued to insist on complete obedience.

As the fieldnote continues, Mr. Kelly, Ms. Smith, and Nyeisha are all yelling, and Ms. Carol points out that everyone at Baker is hollering all the time. Not only is Ms. Smith frustrated by student misbehavior, she is also disappointed when parents do not meet the expectations of what she thinks a parent should do. This disappointment contributes to her increased frustration and to the way she discussed parents in dehumanizing ways as noted in the following fieldnote.

> I walk back downstairs because it is time for the fourth–sixth-grade lunch. I hear Mr. Kelly [lunchroom supervisor] in the hallway screaming, "You don't say nothing to me. You ask me." He screams and repeats this a few times. I then hear Ms. Smith is yelling at Nyeisha because she has a soda. "You don't need a soda." Nyeisha runs away from her to the lunchroom, and Ms. Smith throws up her hands and says, "I've had it."
>
> Ms. Carol, who is in the hallway as well, says to me, "The kids are hollering; the teachers are hollering." She shakes her head. On my way to the lunchroom I stop by the after-school programming room. Mr. James tells me that Kiandra left for the charter school because her mother thinks it is too chaotic here. I ask how Nyeisha is doing in the after-school program. He says, "All of the kids told me not to put her in there because they don't like her. They say she is mean to them. So that was more reason for me to put her in there, so far so good. You know it might be that Ms. Smith doesn't like her and so the kids don't like her." Mr. James and I talk more about the after-school program and students he has kicked out. I hang out with the fourth graders during lunch, and then I leave to go home for lunch.
>
> At about 2 p.m. I walk back into the school through the front doors. I hear music as soon as I get out of my car. It is a nice song that I don't recognize, like the sounds of soul and pop music. I see a car parked in front of the school, and Ms. Crawford, Nyeisha's mother, is sitting in the passenger seat singing and dancing along with the song. There is a young child in the back seat. The driver's seat is empty. She smiles and waves at me, and I think to myself that she looks really happy, and I am glad. This is the third time I saw her at the school so far today.
>
> I walk to Ms. Smith's classroom on the second floor. Ms. Smith seems frustrated and says, "Nyeisha complained of a

stomachache. I took her to the nurse, and the nurse said nothing is wrong with her. Nyeisha, she just lies and lies. Her mother is worthless. And it is so sad. It hurts me. She was awful after lunch. You know I think she is so far gone. She is mentally ill." I ask, "Has she been evaluated by a psychologist?" Ms. Smith responds, "No. But she should be. She is just so far gone, and her mom is really so much of the problem. It makes me so sad when she says she doesn't know what to do, but it is because she doesn't listen." A few minutes later, Nyeisha walks back into the classroom and starts gathering her things. She has been in the behavior support room (BSR) because, according to Ms. Smith, she was awful. Ms. Smith asks Nyeisha, "What are you doing?" Nyeisha says, "I'm not staying in here. I am getting my things and going back to BSR."

After school I see Ms. Smith yelling at Nyeisha again in the hallway. I can't hear what she is saying, but I see Nyeisha walk away from Ms. Smith and into the cafeteria and then Ms. Smith turns around and throws up her hands. Ms. Smith walks up the hallway and sees me and says, "You know I just don't know how much longer I can do this." I ask, "How long have you been teaching?" Ms. Smith says, "Fourteen years. I like this population, and they need it, but it is just so hard. It just hurts me." As we are talking, a parent knocks on the door. It is Nyeisha's mother, Ms. Crawford. Ms. Smith says in a very nice tone, "Hi. Come in." Ms. Crawford asks, "Is Ny Ny here?" Ms. Smith states, "She should be in the cafeteria." Ms. Crawford walks quickly toward the cafeteria, and we see her in the doorway talking to Mr. James. I hear her ask, "How is she doing?" as she enters the cafeteria. Ms. Smith whispers to me while Ms. Crawford is in the cafeteria, "She is worthless. I just don't know. I am not a mother, but I think it is hard to be a mother, I think you have to sacrifice. I know that my sister did for my nephew. She was really strict, and now he is happy and he thanks her. She was tight," Ms. Smith mimics kicking, "and she had to sacrifice a lot." Ms. Crawford walks back up the hallway. I ask, "Is everything OK?" Ms. Crawford states, "Yes." Ms. Smith says, "Nyeisha walks home." Ms. Crawford says, "Yes. She always does. Ny Ny is going to walk to my mom's house after school and then they are going to walk together over to my house." Ms. Smith responds, "OK." Ms. Crawford opens the door to leave. I say, "Goodbye. Have a good evening." (Fieldnotes, February 10, 2016)

Blaming the Parents

As the preceding fieldnote demonstrates, Ms. Smith was frustrated and overwhelmed; she frequently discussed how much she cared about "this population." However, she took out her frustration directly and harshly on students, even though she primarily blamed the parents, whom Ms. Smith considered "worthless" and "so much of the problem." This is an example of blaming individuals instead of recognizing the structural and systematic forces that impact parents like Ms. Crawford (Gorski, 2011, 2023; Kennedy & Soutullo, 2018; Valencia, 2010). Thus, when Ms. Smith's efforts to control students fail, she blames the parents and in turn parentifies her students.

A frequent comment Ms. Smith made to and about her students was "they don't get it." She was referring to life in general and specifically what they needed to do to be successful. Ms. Smith believed that the stakes were higher for the students at Baker because they had so many challenges to overcome. For Ms. Smith, "The parents need to be parents." She stated:

> "They [referring to her students] don't understand how hard it is. They don't understand work because their parents don't work. They think that rent is just based on your income, that utilities are just paid. They don't know that the stakes are so high and they don't know about working for things." I ask, "What can we do?" Ms. Smith responds, "I don't know if there is anything we can do. The parents need to be parents. They are so young and they don't know how to parent. You know, I am not a parent, but I know it is hard. My sister is a doctor, and she was a single mom, and she stayed on my nephew. She rode him so hard, and now he thanks her for it. He is at Harvard getting his MBA. He worked for the NBA in finance. . . . Oh we are so proud of him. My sister did so good, but you know it wasn't easy. She was on him like a hawk. She didn't let him get away with anything. His dad is a doctor too, but he wasn't around and didn't do anything." I ask her again, "So what can we do for students who don't have parents like your sister?" Ms. Smith states, "I don't know. They need to step up. They need to be parents. I don't know. I don't think there is anything we can do. All I know, and I keep telling my students this, is that if Trump gets elected, they better watch out. A lot is going to change. There is not going to be all of this free stuff anymore. I mean I work so hard, and I pay taxes, although I work to not pay that much taxes, but I pay my share. These kids don't understand that all of these handouts are going to stop." (Fieldnotes, April 1, 2016)

Ms. Smith perpetuated negative narratives of parents whom she described as not working and receiving, as she stated, "handouts." She frequently made these kinds of comments to students as well as other adults at the school. Ms. Smith tried to educate her fourth graders about the importance of a career, and she became increasingly frustrated, as the following fieldnote describes, when her students focused on things such as shoes, which Ms. Smith did not consider important.

> As soon as I walk into Ms. Smith's room today, Lamar hollers out, "Ms. Smith is wearing Bobos." He is talking about her shoes. She gets in Lamar's face, and says, "What did you say? What." She throws him out of the class. To the rest of the class, Ms. Smith says, "I don't get this. Why do you care so much about shoes? You have nothing. You know that. Where do you get what you have? Where do things come from?" Marquise states, "Our parents give it to us." Sammy answers, "Things come from our parents." Ms. Smith then remarks, "Why does your community, why do we, talk about shoes? Why do we care about shoes?" Marquise responds, "I know. I know. People want Michael Jordans." Ms. Smith says, "What should we care about?" Students call out things, including, "good credit," "a career," "a house." Ms. Smith explains to her class, "You know all of the shoes are made in China. Your Michael Jordans and my Bobos are all made in the same place. You know how much it probably costs to make those expensive shoes, about five dollars. It is just stupid to care about that." She then says to me, "I don't know what is wrong with my people." She returns to the class and says, "You have to stop caring about this crap. So yeah, Ms. Smith wears Bobos, but I don't care." (Fieldnotes, March 9, 2016)

To Ms. Smith, the stakes were incredibly high for students at Baker. In many ways, Ms. Smith was attempting to provide students with cultural capital (see, e.g., Lareau, 2011) and to help them navigate the culture of power (Delpit, 1995). She said that she wanted her students to be successful, which she thinks of primarily in terms of economic social mobility. She, unlike Mr. Barnes, believed that her students should be learning every day, which contrasted with the way that Mr. Barnes blamed students and focused more on controlling behavior, even if he was not yelling. Ms. Smith also focused on controlling behavior, but she primarily blamed the parents and not the students. Ms. Smith frequently made comments similar to this one: "They [referring to her students] aren't bad. They just drive me crazy. I am trying to keep them from ending up like their parents" (Fieldnotes, May 17, 2016). For Ms. Smith, the parents were the problem, and she had zero tolerance for them. Ms. Johnson explains: "Ms. Smith is trying to save the world. She means well, but she can be really hard on the kids sometimes. I tell her that we can't make parents be parents. We can only do so much" (Fieldnotes, June 14, 2016).

In the following fieldnote, Ms. Smith is "nervous" because Nyeisha, who Ms. Smith, as the previous fieldnotes detail, has a contentious relationship with, is not at school and was seen walking in the street. Ms. Smith appears to be genuinely concerned about Nyeisha, and she then describes how Nyeisha's mother and other "parents need to parent."

> Ms. Smith says, "A woman came to my door this morning, she works with the older students upstairs, and she said that she saw one of my students, she thinks her name is Nyeisha, walking in the middle of the street. This was just a few minutes ago, so around 10. That is the time Nyeisha normally gets to school. She said that Nyeisha told her she was going home. I told her that she has never been to school. I told the woman to tell the counselor, Ms. Johnson, and the front office because Nyeisha has not been to school today." Ms. Smith tells me that she doesn't know what Nyeisha is doing and that she has done this before. I ask if her brother and sister are there, and they are. Her mother is not with her, and Ms. Smith says she is "very nervous."
>
> Ms. Smith states, "Nyeisha's mom, she is overwhelmed. She needs the help honestly. She has six kids with one on the way. Nyeisha needs a mom. Her mom doesn't know what to do. It is chaos in that house. Different dads. Nyeisha and the older kids, two older kids, I think they have the same dad. Then the younger ones have a different one. And the new baby will have a different one. There are at least three dads. The thing is if your mom slacks, you lose. You know she told Nyeisha that if she [Nyeisha] is better, that maybe I [Ms. Smith] would be a mother to her. That is not my job. I am conflicted. You know these are my people, and I am really conflicted. Things are different. The parents. The kids tend to stay in the neighborhood, they don't leave. There are parents who went to school here, there are teachers here who taught the parents. People in this neighborhood tend to stay in this neighborhood. You know I was in this neighborhood once. Yes. My sister went to this school. We lived on [street name]. My parents, my mom and dad, were not educated, but they wanted more for us. We, my sister and brother, are educated. We all have advanced degrees."
>
> She points to Stefon. "You see him there. He is really smart. He gets perfect scores on his PSSA and his benchmark. He is so smart. His dad was in jail for eight years, and he is out now. His mom really tries, and she really stays on him. Stefon is angry at the world. We are working to get him into a better school, but his behavior. I always tell him, "NO one cares that you are angry." I tell my class that. The world does not care that you are angry. He is so smart. My nephew is no smarter than he

is. You know, my nephew, the one who is quitting his six-fig-
ure salary as an analyst at ESPN to go to Harvard. He went to
Stanford undergrad. He is amazing. He takes care of all of us. It
is PARENTING. My sister. She made sure that he did that. He
always used to write her letters, and we go back and read those.
He thanks her so much now for all that she did for him. She was
divorced, his dad is a doctor too, but it really was my sister."
(Fieldnotes, January 5, 2016)

Ms. Smith believed that parenting was key, and although she clearly blamed
parents for the deficits she noticed, her deficit lens was nuanced and complex.
For example, Ms. Smith acknowledged Stefon's mother's efforts in the previous fieldnote. Parents have mixed reactions to Ms. Smith. Many parents like her
"strict" style, and like Danielle mentions in chapter 3, Ms. Smith does "not put
up with any stuff from children." In the following fieldnote, Ms. Carol describes
a different parental perspective.

I ask, "Do you have a favorite teacher here?" Ms. Carol
responds, "NO. But I have a least favorite." "Who's that?" I
ask. Ms. Carol says, "Ms. Smith." I wasn't expecting Ms. Carol
to say this, primarily because she knows I spend time in Ms.
Smith's class, but I don't think my surprise shows. I ask her,
"Why is she your least favorite?" Ms. Carol answers, "I don't
like how she talks to the children. She said to my grandson,
Andrew, in front of me, 'I don't know how she puts up with
you. I would have given up on you.' I was so red. Nicole. I was
so angry. I said to Andrew, 'Don't you listen to that. I would
never give up on you. I love you. Don't listen to her.' If that
is what she says to him in front of me, I can't imagine what
she says to him when I am not there." I tell Ms. Carol, "I can't
believe she said that. What did you do?" Ms. Carol says, "I
talked to Ms. Washington [the principal], and I got him out of
her class. She hasn't talked to me since then. You know what
is weird, the kids love her. Andrew did not want to leave her
class. But now she doesn't talk to him either, and that made me
know that I made the right decision. That is no way to talk to
children." (Fieldnotes, January 12, 2016)

Ms. Carol articulated the disparaging way that Ms. Smith talked to students
as well as the complexities surrounding her presence in the school. Certainly
not all students and parents loved or appreciated Ms. Smith, but neither did all
of them hate or vilify her. Many students and parents appreciated her because
she worked hard to help them be successful. However, her efforts are not without consequences. Her efforts to educate students about the culture of power

(Delpit, 1995) contribute to the deficit default ideology that permeates the school and is discussed in the next chapter.

Summary

Baker School, like many urban public schools, has been unsuccessful in attempts to engage parents and families. These unsuccessful attempts to engage families result in negative and essentialized narratives of parents at the school that tend not to acknowledge the systemic challenges families experience. Surrounding these narratives was the premise that students had been "parentified" because of their family circumstances. Many students at Baker fended for themselves and took care of younger siblings. The chapter describes how Nyeisha is parentified in many respects, and how her mother expressed that she needs support. Despite recognizing ways that Nyeisha takes care of herself and her younger siblings, Nyeisha and other students were infantilized at Baker School and expected to be subservient in the culture of control at the school. Staff at Baker either tend to blame students for what teachers perceive as moral shortcomings or blame parents for not being strict enough. Both ideologies contribute to the parentification and infantilization of students within Baker's curriculum of control, and also to a deficit ideology internalized by members of the school and local community, which I discuss in the next chapter.

Chapter 5

Implications of Internalizing the "Deficit Default"

Teachers and staff at Baker find themselves operating in a survival mode, triaging emergencies and focusing on day-to-day tasks and challenges. The unintended consequence is that everyone is blamed for the problems that arise. It is a vicious circle where teachers, students, parents, the community, and the school are continuously described negatively, and the individuals within these groups internalize the negative messages. The hidden curriculum of control, the systemic lack of resources, and the resulting power struggles and resistance culminate in a *deficit default*, which manifests in internalized deficit perspectives of students, teachers, and parents. This chapter describes how this deficit default ideology develops.

At Baker School, students, teachers, parents, and administrators viewed each other, themselves, and the school negatively. A common narrative was that students attended Baker as a "last resort." If there was another option, students would take it. Students with more involved parents often transferred to charter schools, and many students in the middle grades attended Baker because they were kicked out of their charter school for behavior infractions. As mentioned in chapter 4, when Ms. Smith discussed students in her class who she thought were smart or had potential, the first thing she would say was how she wanted to get them into a better school: "I want to try to help get him [Stefon] into a better school. He is just so angry. I am working with his mom to get him into a better school because he is so smart. He would do well in a different school if he can control himself."

Students who previously attended a charter school described their former schools as more rigorous and having far fewer discipline problems. The middle school teachers, who were all new to the school this year, frequently remarked, "I heard it was worse here last year. I don't know how that is possible." Parent volunteers described this school as far "worse" than previous schools their children attended. Students, primarily in the older grades, also talked about Baker School as "way worse" than their previous schools.

As described in chapter 2, Mr. Barnes and other teachers spent a large amount of their instructional time correcting or attempting to manage classroom behaviors without consistent school structures, interventions, and communication. The narratives that students needed to be controlled, the infantilization of students, the notion that "students don't care" about school, negative associations about parents and parental engagement, and descriptions of how students do not have positive home experiences resulted in a *deficit default* ethos about Baker School, its students, and their families.

Whether they were veteran or first-year teachers, most of the educators generally believed that students "don't care." When asked about different ways they tried to engage students, teachers, as in the example of Mr. Barnes would state, "It doesn't matter what I do. The students don't care." However, adopting the mentality that "students don't care" allows schools and society to not be blamed for students' lack of educational opportunities (Kennedy & Soutullo 2018; Theoharis, 2009).

Students' Internalization of the Deficit Default

The chaotic schooling environment at Baker School, systemic issues of inequality including the underfunding of Baker School, and the disinvestment in the local community contributes to how teachers, staff, parents, and students project and internalize negative messages about themselves and the school. Students, as the following discussion with four eighth-grade students demonstrates, often described Baker School as a "bad school." The students also described the school, teachers, and fellow students as "bad." They suggested that the way to improve the school was to start completely over with "new" students. In addition, the students discussed how any improvements to the school, such as murals on the walls, were entirely superficial and just for show.

> Nicole: What does it take to be successful and what advice would you have? Say you were talking to a fourth grader and you wanted them to be successful, what would you say?
>
> Rashanna: The advice I have is find the right school and no [pause]. What it takes to find the right school and the advice I have is don't go to Baker.
>
> Nicole: OK, so let me hear a little more about that.
>
> Rashanna: Just don't [go] here, it's not a good school that you should be in.
>
> Nicole: Yeah, where did you learn, like how did you know it's not a good school?
>
> Jalayla: 'Cause we go here.
>
> Rashanna: I've been here so long.

Nicole: Yeah . . . What makes it a "not good" school?

Bianca: The kids, some of the teachers.

Rashanna: The teachers.

Renee: The principal.

Jalayla: The food.

Bianca: Of course, your fat self going to say the food. I think the main part that makes this school a bad school is Ms. Washington [the principal]. She needs to go. My mom don't like her.

Rashanna: She is going, we just won't be there when she gone. She's not coming back next year.

Bianca: She should have been gone. You see what this school look like?

Jalayla: She, Ms. Washington, she's not like a . . .

Rashanna: It's like dust on everywhere where dusters next to them.

Bianca: Right, right.

Rashanna: Like the computer has dust on them and there's the duster that's leaning on them. The duster there is literally lean-ing on the stuff with the dust on it, and they're not using it. It's just like dust everywhere. How does dust get stuck to the floor like that? [Rashanna points to the dusters on top of the broken, dusty computer monitors and is laughing.]

Nicole: Say more, do you all agree with Rashanna's advice?

Jalayla: Mm-hmm [affirmative].

Bianca: I do. Renee?

Renee: Ummm. Well, yeah, I agree.

Nicole: You agree? The main reason you think this isn't a good school is because of the teachers and the principal.

Renee: Mm-hmm [affirmative].

Bianca: The principal. And some of the students because we can't just blame it all on the teachers and the principal because some of the students here are bad here.

Jalayla: Ms. Washington's not, she's not really like a real tough, tough principal like that is what this school needs, like a real mean principal.

Rashanna: No, she too mean, that's why don't nobody like her, don't nobody listen to her.

Bianca: No, she's not . . .

Rashanna: She don't do nothing, like . . .

Bianca: She not mean, she just . . .

Rashanna: Somebody, she is in her office all day and she won't do nothing. We don't see her most of the day.

Bianca: She's tough on like small things, but on the big things, she don't do nothing about it, but on the small things, she wants to do things about it. It's no big deal.

Jalayla: Like don't wear uniform, it's a whole big deal.

Bianca: Yeah, big problem, but if somebody's phone goes missing or somebody goes missing out the school, she won't make a big deal out of it. "Oh, it's not my fault."

Rashanna: She don't care. Ms. Johnson and them are going to be the only ones asking, "Did you see the child?" Ms. Washington, we don't see her. She's going to be at home or in her office. She got a sign on there that says, "Don't enter without permission."

Bianca: Yeah just like when my mom was coming because she [the principal] was getting smart with me and stuff, so my mom came down here and she was not trying to talk to my mom. They were like Ms. Washington is in her office and all of that. My mom was like, "Well tell that 'b' to come out" and she was not trying to come out.

Jalayla: She don't like sitting there talking to parents.

Rashanna: Every time my mom comes to get my phone from her, she doesn't want to be coming out, she be saying that we got to schedule a meeting and all that.

Bianca: Or if not, she sends other people to sit there and talk to the parent.

Renee: Yeah, like Mr. Dixon or Ms. Forbes.

Rashanna: The girl's parents were up here snapping. They were saying she was dumb, just because she has a degree, that don't mean she got no sense. They were waiting for her. They said she didn't get here yet, they still sitting in the office waiting for her.

Jalayla: Not Ms. Washington, she would be in a meeting.

Bianca: She makes excuses.

Rashanna: She don't let nobody in her office though.

Bianca: She's like, "Don't make me call your mom." She'll talk to your mom over the phone, but not in person.

Jalayla: You have to pay attention, the only time she lets them in her office is when they have food or something.

Rashanna: Yeah, when they dropping her food off. Her whole freezer is filled with food, we went in there to get something before — she had all these frozen dinners and stuff in there.

Jalayla: She has jars of candy and stuff.

Rashanna: Yeah, jars of candy on the table.

Renee: Who that?

[Students are banging on the library doors and peering through the window.]

Bianca: Who's that Deshawn, his little ugly self, and Edward. They need to go somewhere.

Jalayla: They're not even in Ms. Dockett's classroom right now.

Bianca: Right, like they're just on the school.

Nicole: That's not . . . ?

Jalayla: That's Ms. Roberts's classroom [referring to the screaming coming from next door].

Nicole: Let's talk more about what Rashanna said. Is there a way to make Baker a better school?

Bianca: Get rid of the principal.

Rashanna: I think they should just let go all the students and just start over with new applications and stuff.

Jalayla: They need to for real do this school over.

Rashanna: Just take everything, start over. They need to repaint it, paint the floor, the ceiling. The ceilings look like some floors or they're just all bulked in and stuff. I don't think no school honestly got this type of ceiling no more.

[Students are chiming in and adding things that also need to be redone.]

Bianca: There's a hole, almost the whole ceiling in every room is messed up.

Rashanna: No school really got no ceilings like this no more.

Jalayla: They need to fix the lights.

Bianca: Yeah, like nobody has ceilings like this no more.

Rashanna: Or lights.

Nicole: I do like how you guys have a lot of nice murals on the walls. My school didn't have that.

Jalayla: Yeah, they just started putting . . .

Rashanna: They just mainly focus on the walls though.

Bianca: Yeah, they don't clean . . .

Rashanna: Like the ceiling is leaking water, but the walls got posters all over, make it look like it's a good school.

Bianca: Right.

Rashanna: It's pictures of the students with books in their hands, I bet none of those students don't know what them books is about, or anything else about those books. Most of them probably, yeah, they probably don't know how to read, most of them holding them.

Bianca: Or don't know how to read.

Nicole: You think it's just for show?

Renee: Yeah.

Bianca: Yeah, I think it's just to make the school look good, but for real, for real, it's not good. They just want the visitors and stuff to think it's in here. They . . . .

Rashanna: The visitors who came last time, they got all the students out the classroom with uniforms and told us to walk around with the visitors.

[The loud speaker is going off: "Pardon the interruption. Ms. Johnson call the main office."] (Group Interview, May 25, 2016)

As this conversation highlights, students internalized a deficit default surrounding the school and themselves. For example, the advice they had for younger students to be successful was "don't go to Baker." Baker was "not good," according to these students, because of "teachers," "kids," "the principal," and "the food." The students also commented on the state of the physical building: "Like the ceiling is leaking water, but the walls got posters all over, make it look like it's a good school." The students articulated that many efforts are primarily for appearances. The students also internalized the hidden curriculum of control when they made comments like "this school needs a real mean principal." I heard many other students make similar claims. Finally, when I asked the students how Baker could be better, Rashanna's answer, "I think they should just let go all the students and just start over with new applications and stuff," is a powerful example of how the deficit default becomes internalized. The internalization of the deficit default is an example of *symbolic violence*, which is discussed in more detail in the next chapter. Students' perceptions center around how the school is not good and the people, including students in the school, are not good. The negative way that students talk about themselves and other students in the preceding example demonstrates how the deficit default is internalized by students. Part of that internalization is reflected in how students talk about teachers, who, as the next section describes, are operating in survival mode, which contributes to how teachers have also internalized the deficit default ideology in the way they discuss students, the school, and the community.

Operating in Survival Mode

In a similar way to how students coped with the stressful environment of Baker with a habitus of fierceness, teachers also coped by operating in a survival mode. Prolonged exposure to stressful interactions in high-poverty schools can be mentally and physically toxic for students and teachers (Bottiani et al., 2019; Madigan & Kim; 2021; Paulle, 2013). The stressful environment at Baker School generated negative or maladaptive behaviors that both teachers and students demonstrated. Baker was generally considered a hard place to teach, and students recognized this. For example, Rashanna stated, "It is hard to be a teacher here." Teachers felt disrespected by students, administrators, and parents. To make matters worse, teachers were also frustrated because they had not had a raise in years due to stalled contract negotiations (Graham, 2016). Another more recent example of this frustration is reflected in the high (16.4%) teacher attrition in Philadelphia, which is more than double the state average of 7.7 %, and teachers cite low pay and high workloads, among other reasons, as the causes for leaving (Fuller, 2023).

Every month, teachers described how they were told to try a new teaching approach, and they were so overwhelmed by the constant focus on test preparation that they often said they couldn't really teach. Teachers did not find the school's professional development helpful, but teachers did support each other through informal networks. For example, teachers who taught the same grade, sometimes called a "grade group," often supported each other.

The fourth-grade teachers developed lesson plans together, with each teacher maintaining responsibility for different lessons (e.g., math, reading, social studies, science). These teachers also had lunch together in Ms. Smith's classroom. They took turns hosting the students who had lunch detention, and they would watch each other's students if a teacher needed to send a child to another class for a "break." Ms. Smith reported that if someone from the fourth-grade team had to cover, which means lose one's preparation period to watch another class, a middle school class, they would "go together to help each other." This was because the teachers and other staff in the school considered the middle school students and that entire wing of the school to be the "worst" and "out of control." This was the same mentality at the school where I taught for many years, and the lower grade teachers ostensibly refused to cover the middle school classrooms.

The middle school teachers each taught a different subject, so lesson planning support was not a part of their informal network. However, the middle school teachers described relying on each other to "bitch and vent." For most of the year, the middle school team consisted of three first-year, White male teachers, who were, as one student described, "new to the game," and one veteran Black female teacher, Ms. Jenkins, who was new to Baker. The English teacher was not hired until November, and there were two teachers in that role before they hired him. Another first-year teacher was hired to temporarily replace Mr. Barnes, who left in May following the student assault described previously. All the middle school teachers relied on Ms. Jenkins for insight, mentoring, and support.

The teachers at the school, and especially the first-year teachers, did not believe that they received adequate professional support from the principal. At best, they said they were happy when she "left them alone." Veteran teachers also expressed this sentiment, and many teachers stated that they were relieved when the principal was absent. For example, Ms. Smith stated: "'Ahh! Today is Wednesday and we have grade group and have to show her [the principal] all of this data. I hate grade group. When it is canceled, we dance.' Ms. Smith danced for a few seconds. 'When she is out, we do a dance.' Ms. Smith does another dance" (Fieldnotes, March, 16, 2016). In general, teachers believed that they were not supported by the school administration, especially related to student discipline. One example of this was that, according to many teachers, the principal stopped allowing students to be suspended in November because by then the school had already suspended the total number of students it had suspended the previous school year. This, teachers believed, allowed students to internalize that they could do whatever they wanted.

Schools in Philadelphia are rated each year, and one of the factors that goes into the rating is the number of suspensions. As Rashanna and other eighth graders articulated, many aspects of schooling at Baker were done for appearance purposes: "to make it look like it's a good school." Mr. Webster affirmed this: "All of the data, attendance, behavior, test scores, are manipulated so that the school looks like an OK school on paper, and it is not. It is one of the worst schools. When I came here, I was shocked because I thought the school looked OK on paper" (Fieldnotes, June 20, 2016). Comments teachers frequently made when asked how they were doing included, "I'm hanging in there" or "I'm trying to make it through the day." These statements, said with visibly fraught affect, come from both new and veteran teachers. Mr. Dixon, the school disciplinarian, once said: "I am just burnt out. I'm not sure if I'm going to make it. I am drained" (Fieldnotes, March 30, 2016).

The burnout and frustration that teachers experienced had unintended consequences that impacted students' schooling experiences. One of these consequences was that teachers talked to and about students in disparaging ways. Ms. Johnson, the school counselor, commented on the impact this can have in the following fieldnote.

> Some teachers just talk to kids any kind of way. They say things like "You are ignorant like your mom." I've heard a first-grade teacher say "you're stupid" to a child. That student will never listen to you. There is one White student in the school, Matthew.

> He was in Ms. Anderson's class, and she is White. She was so mean to him. I don't know if that is about him being White. We had to switch his class. He is now in another class. He does have a lot of issues. His mom is a drug addict, and he lives with a foster family. I don't know what the deal was. Ms. Anderson just really did not like him. I remember actually hearing her say in front of Matthew, so I know he heard it too. She said, "Now that Matthew is gone we can have a party." (Fieldnotes, June 14, 2016)

Ms. Johnson pointed out that Matthew would never listen to that teacher, Ms. Anderson, because of how she repeatedly disparaged him.

Teachers' frustration, stress, and operating in survival mode were part of how a deficit default became normalized at Baker School. Consequences of this survival mentality are that teachers tend to project frustrations onto students and/or parents, which in turn perpetuates the deficit default at the school.

The Disconnect Between Students and Teachers

Operating in survival mode at the school often leads to teachers misunderstanding student behavior and experiences. Whether or not the teacher is from the local community (e.g., Moll, 2000), there often remains a disconnect between students' and teachers' lived experiences. This disconnect contributed to and reinforced the deficit default at Baker explained in the beginning of this chapter. In the following excerpts from a conversation, Bianca, Rashanna, Renee, and Jalayla, all eighth-grade students, discuss how many teachers do not understand them. They begin by discussing how caring about students is a part of understanding them (Lavy & Naama-Ghanayim, 2020; Noguera, 2009).

Specifically, the girls state that some teachers, like Mr. Crowley, a first-year White male teacher, do not understand "where we come from" or "that we are do or die." What they say teachers need to understand is that, for them, "tomorrow isn't promised. You can't be threatening us with our grades and things like that." Furthermore, students point out what they perceive to be a disconnect between teachers who have "degrees" and their parents, many of whom do not.

Nicole: We're talking about Mr. Crowley.

Bianca: I don't like him.

Nicole: How come?

Bianca: 'Cuz, he want everybody to get kicked out of graduation.[1] I don't like him. I don't know about them [other students], but I don't like him.

Nicole: Tell me the difference between Ms. Jenkins and Mr. Crowley.

Rashanna: Ms. Jenkins care.

Bianca: Ms. Jenkins care yeah and Mr. Crowley don't.

Renee: She don't be like, I don't want you all in graduation.

Bianca: He be like I'm going to do everything I can to get you all kicked out of graduation.

Nicole: Do you think that Mr. Crowley just doesn't understand that you all take what he says seriously?

Jalayla: He don't understand where we come from.

Nicole: You don't think he understands where you come from?

Jalayla: Nope.

Rashanna: That we are do or die.

Nicole: What does that mean?

Bianca: He don't understand what we try to tell him.

Jalayla: Basically, we live in like a tough neighborhood, right?

Renee: So, we take everything to the heart.

Jalayla: Exactly.

Rashanna: Do or die.

Renee: Right.

Jalayla: Basically.

Nicole: Give me some more examples about that. Ideally, my research could help teachers to better understand. What does he need? I'm not going to tell him specifically, right? What does a teacher maybe like him . . .

Renee: He need to understand tomorrow isn't promised. You

can't be threatening us with our grades and things like that.

Jalayla: Exactly.

Renee: Some of our parents didn't go to college. That's probably going to be the first time . . .

Jalayla: That's the thing I hate about teachers. Y'all sit there. They constantly throwing at us how they got they degree and that high education.

Rashanna: They be like we got to respect them.

Bianca: They are like I got my teacher's degree. What you got? You don't got nothing.

Rashanna: There's no respect for us. They say, we got this many degrees, this, that, and the third. They don't know. Most of us can make more money in a day than they make in a year. They just expect when they look at us to not think that.

Jalayla: I hate when they do that.

Renee: They always try to do that.

Bianca: Yeah.

Renee: They are always like . . . What if you all didn't get your degree?

Jalayla: Exactly. I hate when they throw that in our faces. Oh well. You all so hype because you all got you all's teacher's degree. You all's master's degree. All that other type stuff. What we supposed to care for? We not worried about what you all got? We trying to worry about what we need to have.

Nicole: Mm-hmm.

Jalayla: I hate when teachers always say that. That's their favorite thing. "What do you all got? Because I got this."

Nicole: They say that to you specifically?

Jalayla: Yes.

Bianca: Yes.

Renee: They are like "I got my teacher degreeeeeee."

Bianca: "I got my teacher degree. I got a master's degree. What you all got?"

Renee: But y'all working as a teacher though. You all could've been a nurse, anything else, but you all a teacher teaching us so . . .

Jalayla: They be like, well since I got all that. I don't really got to teach you all. I can let you all sit here . . .

Bianca: Yep.

Nicole: You hear a lot of teachers say things to you, like I have this, right? How does it make you feel when they say that?

Renee: Be like "Okayyy . . ."

Jalayla: It makes you want to punch them in they faces.

Bianca: No, I just be like, OK? You're telling me for? I don't care.

Renee: Watch this when I go to college and yep.

Rashanna: I think they expect for all our houses to look like crack houses or something the way they talking.

Bianca: Right. This why I think Mr. Crowley think he better than us or something.

Jalayla: I think he racist.

Bianca: Probably is.

Rashanna: I'll take pictures of my house and show him.
. . .
Nicole: What does it mean to say that your teachers think that you live in a crack house? They don't understand you. They have these stereotypes, or what do you think?

Jalayla: Don't you know how some people think about how you dress and all that stuff. So they go with the way we act and all that. They take that as, oh well you probably live in this such a house and your house is probably not all that. And your house is probably not that nice looking. It probably look dirty. Just because by the way that we dress or we act.

Nicole: Has a teacher ever said anything like that to you?

Renee: No.

Jalayla: But I can tell they probably be thinking it. (Group Interview, June 15, 2016)

Perceptions and Misperceptions About Social Hierarchy

These students are angry about the perceptions of social hierarchy based on credentials, which in this case is the symbolic capital of having status conferred as a result of a diploma (see Bourdieu, 1989). Teachers are "throwing at us how they got they degree and that high education," but as the students describe, that does not mean that students respect them. In fact, in the local community, higher education does not have the same status. Instead, students note the way that teachers disrespect them by making comments about what they (teachers) have that students do not. Students interpret this as a lack of respect and care, and this is an example of how teachers' misunderstandings can translate into a disregard for students as persons (see Lavy & Naama-Ghanayim, 2020; Noguera, 2009). In the following excerpt, the students bring up a teacher, Ms. Jenkins, who cares. Although Ms. Jenkins also makes comments about having degrees, the students describe how Ms. Jenkins shows that she cares about them and their education.

> Renee: We'll say we don't care and he'll [Mr. Crowley] be like, "OK you don't have to care." He be like, "I got my degree," and we were like we don't care. OK.

> Jalayla: Ms. Jenkins probably said that probably once.

> Rashanna: That's like when they say stuff like you already got through school. No, duh, you already got through school. You're stating the obvious. Ain't you all here teaching us?

> Jalayla: Ms. Jenkins probably only said that once, right? One time before . . .

> Nicole: You've heard other teachers say it besides him.

> Jalayla: Mm-hmm [affirmative], but he say it often.

Bianca: He say it often.

Rashanna: Ms. Jenkins say it all the time.

Nicole: Ms. Jenkins says it all the time?

Rashanna: Yeah, she say she already got through school a lot. She might not say it to her class a lot. They said Ms. Jenkins be letting them make dust mansions and all. She do not let us barely pull out our hand.

Bianca: She don't even let us get up out our seat.

Jalayla: This is what Ms. Jenkins I think she do care about our class education and stuff . . .

Renee: It's the way that we be acting.

Jalayla: Yes. I think that's why . . .

Renee: You know how we got Kwame.

Rashanna: They said she admitted to her class that she show favoritism.

Renee: Yeah Tanisha told me that.

Jalayla: Yeah, but she probably do show favoritism, but I just think that she know our class. Our class was for real, for real. We got really smart kids in our classroom. That's why I think she . . .

Renee: We're higher than them in math.

Jalayla: For real, for real. So that's why I think she always putting pressure on us and want us to do more work than her class could.

Renee: Right, we're higher than them.

. . .

Nicole: At the beginning of the conversation you said that Mr. Crowley doesn't understand you, right?

Jalayla: He don't.

Nicole: What specifically does he not understand?

Renee: It's hard!

Jalayla: It's hard to be us.

Rashanna: At this point of the year, all I want is these teachers to understand if they say something to me on Monday, I'm going to hit 'em. I don't care.

Bianca: No, because they going to try to kick you out of graduation.

Rashanna: I don't care. Let them. I'll wait until Tuesday and hit them right after the graduation while we walking up. Hit them right while we walking down the aisle. I don't care. (Group Interview, June 15, 2016)

As the eighth-grade students discuss, students pay close attention to things teachers say. Comments that may seem to teachers as "throw away" lines can influence students' interpretations about teachers and themselves. The difference in the preceding fieldnote about Mr. Crowley and Ms. Jenkins is that students think Ms. Jenkins says things to them because she truly wants them to be successful; whereas they think Mr. Crowley is just trying to punish them. Mr. Crowley, on the other hand, was frustrated for what he perceived to be a lack of consequences, and I have taught in a school similar to Baker and experienced Mr. Crowley's frustration, in particular related to graduation. What I did not understand when I was a first-year teacher was how important eighth-grade graduation is to students and their families. The students discuss how Mr. Crowley wants to kick them out of graduation. This is an extreme affront to students, because as Renee states, their tomorrow is not promised. There is no guarantee that they will graduate from high school. Mr. Crowley did not see this larger picture, as a first-year teacher, a White, male teacher, who was frustrated by what he considered student misbehavior and a lack of consequences at the school.

Students Blaming Their Teachers and Themselves

When Rashanna says, "I think they expect for all our houses to look like crack houses or something," she is discussing ways that students feel degraded because of assumptions teachers sometimes make about students' lives that largely stem from a lack of understanding of the multiple worlds that students navigate, an understanding that is informed by stereotypes (e.g., Phelan et al., 1993; Phelan et al., 1994). Jalayla expands on this and states how she believes that teachers like Mr. Crowley judge students based on "the way that [they] dress or [they] act." The students also discuss how they feel and would like to respond when teachers disrespect, misunderstand, and demean them. Students' desired responses connect to their habitus of fierceness in which they do not want to show weakness. In the following excerpt, the students' discussion demonstrates an internalized deficit default about themselves and their community. Renee, specifically, articulates an internalization of the need for students at Baker School to be controlled.

> Nicole: Renee, you said that they don't understand that it's hard. Explain more about that.
>
> Jalayla: It's shooting . . .
>
> Renee: We're from the hood. So, every day is shooting, this, that, and a third. Of course, we going to come here and act how we do. Run around. We're not used to sitting down, being proper, and this, that, and a third.
>
> Bianca: Yeah.
>
> Renee: We going to run around. Be . . .
>
> Jalayla: We going to want to have fun, but . . .
>
> Renee: Exactly.
>
> Jalayla: They think they'll . . . like we . . .
>
> Renee: That we're just supposed to sit and do our work and be quiet. Not say something back. We're not from where he from. We're going to get smart. We're going to want to hit you. We going to do this and a third. We're going to act up. (Group Interview, June 15, 2016)

Bianca, Renee, and Jalayla discussed how many teachers don't understand their lives and the many challenges they often experience in their neighborhood, and the students commented on how frustrated they were when teachers expected them to sit quietly and tell them everything they should not do. However, Bianca, Renee, and Jalayla also show how they have internalized a deficit ideology about themselves and their neighborhood, as evidenced when Renee says, "We are going to act up."

Teachers Giving Up

Mr. Barnes was a first-year White male teacher in his early 20s. After finishing his undergraduate education degree and student teaching, he started his first formal teaching position at Baker. Mr. Barnes explained that he had wanted to be a teacher since he was in high school.

> It [school] was like a meritocracy, like if you were doing the correct thing, you'd be rewarded; if you weren't doing the right thing, you'd be punished. So I loved getting the praise from my teachers, I loved getting the attention I wasn't getting at home, and I don't know, just something about that like it seems like a very just sort of system when it's done right to me. It seems like it's one of the few places where justice can truly operate. (Interview, February 1, 2016)

As described in an earlier chapter, Mr. Barnes was assaulted for the fifth time by March, and he became demoralized. He stated that the assault and the subsequent bureaucratic hoops he had to jump through to feel safe as an educator contributed to feelings of despair. He posited, "The educator's safety is not taken very seriously at all. Yeah, you have to get the police involved, it seems like, to actually get something done, and even then it seems like it's a slow process." We continued our conversation.

> Nicole: Why do you think that is?

> Mr. Barnes: It makes you feel very defeated to see that even something as serious as this [the assault] is — it gets run through like this bureaucratic system that just takes forever you know. I think our district is too big, I don't think we have enough staff, I don't think we have enough resources to actually have any of these things dealt with efficiently.

> Nicole: So at one of our first interviews, you know you talked about just like how really committed you are to teaching.

> Mr. Barnes: Yeah.

> Nicole: Do you still feel that way?

> Mr. Barnes: Oh, absolutely, yeah. I mean, I'm just [I] still haven't missed a day, haven't come in late. Even in the wake of that like [the last assault] I didn't go home early, so my commitment I think is stronger than ever. I think I need to reevaluate where I'm teaching because this is too much, this is just too much for me to handle. (Interview, March 4, 2016)

Mr. Barnes discusses the systemic issues that make teaching at schools like Baker more challenging, and chapter 6 builds on the systemic complexities of teaching and learning in large urban cities. While Mr. Barnes acknowledged the bureaucratic challenges, he also deficitized students. He stated that he did not believe that teaching at Baker was actually teaching. For Mr. Barnes, the particular challenges at Baker and his personal traumatic experiences influenced how he eventually gave up on teaching at Baker or on trying different approaches to engage students.

> Nicole: Do you think maybe they're just like not interested in school? Maybe we need to change schooling a little bit to . . . ?

> Mr. Barnes: Oh, I'm always for that, yeah. I think — when so I mean they all know the stakes of the PSSAs [statewide standardized test] and everything and that alone seems wrong to me, and I think we have systematically made school more boring. But when you do have people, like I would argue that the majority of teachers here do try to go outside the box and still deal with the PSSAs, still play ball there, but also try to make it entertaining and engaging to them, while imparting those skills that they still need to develop at this age. I think people are trying to do a really good job here, like I'm very impressed with the staff at the school, but it just doesn't seem like there's much — anyone is really being receptive to it like in the student body.

> Nicole: Do you think — have you ever thought like, OK, I'm just going to try something completely new. This isn't working; I'm going to try something brand new?

> Mr. Barnes: Oh yeah, yeah, like sometimes I would just like drop it and like I'll have them just analyze song lyrics, just hook them into something you know, and then try to tie it back in. And it doesn't seem to be much interest. And I'm just like at the end of my rope, like I've — this is all in my first year and that's a hard thing because I don't have all the resources that a seasoned teacher has. And even when I talk to Ms. Jenkins, who's been in the education field for like two, three decades now, she's had all those different things at work and she is running out of stuff.
>
> So it's hard for me to be like, as a first-year teacher, I'm going to, you know, reinvent the wheel and come up with something. This lady, who I admire greatly and who I would imagine would have the most control over these kids, she's saying that she's losing control over them. So it's difficult for me to produce these resources that I don't even know exist yet. So yeah, I'm constantly like I'm on Pinterest all the time trying to look

> for stuff because it's just — I'm not coming up with it on my
> own, you know, whereas I try it and it's just not working out, so
> I need outside help. (Interview, March 4, 2016)

Mr. Barnes stated that he was "burnt out." He also repeated several times that he and other teachers felt "defeated." Although he was trying hard and had yet to miss a day of school, it was quite clear that he was projecting his negative conclusions about motivation onto the students instead of thinking about different ways to engage students. While he acknowledged that the school lacked resources, he did not see how the entire system contributed to the problems he faced at Baker. He was unable to see how his beliefs about students lacking motivation and his pedagogical practices potentially influenced how students engaged with him, the course content, and the school. Instead, he described the school and students' behaviors as the problem, which contributes to deficit narratives of students at Baker and, as the next section discusses, erodes the trust between students and teachers that is necessary to foster relationships and to create positive learning environments.

The Need for Trust

In the next excerpt, students discuss what it would take for teachers to understand them. They suggest that teachers like Mr. Crowley get to truly know them and the community and that teachers try to empathize with students without demeaning them. This means understanding, as the students describe, that their lives are "hard." However, this also means letting students know they genuinely care by trying to understand their experiences and not forming deficit assumptions based on stereotypes. Furthermore, the students reference a need for additional support to help teachers do these things.

> Nicole: Basically, you're trying to say . . . tell me if I'm characterizing this correctly. Some teachers don't understand [the local neighborhood]. They don't understand . . .
>
> Renee: Philadelphia, period.
>
> Nicole: Philadelphia, period.
>
> Nicole: Let's go back to Mr. Crowley, using him as an example. He doesn't understand that sometimes your life is hard. You might go through some things before [you get to school]? How can he better understand you? You might not want to come in and sit like this [hands folded]. I don't know many eighth graders that want to come in and sit like this, right? No matter where they're from, but [this neighborhood in] Philadelphia is

a different place than he grew up. How can he teach you better? How can he understand you? Be a better teacher?

Bianca: He need to find somebody that teach teachers because he need help.

Nicole: He does have someone, right?

Bianca: No. He ain't teaching him right.

Nicole: What do you think, Renee?

Renee: What you say?

Nicole: How can Mr. Crowley have a better understanding? Understand that it's hard?

Renee: Let him stay down in [this neighborhood] for about a month. He going to start acting like us and being like we do. Acting crazy and stuff.

Bianca: No, I say two months. Two months.

Renee: Yeah.

Jalayla: Let him stay down here for two years and I bet you he going —

Rashanna: He going to be dead.

Bianca: Right. He ain't going to be able to survive out here.

Renee: For real.

Rashanna: I bet he already going to be hung by the time he walked out the building. I don't like him.

Nicole: Tell me about Ms. Jenkins. Does she understand you?

Jalayla: Yeah, Ms. Jenkins understands us because . . .

Renee: She from down here. (Group Interview, June 15, 2016)

In the final excerpt of this conversation, the students discuss how teachers, especially Mr. Crowley, call their parents to report negative student behavior.

The students characterize report card conferences by saying, "It's like they're out to get us." The crucial relationships between teachers and students cannot develop because of a lack of trust students have in their teachers, the complicated relational dynamics and resulting power struggles, and the deficit ideologies teachers have about students and their families. Furthermore, this excerpt also highlights the complicated relationship between the school and parents that is often informed by the negative feelings parents have about the school and staff.

Nicole: What about Mr. Crowley?

[Ms. Roberts is yelling in the background. Her classroom is next to the library, where we are meeting. The students and I often meet during a missed prep in which students have free time and often sit and talk or play cards.]

Jalayla: He just call our parents. That's all he do.

Nicole: Does he only call for things negative?

Bianca: Yeah.

Renee: Yep.

Jalayla: He don't never call for nothing positive.

Rashanna: He'll say it to us, but he won't call.

Nicole: He will say positive things to you?

Jalayla: Watch when report card time comes. He'll say positive things when we by ourselves, but when we [with our parents] . . .

Rashanna: Then we the worst kids in the damn world.

Jalayla: Yeah, but when it comes to our parents, "Oh your child does this and she needs to learn this and she needs to learn that."

Nicole: I have sat in on those report card conferences. What do you all think about those?

Rashanna: They lie. They say a lot of stuff that's not true.
Jalayla: They really do.

> Rashanna: It's like they're out to get us.

> Bianca: I mean, you see us run around and stuff like that. They
> make it bigger than what it really is. They make it seem bigger
> than what it is. (Group Interview, June 15, 2016)

An important basic concept of teaching is that students want to know that their teachers care about them. For Bianca, Jalayla, Rashanna, and Renee, that involved trying to understand their lives and what they go through at home and in the community. Instead of thinking about students' home lives through a negative perspective, other ways to consider students can include thinking about how they are problem-solving at school and at home and the adaptive way that they respond to often-challenging environments. For example, when students fight other students, they often do so as a means of surviving and establishing a habitus of fierceness. When students state that they "don't care," this can be a way of not showing investment in something or someone to protect oneself. Bianca, Jalayla, Rashanna, and Renee articulate their understandings and frustrations about schooling at Baker, and they offer important insights that teachers, and other educators, can learn from. Our conversation also highlights the importance of paying attention to systemic inequality, which is discussed in the next chapter.

Students did not perceive that Mr. Crowley and Mr. Barnes demonstrated that they cared about students. Instead, students believed they blamed students and wanted to punish them. Blaming students is a direct embodiment of deficit ideologies in which systems of oppression are not recognized (Gorski, 2011, 2023; Valencia, 2010, 2019). Deficit ideology, as articulated by Mr. Barnes and Mr. Crowley in the preceding excerpts, blames students as not being motivated. This ideology, which is woven into schools and other institutions, is a way of noting "deficiencies" in marginalized communities or individuals and indirectly justifies oppression by placing those being oppressed as the problem (Gorski, 2011, 2023; Valencia, 2010, 2019).

In addition, as a first-year teacher, Mr. Barnes noted how he was in survival mode and often struggled to make it through each day. Mr. Barnes projected his struggles on students. Instead of thinking about his teaching, the school, or the broader system, he considered "these students" to be the problem (see Nygreen, 2013). Although educated in more progressive educational approaches that reflect a middle-class habitus, Mr. Barnes, influenced by the violent and controlling nature of Baker, reacts to students in ways that run counter to the progressive approaches to education he espouses that value listening to and learning from students. For their part, students tend to view Mr. Barnes as "boring" and a "pushover." Although he does not yell at students, he reverts to more behaviorist and less progressive pedagogies based on assumptions about what students need and who should be controlled. Mr. Barnes, for example, engaged in pedagogical practices that do not align with his beliefs about education and the more progressive schooling experiences that inspired him to become a teacher. Instead, he has adopted a different type of habitus to survive at Baker School, and the consequences of this are that he quit teaching at the school and was not, according to his own words, an effective teacher at Baker. It is also important to note the potential cultural, racial, and socioeconomic differences between Mr. Barnes and his students that may have contributed to his students' perceptions of him not caring about them.

Ms. Smith, while more assertive in her actions toward students, was perceived by students as caring about them and appeared to be more successful in teaching at Baker than Mr. Barnes. Although Mr. Barnes did not yell at his students, those students did not appear to believe he cared about them. Ms. Smith yelled at students, yet they perceived her as caring about them. Both teachers contributed to the hidden curriculum of control. These two complex narratives provide insight into the deficit default that surrounds parents and students at Baker. Ms. Smith was attempting to educate her students about the culture of power (Delpit, 1995). But this comes with unintended consequences, such as contributing to the deficit default. Even though Mr. Barnes believes his not yelling at students is evidence of how he respects them, he often speaks about his students in disparaging terms. Ms. Smith, on the other hand, frequently yells at the students, but many students love Ms. Smith because they believe she cares about them. She also has many conversations with me about how much she cares for her students. Thus, Ms. Smith, Mr. Barnes, and Mr. Crowley internalize and perpetuate the deficit default ideologies in different ways, and while operationalized differently, they all contribute to the curriculum of control and deficit narratives.

Summary

In chapter 5, I show how the deficit default surrounding Baker School and its students became internalized by students, teachers, and their families. Baker School is seen as a "last resort" by many, including students and teachers. While students internalize the negative perceptions, they also try to push back against them through behaviors and language that demonstrate a habitus of fierceness. Teachers, often because of frustration and stress, perpetuated the deficit perceptions and blamed students for what they perceive as a lack of motivation instead of recognizing the systemic and structural factors that directly impact students at Baker School, which is discussed in more depth in the next chapter. Students also blame teachers for not understanding them and their experiences, and students note how the principal perpetuates the deficit ideology by not being involved and dismissing their concerns. The frustration of both students and teachers, who are operating in survival mode and experiencing burnout, continues to perpetuate the negative perceptions of the school. Teachers feel burned out and are exasperated by what they describe as a lack of support from the principal and administration. These tensions between students and teachers make it difficult to form relationships, as described as in chapter 3, because students believe teachers do not care about them. A consequence of the deficit default is that everyone is blaming each other but no one is connecting the challenges that Baker faces to larger systemic issues, which are discussed in the next chapter.

Chapter 6

The Realities of Systemic Failure

Students, parents, teachers, and administrators tend to agree that Baker is not a "good" school. But it is important to explain that Baker School functions in, is a part of, and is affected by other systems that contribute to Baker's status as a "failing school." These systems include, for example, the local and national public education system, tax revenue systems, the job market, the justice system, health care, child protection agencies, as well as systems of oppression and structural racism. However, the ways in which a variety of other systems and policies affect Baker are often ignored or denied, and instead, individuals (primarily students, teachers, and parents) are blamed for the school's "failure." In this chapter, I describe the disinvestment in urban public schools by beginning with the lack of basic resources and how this lack of resources impacts students and teachers at Baker. This chapter also builds on the discussion of teacher burnout discussed in the previous chapter and shows how systemic issues contribute to this burnout. In chapter 7, I show how these macro-level inequalities, which are often invisible, result in teachers and students struggling for their humanity at Baker School.

Lack of Funding and Resources

A central component of the systemic failure of urban public schools is a lack of funding and resources. It is challenging for schools to operate effectively when broader issues of poverty and structural racism have not been addressed (Anyon, 1997; Silva-Laya et al., 2020). As discussed in chapter 1, income and wealth disparities in the United States have increased since the 1970s (see, e.g., Hanushek & Lindseth, 2009; Hoffmann et al., 2020; Reardon, 2011, 2018), and while there is not a consensus in the literature, recent research (Jackson, 2020; Jackson & Mackevicius, 2024; Miller, 2018) has found that increased school spending improves student achievement outcomes. The disparity in school funding in Philadelphia that chapter 1 overviewed is evident in Philadelphia schools such as Baker. Physical aspects of the building needed repair, including the plumbing and the roof, which frequently leaks. When students were asked questions about the school, physical appearance was usually one of the first things they mentioned. Students particularly lamented the leaking roof, missing ceiling tiles, peeling paint, trash around the school, dirty floors, and the state of the bathrooms.

Building Disrepair

Students described the school as "dirty" and "falling apart." By "falling apart," students often referred to the peeling paint on the walls, which was chipped in many places, revealing the multiple layers of peeling paint of various colors. Students also lamented the missing ceiling tiles in classrooms and hallways and commented on how these were not replaced or frequently fell during class. Other common observations students made included noting that trash was strewn about the hallways and classrooms, that the bathrooms were missing toilet paper and soap, and the plumbing and roofing leaks that occurred throughout the building. "Why can't this school just look like a good school?" Jalayla, an eighth grader, asked. Her friend, Bianca, added to the conversation: "They could try to make it look bright and happy instead of depressing." As discussed in a previous chapter, Rashanna, a fellow eighth grader, stated, while laughing at the irony: "Like the computer has dust on them and there's the duster that's leaning on them. The duster there is literally leaning on the stuff with the dust on it, and they're not using it. It's just like dust everywhere. How does dust get stuck to the floor like that?"

Lack of Cleanliness

In addition to the general sense of the physical building needing repair, students and the principal, Ms. Washington, agreed that the school, in particular the school bathrooms, needed to be cleaner. Ms. Washington stopped me one morning as I came into the building and asked,

> "Nicole, do you see this dirt?" She is pointing to a picture she took on her phone of one of the bathrooms. "Would you let your house be that dirty? No, of course you would not. This is unacceptable. They mean to tell me that this is one day's accumulation of dirt? I don't think so. I am so tired of trying to force people to do their jobs around here. One day's dirt and it looks like this? I don't know, Nicole, I am so tired. I am so tired of this." (Fieldnotes, January 29, 2016)

I cannot comment about the dirt in the other bathrooms, but the staff bathrooms were so dirty that I tried to avoid going to the bathroom at the school even when spending full days there. I remember thinking Rashanna might be partially exaggerating when she told me during one of my first visits to the school, "I don't go to the bathroom here. I wait. There is no toilet paper, no soap, no paper towels, and they are so dirty." However, I soon learned that she was not exaggerating. I adopted a similar approach to try and avoid using the bathrooms after nearly vomiting while washing my hands in the staff bathroom. The utility sink, which is right next to the hand-washing sink, was filled with foul-smelling, mildewed, brown water.

Limited Educational Offerings and Staffing Constraints

Another aspect of the physical building that impacted students was that it did not have an official gym. The cafeteria and the gym were the same area; thus, gym classes, which students had once a week, either took place outside when it was warm or in the students' homeroom classes during the winter or on rainy days.

Other specialty classes, in addition to gym, were generally referred to by students and teachers as "prep classes" and included art, gym/health, science prep, math prep, and computer/writing prep. Teachers would have their "preparation period" when students went to these classes, and thus art, gym, and other classes were referred to by students and teachers as "prep classes" or "prep." These classes were much preferred by students and teachers alike. When they did not have one of these classes, students and teachers would comment: "I didn't get my prep!"

Some groups of students, such as one of the eighth-grade classes, never had art all year because of a scheduling issue. During the many gym classes I sat in on, which took place in the students' homeroom classroom, students watched videos from the 1980s and were asked to complete worksheets that, for example, included labeling body parts and organs in the respiratory system.

The science prep classes were taught by a man on his way to retirement, Mr. Phillips, who was also absent for several months during the year. Mr. Phillips was generally respected by teachers and students. He was a tall Black man in his late 50s. Despite being absent for so much of the year, he was not disliked. Teachers, with a kind of reverence and empathy, would say, "Mr. Phillips, he is tired. He has been at this for so long. He is just tired." Students would also listen to him and seemed to respect him largely because he had been at the school for many years. However, his pedagogy appeared to be lacking. For example, during one of the days Mr. Phillips was present, he came into the eighth-grade students' homeroom classroom, pulled up a video on YouTube about magnetics, and told the students to watch it.

Other schools' specialty classes might include art, music, a foreign language, theater, computer programming, and so on. But Baker's offerings of specialty classes were limited and primarily focused on test preparation. During computer prep, students were expected to spend a significant amount of time taking practice standardized tests online instead of learning computer or technology skills.

The computer prep was taught by a teacher that students loved, Ms. Roberts. Ms. Roberts was a Black woman in her 50s. Students always tried to stay and help Ms. Roberts; they came to her class as often as they could. She had been teaching at the school for 10 years. Although the students loved her, they frequently said she "does not know anything about computers." For example, Rashanna stated: "She is not qualified to teach computer. She was supposed to teach writing, but they told her to teach computer. She doesn't even know how to turn the computers on" (Group Interview, June 7, 2016). However, despite not learning anything about computers or technology in her class, the students thought that Ms. Roberts was a good teacher, and they respected her. They went to her for advice, comfort, when they needed a break, to hang out, or to avoid being in another class.

The math prep class, taught by Ms. Myers, a middle-aged Black woman with ties to the community, tended to involve remedial math. During one math prep class, the eighth-grade students were instructed to answer two problems and then sit and talk quietly. Most of the students skipped the class. There were two students who came to math prep on time, and six more students joined by the end of the period. The eight students completed their two math problems and then two students slept while the rest played a card game.

When I asked the students why they did not go to math prep, a common response included: "We don't do anything in there." In addition to the eight students who attended class, a few other eighth graders ran in and out of the math prep classroom. Kwame ran into the room for a few minutes, got into an argument with another student, picked up a broom and started chasing the student around the room, dropped the broom, and then ran out. Ms. Myers reflected on this experience to the remaining eight students: "You know it doesn't hurt me if you don't come to class and do your work. I get paid either way." As discussed in the previous chapter, these types of comments were especially jarring to students. Students would say that these statements made them "want to punch them [teachers] in they faces" (Jalayla, Interview, June 15, 2016) and contributed to feelings of disconnect between students and teachers as described in the previous chapter. Furthermore, staffing constraints, scheduling conflicts, inadequate preparation, and feelings of burnout contribute to the limited educational offerings and experiences that students have at Baker. As a result of these issues, students are not getting a chance to have art, learn about computers, experience different sports, or learn about science.

Little or No Educational Materials

Teachers and students were also significantly impacted by a lack of basic educational resources, such as textbooks. For example, the seventh-grade social studies class had a small set of extremely out-of-date textbooks. Other Philadelphia schools had social studies textbooks that had been published within the past three years. The social studies curriculum that teachers were expected to follow referred to these textbooks, so this was just another challenge for teachers at Baker. Mr. Barnes discussed the textbook situation in which there was one textbook for all of the eighth-grade students.

> Mr. Barnes: Yeah. They had one book so occasionally I would scan things out of it and make copies of that, which I do not think is legal, but . . .
>
> Nicole: They had one textbook for the entire seventh and eighth grade for social studies?

Mr. Barnes: It was eighth grade, yeah. There was a small set of seventh grade, but they were also so dilapidated and old that it was actually more harmful to use those.

Nicole: OK.

Mr. Barnes: That I just clearly made my own.

Nicole: OK. Wow. I can't believe I didn't know that.

Mr. Barnes: It was like those books were made as the Soviet Union was falling apart. A lot of those countries don't have those names. It was bad. It was really bad so I made it. Yeah, for eighth grade we had a singular textbook. For seventh grade there was maybe half the class set so you could probably pair people up. Actually, what I did was I went to my old teacher supervisor at [another Philadelphia school] and asked if I could borrow her textbook and make copies out of it and stuff.

Nicole: OK. The students at [another Philadelphia school] in the seventh grade have textbooks?

Mr. Barnes: Yeah. It was a different textbook. It was updated and fine.

Nicole: In your scope and sequence if you had one, it would have been referencing the textbook that students had at [other Philadelphia schools]?

Mr. Barnes: Like the more recent one, yeah. Ours was outdated so, again, the scope and sequence naturally didn't reference things in our book. It would be like, "Go to page 42 and it would just be a totally different section."

Nicole: Wow. Was [the principal] aware of this?

Mr. Barnes: Oh, yeah. That was like before school had even started. She was like, "Just so you know there are really no textbooks." I don't know. I think going to school for history these days they instill in you that textbooks are not great so you should really be reaching out. It wasn't like the end of the world. There were some days where it probably would have been nice to have it as a reference point, but we didn't. That was certainly not a deal breaker or anything, but looking back it's kind of, I don't know. It's sad, but it's also a little funny that it

> worked out as well as it did just with really no tools. But I don't know. I guess that's the way it's going because now you have to do more investigative research to make sure that what you're finding isn't either myth or whitewashed. That sounds like kind of the skill I was trying to teach them so it did kind of work perfectly with how I was going about it. (Interview, July 29, 2016)

Teachers at Baker had to buy many of their own materials, including copy paper.[1] There was a library at Baker, but like many schools in Philadelphia, there was no librarian; so the library did not function as a library that students could use. At Baker, the library was a place where meetings were held because it had an air conditioning unit. Baker had a nurse at the school two days a week. On the other days, the job of nurse fell to the principal. The school's only counselor often filled that role as well.

The limited number of nurses in some of Philadelphia's schools had been a problem since the 2011 budget cuts and layoffs. In 2014, two students died in Philadelphia schools that did not have a nurse assigned to them at all (Strum, 2015). The lack of school nurses is seen across the United States, and a 2017 study found that only 40% of public schools have a full-time school nurse (Jean, 2022), and the nurses that remain are experiencing burnout. In addition, when teachers and other staff take over additional responsibilities such as serving as a nurse or a counselor, it can lead to increased stress and contribute to feelings of burnout, which is discussed in the next section.

Faculty Burnout

In addition to Baker's physical appearance and limited materials, the lack of funding and financial resources were evident in staffing issues. On the first day of the 2015–2016 school year, Baker did not have a secretary or a middle school English teacher. It was not until November that there was a permanent teacher hired for the middle school position. Before that, there were three other teachers in that position who left prior to the teacher who was finally hired. It is also important to note that all four of the middle school teachers were new to the school that year, and three of the four were first-year teachers.

During the previous school year, there had been considerable turnover of middle school teachers as well. There were seven different teachers that school year. Thus, in two years, there were 15 different teachers in the four middle school teacher positions. At Baker, teacher turnover and the constant stream of inexperienced teachers created additional problems, including potentially contributing to the power struggles between teachers and students discussed in previous chapters. Issues of teacher turnover are not unique to Baker School or Philadelphia. Using national statistics, scholars have found that teacher turnover in schools with high percentages of low-income students is almost 50% higher than schools not categorized as having low-income students, and teachers at schools serving predominantly students of color leave with 46% more frequency than teachers at schools serving mostly white students (Carver-Thomas & Darling-Hammond, 2019).

In addition to this high teacher turnover, the school had difficulty getting substitute teachers. This was a phenomenon that occurred in many Philadelphia public schools, including the one I taught at for many years (see also McCorry, 2016). Demand for substitute teachers has always been higher than supply, and in other urban cities like Chicago, researchers have noted the disparity between increased substitute shortages in schools with lower socioeconomic statuses (Roach, 2023). When a substitute position is not filled, teachers lose their 45-minute preparation (prep) period and instead have to "cover" or teach another class during that time. For many weeks at a time, the teachers at Baker would not have a single prep period. At Baker, it was not uncommon for approximately six to seven teachers (out of a staff of 28 classroom and specialty teachers) to be absent each day. There never was a day I visited the school when all teachers were present, which means that teachers' already challenging jobs become more exhausting, as reflected in comments many teachers and other staff members made about being mentally and physically "tired."

Depersonalization

The consistent lack of substitute teachers, the increasing disciplinary issues, and the general chaos at the school contributed to the faculty exhibiting signs of burnout, which included, among others, emotional exhaustion and depersonalization (see Bottiani et al., 2019; Camacho et al., 2021; Camacho & Parham, 2019; Madigan & Kim, 2021; Maslach & Jackson, 1981; Maslach et al., 1996; Schaufeli & Salanova, 2007; Schultz, 2018; Skaalvik & Skaalvik, 2017). Depersonalization includes "negative, cynical attitudes and feelings about one's students or colleagues" (Skaalvik & Skaalvik, 2010, p. 1060).

First-year teacher Mr. Barnes described, multiple times, how he was extremely burned out.

> Nicole: Yeah. So are you planning to teach somewhere else next year?

> Mr. Barnes: Yeah, I'm going to try site selection, but I'm open to whatever, it's like just I don't feel like it would be any better. And this is — but I have no desire to do administration, I have no desire to do anything but be a classroom teacher. And I think if I were here again next year, I would not be in that mindset anymore because this alone is like, I'm burned out, like I'm just outright burnt out at this point and you can only do that to yourself for so long. I still have to — I'm burned out now and I still have 73 days to go, and that's a considerable amount of time but

> not many breaks or anything in between. . . . My philosophy on this job will be my philosophy on life in general, like it's like a movie, you only get to see it once and that's to just try to take it all in as much as you can. So I'm not going to be absent if I can physically get out of bed, or I'm not going to be, you know, late or anything if I can help it because I'm just going to give it my all and try my very best. But I think this year is the most I can do. I really think if I try to come back next year I would just probably quit, I don't think I can make it. I don't think I can make it through this year, you know, to be totally honest with you, every day it's like inconceivable that there's more, that we're not at the end yet, you know. And that's the toughest thing to try to find ways to keep moving, and like occasionally I'll have like an epiphany. Like I was in the shower the other day, and I thought of what they could do for the quarter three project, and it's like in the beginning you're planning that stuff out before they're here, but once it hits, it's so hard to plan ahead because like just your day-to-day plans don't go well. So the fact that you have to plan weeks in advance it's really tough to do. I feel like I trained for a five-mile run, and I still got 15 to go, you know, like I hit the wall.
>
> What I felt coming in here today, just like that knot in my stomach, just feeling nauseous and everything, dissipated because of how that first class went. I mean when I like take the train or drive in like sometimes I like almost I miss stops and stuff because it's just like I can't accept that I'm voluntarily coming back,[2] you know. But I'm trying. (Interview, March 4, 2016)

As described in chapter 5, Mr. Barnes believed that the student population at Baker School was "unmotivated" in general and "hard to teach." This was evidence of how he demonstrated the signs of "depersonalization" associated with burnout — having negative opinions of one's students (Skaalvik & Skaalvik, 2010). Mr. Barnes was, like most first-year teachers, struggling. However, he was trying. He had not missed a single day of school and was often at the school more than an hour early. Consistent with the other signs of burnout he demonstrated, Mr. Barnes did not feel like there was anything he could do, and he received little support from the school administration. While the principal was not the focus of this research, it is important to contextualize that she was busy putting out fires. I had many meetings with her, and she seemed to care very much about her school and students, but she also seemed overwhelmed and that her hands were tied. She also expressed signs of frustration and exhaustion.

Too Many Responsibilities

In addition to the lack of support teachers experienced, many staff members, like Ms. Johnson, took on additional responsibilities. As described previously, there was a nurse at the school two days a week. This meant that other staff had to take over these responsibilities. There was one counselor for over 500 students, and the counselor ended up taking on the roles of substitute teacher, de facto principal, nurse, secretary, and counselor. Ms. Johnson, the school counselor, taught two classes, covered at least one class a day, and recited the morning announcements. She also acted as the school nurse, met with parents, was responsible for the eighth graders' high school applications, was the eighth-grade sponsor who planned trips, the dance, and the graduation ceremony.[3] She was supposed to meet with students, but that part of her job was often limited because of the multiple roles she had to play.

Ms. Johnson was a middle-aged Black woman with two young children in grade school. She had been at Baker for five years, and before that she worked at several other schools in Philadelphia. Ms. Johnson was very well liked by teachers and students. She exuded kindness and openness, even though she frequently demonstrated signs of being overwhelmed. She cared about the school and the students. Her colleagues often described her as doing "everything." When I first met her in 2014, another teacher told me, "She is the principal, nurse, disciplinarian, substitute, and counselor. You name it; she does it."

When Ms. Johnson and I spoke one-on-one, she was often trying to multitask. This included prepping for two of the classes she taught each day by looking on YouTube for a video to show the students. All teachers had school-supplied computers, and there were screens and projectors in each of the classrooms. Thus, showing a video was a common approach by many teachers in a pinch. But "pinches" seemed to happen with regularity at Baker. Ms. Johnson would read the morning announcements every morning over the loudspeaker, which also included reciting the pledge of allegiance and the daily affirmation.[4] She also had many meetings with parents and wore a walkie-talkie so that she could be contacted immediately. Other staff also frequently used the walkie-talkie or loudspeaker to request Ms. Johnson report to another meeting, the office, or a classroom.

> Today Ms. Johnson and I had about five minutes alone when I found her in an empty classroom on the third floor. She was making coffee and invited me to sit with her. We spoke about being moms, and she was relishing the quiet of this classroom. Of course, after five minutes, her name buzzed over the walkie-talkie, but she didn't need to go far as we heard the yelling on the other end of the hallway soon enough. Two eighth-grade students were yelling at each other, and it escalated into a physical fight. Ms. Johnson counseled one of the students afterward while another teacher spoke to the other student, and the other

> staff members tried to usher the other students back into their respective classrooms from the hallways. (Fieldnotes, February 16, 2016)

Ms. Johnson understood the many struggles that students went through daily, often before they got to school. She tried to mentor and counsel students like Bianca, Jalayla, Renee, and Rashanna, but her interactions were often rushed because Ms. Johnson had far too many critical roles, and she was in a constant state of triaging emergencies that resulted from these roles. Thus, her dealings with students primarily involved "putting out fires" rather than being intentional and prepared in her primary role as counselor.

Just "Putting Out Fires"

One example of these "fires" included when Ms. Crawford told Ms. Johnson that Ms. Sanders "grabbed Nadira [her daughter in second grade] by the shirt." I was standing with Ms. Crawford when she told Ms. Johnson: "I don't buy clothes for the teacher to be grabbing them. I saw her grab Nadira's shirt." In addition to speaking with angry parents when the principal was not available, other roles included dealing with emergency student situations (e.g., a missing student), serving as the nurse, overseeing dismissal for the many different buses, mentoring a counseling intern (Denise), running programs and partnerships with local organizations and universities, hosting a high school fair, helping eighth graders apply to high school, serving as the eighth-grade sponsor planning graduation and trips, and filling out a large amount of required paperwork. (Ms. Johnson's roles were like those of other counselors in the schools I worked and researched in; however, many counselors did not also teach classes, although it varied depending on the school.)

Ms. Johnson did a great deal for the students and school. As mentioned earlier, she was universally well liked by students, teachers, and parents. However, on several occasions later in the school year, Ms. Johnson reacted explosively by screaming and throwing papers, her walkie-talkie, and anything else within reach. The counseling intern, Denise, spent considerable time at Baker with Ms. Johnson and described an incident that, according to Denise, "illustrates Johnson's burnout."

> Denise: She was always being pulled out of things, and there was just one defining moment and I talked about it in class for a while. Basically I just saw the manifestations of burnout by Ms. Johnson and she got very, very upset with Ms. Mercer. They were pretty good friends and Ms. Johnson was just very candid with me all the time and telling me her true opinions about people to me. I knew she was very close with Ms. Mercer and basically they were like the two teachers who take on many of

the principal's responsibilities and when she was out, would take over her [the principal's] roles. Ms. Johnson was being put into a meeting with a teacher and then with a student issue, but then she had to cover a class. She was like a permanent substitute teacher, and she was supposed to cover a class for Mercer, but Mercer ended up having the class two periods in a row and apparently it's a very challenging class. Ms. Mercer came down and wasn't happy about it, and Ms. Johnson was like, "I don't know which one to deal with, I'm doing ten different things." Then she, to put it in short, just freaked out. She cursed and threw her walkie across the hall and then stormed out the office and she went to her office, which obviously wasn't far, and just was like not yelling *at* me but *to* me type of thing. She was like, "I hate this school," and there were people, I could hear people coming in the hallway and listening and she was like, "I hate it here, like the last thing I needed was something from her, someone like her yelling at me."

Nicole: Ms. Mercer was yelling at her?

Denise: She wasn't really yelling at her, well she didn't raise her voice but there was strife between them and Johnson felt that from Mercer. Then Johnson is like, "I don't need that from her — we were supposed to be a team. I had stuff to do." And she was really saying how she didn't like the school, and there were at least two students in the hallway. She was in her office and I kind of left the door open. I was in the doorway. I followed her into her office, but I left the door open because when she came in there she threw her laptop, threw a chair so I was like oh God. I was like oh God and then so Mercer comes up, she looks at me she goes, "Is she talking about me," and I'm just silent I was like ah, and she was like, "Are you talking about me," she [Ms. Johnson] is like, "Get out of my office. I don't want to see your face. Get out of my office." While this is happening I go get the walkie she threw across the hall literally from almost from her office like a little bit far [points] into that doorway.

Nicole: Which one? The one where you go into that open stairwell where the benches are?

Denise: Yeah.

Nicole: All that way like down past the restrooms?

Denise: Yes, yes, yes. So she threw it so I went to go get it and then by the time I came back, Mercer had closed or Mercer had left, and the female school cop was in there. I don't think the lady knew who I was, and half the time they think I'm a student anyway, so she kicked me out. She shut the door kind of, and I'm just like OK, so I'm standing in the hallway hearing her yell, like going off.

Nicole: She is yelling now at the officer.

Denise: Yeah, but it was that yelling not *at* but *to* type of thing, and then Washington [the principal] comes out because some-one went and told her and Washington knocks on the door. She is like, "It's like me can I get in." And they are all in there. Then Mercer gets pulled in. Then this was the best part. So OK, then the principal, Mercer, and Johnson are all in there — Who is doing the buses?

Nicole: With the security officer?

Denise: Yes, who is doing buses? Those are the four people you would call for buses, so I'm with her every day, so I'm trying to do it. There is one parent who is there in Ms. Forbes's room all the time.

Nicole: Yes, Ms. Redmond [parent volunteer].

Denise: Yeah, so she is kind of trying to help but I'm standing out the door, buses are showing up, and I'm telling kids, and I'm like I have no idea what kids go where. There is so many kids I was like no one can leave. So I was at the door and I'm like, "No one can leave yet I'm sorry but I can't like this is going to be on me. No one can leave yet." Except there were [a] few people that I knew because they would be a part of the school's different day cares and I knew them. A few kids left and then what's her name Mercer comes out and you could tell she had been crying and she was like, "I got it from here," she went actually, "Thanks, I got [it] from here." Then Ms. Redmond comes up to me, and she was like, "Johnson wants you," and I was like, "I'm doing this. I can't leave because no one else is here." I didn't, no I was like, "What do you want me to do? These kids are just going to literally leave." There have been times when 6-year-olds were like, "Oh I'm going to walk home," and I'm like, "No you are not. Wait for your mom, your mom is coming." I knew there were kids who leave and they shouldn't. And then you obviously have the issue of what if someone tries to take a child. I was like I can't leave and then Mercer finally comes back. But then there is no one in the auditorium, so I go to the auditorium, and then a little bit later Johnson finally comes out and she sees me and as far as I can remember she actually touches my, like rubs my shoulder and she is like she just says sorry in passing. I was just like I don't think I even said anything, and then she was joking with other teachers and one of the other teachers I forget who, I forget her name, joked with her about her going crazy or something real quick and she was like, "It's been a bad day." Then before we left once the kids had left she was like, "I'm really sorry." She apologized. But one, she was like clearly burned out, two, it was also very dangerous for her to throw a freaking walkie because a child could have been walking by. Three, it's irresponsible that you had no one there to run dismissal, but there was a lot of things at play. But that was my craziest, I think, incident at Baker. But it was like, still on one hand it was just like the school has so much need. I feel like what do you do when a lot of issues come down to resources. Resources for I think they need more than, well that's another issue having officers in schools but they need more support for behavior and keeping kids out of the hallway. I think they also need more trainings for how to better understand and deal with the many issues. (Interview, July 25, 2016)

Denise's description of Ms. Johnson's burnout also highlights how a lack of resources, including understaffing and insufficient training and professional development, impacts faculty and students and could potentially cause harm. The lack of resources contributes to the burnout that educators like Ms. Johnson experience and the extreme stress that Ms. Johnson and Mr. Barnes exhibit. However, as Denise points out, children are potentially harmed as a direct result of the lack of resources and associated burnout.

I observed a similar scenario to the one Denise described. During one of the final graduation practices with the eighth-grade students that Ms. Johnson led, she became increasingly frustrated with students who were running around the auditorium, did not know the lyrics to the songs they were supposed to sing, and were not taking practice seriously. Ms. Johnson threw her walkie-talkie across the auditorium and screamed, "Shut the hell up!" She then started crying and told the students that the principal just told her that some of them would not be able to participate in the ceremony. Ms. Johnson yelled, "I fight for you. I do so much for you. But I can't argue on your behalf when you don't do what you are supposed to do." She was screaming for so long and so loudly that the principal walked in and beckoned Ms. Johnson into the hallway. The principal then told the students that practice was canceled for the day and told the teachers to take the students back to class (Fieldnotes, June 17, 2016). As the counselor,

Ms. Johnson's primary role was to support and advocate for students, which she clearly was trying to do. However, she was overwhelmed, ended up doing multiple jobs in the school, and she, as well as the students, suffered.

Ms. Johnson, Mr. Barnes, Mr. Dixon, and many other teachers at Baker were burned out and struggling. Part of this burnout was related to the lack of resources and disinvestment in schools like Baker. Other components of this burnout were the stressful and toxic (e.g., Bottiani et al., 2019; Camacho et al., 2021; Paulle, 2013) environment of Baker and their continuously trying and failing to control students' behavior. These components, including the curriculum of control, the parentification and infantilization of students, and the deficit ideology that results in blaming students and parents, combined with the systemic disinvestment in schools and communities like Baker creates a toxic schooling environment that has a profound impact on students' lives and prospects.

In the next chapter, I focus on the student experience at Baker and highlight the daily experiences and struggles of an eighth-grade student, Rashanna, and a fourth-grade student, Nyeisha.

Summary

This chapter presented examples of systemic failure that contribute to the status quo of urban public schools like Baker and how these are connected to broader systems as well as the historic disinvestment in urban schools in cities like Philadelphia. The systemic disinvestment in Baker School is demonstrated in how the school was literally and physically falling apart, as evidenced by the deteriorating school building, cleanliness issues, the course offerings (or lack thereof) for students, the lack of instructional materials, limited training and support of teachers, the influx of new and/or inexperienced teachers as a result of teacher turnover, and teacher burnout and depersonalization, which are connected to how opportunity gaps manifest in schools (Gorski, 2018). This disinvestment impacts students and teachers, in particular highlighting how even a caring and hardworking counselor, like Ms. Johnson, cannot compensate for the failing system. Chapter 6 put into context the many struggles that teachers and counselors are facing to humanize teachers and contextualize their experiences. In the next chapter, I focus on students and how they, like teachers, are struggling for their humanity at Baker School, and how they are still children whose futures and dreams are directly impacted by the systemic failures that this chapter discussed.

Chapter 7

Struggling for Humanity

This chapter focuses on two students, an eighth grader and a fourth grader, to contextualize their experiences of schooling by highlighting how the systemic realities, the curriculum of control, and the parentification and infantilization directly impact students. I describe the *symbolic violence* that occurs at Baker and how students and the broader society internalize this. I conclude the chapter by articulating the resiliency that students and teachers have as they navigate the challenging, stressful, and at times toxic schooling environment of Baker (see Boen et al., 2020; Paulle, 2013).

As the previous chapters describe, the curriculum of control, the resulting power struggles and resistance, as well as the systemic lack of resources culminate in a *deficit default* based on negative feelings of students, teachers, parents, and the entire school. Teachers, as the previous chapter illustrates, are burned out. Much in the same way that teachers are burned out and struggling, students are also struggling. Many students at Baker navigate complex challenges daily, as well as taking care of themselves and younger siblings. This chapter focuses on the contextualized experiences of two students to remind readers that these are real students at a real school, not simply abstract facts or stereotypes.

Schooling and the Community: A Glimpse into Rashanna's Experience

Rashanna is an eighth-grade student who has attended Baker since kindergarten. According to Rashanna, the "categories of people [students] include cool, nerdy, stinky, weird, and just like outcast. No one talks to them" (Interview, May 31, 2016). She describes herself and others describe her as one of the "cool" and popular students. Rashanna discusses wanting to be an investigative police officer. She also loves art and is a talented artist. Rashanna missed out on opportunities to explore her artistic talent and to participate in the mural club because she wasn't able to take an art class all year when her eighth-grade class was never put on the art teacher's schedule. Rashanna explained, "Yeah. I came back to the school this year because I thought we was going to have her [the art teacher], but we didn't." She continues, "I don't know [if we will have art]. First, it was supposed to be the second marking period. Then they switched it to the third. Now they switched it to the fourth. And we still haven't had art" (Interview, May 3, 2016). Rashanna often skips her other classes and goes to the art room. She describes how she skips English: "I don't go to his class. [pause] He actually tells me that he likes it better when I am not there, so I don't go. But he better give me a good grade since he told me not to come to his class" (Interview, May 3, 2016). Rashanna was not deeply invested in grades, but she pointed out that Mr. Webster encouraged her not to come to class, and thus she believed it would be unfair for him to fail her. I have observed the English teacher, Mr. Webster, tell students to leave his class. As mentioned in an earlier chapter, other teachers, school leaders, and staff often made comments about how they were glad that there were few students in attendance or that they hoped a certain student would not come to school. Rashanna was one of these students. She was frequently in trouble with teachers and other adults. My experience of Rashanna was that she was a smart, caring, and intelligent young woman. However, based on comments from teachers and other staff members, this was not the impression other adults had. Mr. James, the director of the after-school programming at Baker, told me that Rashanna was "terrible": "Mr. James mentions that he saw me talking to Rashanna in the cafeteria. He says, 'Well, yesterday when you weren't here, she was cursing out Mr. Kelly. They were in a screaming match. She is always going off on somebody. It must be learned behavior. If you had seen Rashanna yesterday. She cursed him out like there was no tomorrow and then she just walked away'" (Fieldnotes, February 10, 2016). I had never seen Rashanna behave this way. I would often see her put her head down in class, and she seemed to rarely complete assignments, but I had never seen her yell at an adult. Ms. Johnson, the counselor, knew Rashanna well and thought that she had a lot of potential. Ms. Johnson, like Mr. James, suspected that Rashanna had very limited parental involvement.

Limited Parental Support

Rashanna tried to avoid going home; she was either at dance at the recreation center, at Deana's [another student] house, or with her cousin. She respected her mother because she worked several jobs, but Rashanna was angry that her mother was never around. In the following excerpt from one of our conversations, Rashanna described how she raised herself and her nephew, who is four.

This is another example of how the students at Baker were parentified and of Mr. Dixon's argument (chapter 4) that students did not listen to their parents because they had lost respect for them. Rashanna discussed her disappointment in her family when they did "dumb" things, when they "leave," or are taken from her. She cited these aspects as reasons why she said she "doesn't care because no one cares about" her.

Nicole: When you said you thought your life was going to be the same forever, what do you mean the same? What's changed?

Rashanna: Like when I was younger, I thought I was always

going to wear ballies and barrettes and always have the same friends, and always feel the same way about people now. I used to like think everything was joyful. I used to always have hope. At this point, I don't really know what hope is. Sometimes I have it. Most of the time I really don't care about a lot. Like if you ask Mr. Dixon, he'll say that most of the time I say I don't care a lot. For the most part I don't. I don't really feel as though I need to. I'm not going to act like I care if I don't. I don't give them excuses because I still don't care.

Officer Perry: Excuse me real quick. Is Edward in your class?

Rashanna: No.

Nicole: Let's talk about two things you said. What do you mean when you say you don't have hope?

Rashanna: I don't. I don't really like believe most things people say, I know it's not true so I just don't listen. I choose not to. I like close my ears and my mouth. I just don't talk. I just completely zone that person out. I don't like advice very much.

[Students are yelling in the background.]

Nicole: So a lot of people try to give you advice. What kind of advice are they giving you?

Rashanna: They don't think that I should act the way I do. I don't really feel like my mom and dad should be telling me anything. My mom was at work most of my life. My dad was locked up most of my life. I learned from the streets, just like most of the other kids in this school. We all taught ourselves.

Nicole: What did you learn?

Rashanna: I learned not to care and don't listen. Listen to yourself 'cuz [pause] nobody will give you better advice than yourself.

Nicole: When you say you need to learn not to care, what made you stop caring?

Rashanna: Other people didn't care about me.

Nicole: Like teachers, family?

Rashanna: Most people in my family, they said they would never want to leave me [pause] this that and a third, and then they did something dumb. They either got took from me or left me. I mean [pause] most people I can't really blame for it. For some reason, even the people who are here I feel like they left me. It just made it even worse when my grandma died two days after my 10th birthday. So, after a while [pause] I just stopped caring. I don't get attached to a lot of people. Only person I'm really attached to now is my nephew. I basically raised him. His mom never really was around. (Interview, May 11, 2016)

Learning from the Streets

Rashanna stated that she raised herself and "learned from the streets." One of the things she learned was to "to run and hide 'cuz that's what we all do" (Interview, May 11, 2016). This running and hiding was often in reference to the police. Rashanna stated that she frequently worried about getting killed or going to jail. After the eighth-grade dance, which I attended along with Ms. Washington, Ms. Jenkins, Ms. Mercer, and Ms. Johnson, Rashanna told me the following Monday morning, "The other night, Friday night, we literally almost got killed" (June 20, 2016). Rashanna described how the peers she was with threw a bottle at a man's truck. They didn't know the man was outside, but then he started yelling and went into his truck and pulled out a gun. She and her peers hid behind other cars, and then Rashanna said that the cops came, and everyone started running. Rashanna frequently told me about events like this one. This event and others are examples of the situation that adults at the school do not understand. They have no idea of what students go through on the "streets." I asked Rashanna if she was scared.

Nicole: What did it feel like on Friday night? Were you scared?

Rashanna: Yeah, but it's something that we're used to. 'Cuz is like a everyday thing for us.

Nicole: Worrying about getting killed is something you worry about every day?

Rashanna: Yeah, or going to jail.

Rashanna described being scared but also familiar with her fear. She stated that many of her peers were not as scared, like Destin, because he had a gun. I asked if it was common for people to have guns, and Rashanna answered:

Rashanna: Yeah. Most of the boys in this school got guns. They won't bring them into the school but they do got guns.

Nicole: Why do they have them?

Rashanna: Because they get them. [pause] Some people's parents give them to them. The boy last year, everybody in the eighth grade jumped him last year. His mom gave him a gun and brought him back to school. (Interview, June 20, 2016)

Rashanna told me that her mother got a gun many years ago as soon as they moved to this part of Philadelphia. Rashanna described being afraid and glad they had a gun at home.

Our dog went missing out the house. Then, my brother called her [Rashanna's mother] one day and said that the men were sitting in our yard. [pause] They opened our gate and sat in our yard. Our steps are like. [pause]This is the steps to get in the gate and our door is all the way back here. My brother called her one day and said that the men were sitting in our yard. [pause] They opened our gate and sat in our yard. (Interview, June 20, 2016)

Although Rashanna stated that she is used to being afraid and often presented herself as unafraid, in many of our conversations, she appeared frightened. She said she wanted to learn how to use a gun: "She [Rashanna's mother] said she would teach me how to shoot it, just in case someone come in here or something" (Interview, June 20, 2016).

On multiple occasions, Rashanna made comments about how the students at Baker bring the community into the school: "We bring the outside into this school." Rashanna describes how certain behaviors became ingrained in her peers and her family.

Like Haakim, he think that he can do what he want. He think that he can. He says don't fight, he will kill you, or he'll shoot you because I know Haakim's uncle. That's just how his uncles were. Haakim's uncles hung with my brothers. That's how they are. Haakim uncle went with my sister. That's how she is. All his friends, that's how they are. It's just like their natural instinct after a while. And then gangs and all that, if they want you, you don't really have a choice. (Interview, May 11, 2016)

Rashanna was part of a well-known family in the community. Her dad and older siblings belonged to a local gang and were either currently or had already served time in jail. Rashanna was 13 years old, but she looked like she could be at least 16 or older. She stated that when she and her friends were chased by the police, that did not bother her because she looked like she was so much older and not with the younger kids.

The Impact of the Justice System

Rashanna had an interesting relationship with the police. She was frequently involved in negative situations with them or running away from them. However, she would say that she wanted to be a police officer. Rashanna described one time when officers came looking for her at three in the morning. Rashanna was at her friend's house, where she frequently spent the night, and the police could not get anyone to answer the door after banging for some time. Rashanna stated that they were asleep and did not hear anyone. The next day, the police came to Rashanna's house and questioned her about a phone call a male student made from her phone threatening to kill an officer: "So he basically said they killed his brother, so he's going to kill one of them. They didn't know who it was from the voice. They wanted me to tell. They basically said they were going to lock me up if I didn't tell. But I still didn't tell 'cuz I wasn't going to" (Interview, May 31, 2016). Rashanna stated that the "cops" were playing "good cop, bad cop" with her. Rashanna said, "The lady was the good cop, the one who sat down. The man was the bad cop. He just stood there staring at me. I just was laughing. So after a while, they had to get rid of that act" (Interview, May 31, 2016).

The justice system had directly impacted Rashanna's family. The adults in Rashanna's life were never around primarily because they were or had been in jail.

> Rashanna: I think I'm more so mad at my dad when he goes to jail than my brothers because my brother was like locked up six years. That's another reason that like me and Haakim aren't like super close.
>
> Nicole: Why?
>
> Rashanna: Like, when me and Haakim were younger, we used to be like super close. We used to play games and stuff because he used to always be at my grandma's house or his uncle's. After a while, we just realized that his uncle was the reason that my sister got locked up and my brother got locked up.
>
> Nicole: I didn't know your sister got locked up, too?
>
> Rashanna: Yeah, my sister got out of jail at the beginning of last year.

Nicole: Why did your sister and brother get locked up? Did they get locked up at the same time?

Rashanna: No. My sister got locked up a little bit after my brother. My brother turned himself in after the cops came looking for him the day that they locked up Haakim uncle. When he came home from work and found out he just turned himself in.

Nicole: What did Haakim's uncle have to do with it?

Rashanna: Haakim uncle the one who got my brother into doing dumb stuff.

Nicole: Do you want to tell me what kind of dumb stuff?

Rashanna: Like, selling drugs and dumb stuff like that. Now my brother, he like, I mean he didn't no more, but after a while his name was still somehow found in it.

Nicole: He's still in jail?

Rashanna: No, he got out of jail two or three months ago. My dad got out like February. My other brother's in jail now. I don't know what he did.

Nicole: How long has he been in jail?

Rashanna: A few months. (Interview, May 31, 2016)

The experiences that Rashanna describes, being chased by the police, feeling abandoned by her family because they are dead or in jail, learning how to fire a gun, raising her nephew, and raising herself, are in stark contrast to how she is expected to behave at school and perhaps explains why she sometimes yells at adults who try to tell her what to do. She is 13, which is a challenging age for many teenagers, but also she is dealing with complex challenges that many adults have not experienced. At the same time, she is at a school that is chaotic and infantilizing, and she is not able to take the one class — art — that she enjoys because of scheduling failures.

Being Tough: The Habitus of Fierceness

At Baker, Rashanna was feared and respected. She embodied such a habitus of fierceness that other students and often other adults did not bother her. I never saw Rashanna fight. Rashanna told me that she used to fight, not necessarily in school, but in the community. However, she stated, "But at this point I don't feel like fighting. It's not something that I need to do. It's like immature." She would only fight "if you put your hands on me or my family" (Interview, May 31, 2016). Rashanna stated that teachers did not understand students' experiences and that is part of why Rashanna and her peers would say that they did not care about schooling.

Rashanna, however, did care about school, as she discussed in the following excerpt. Here she stated that fighting was "dumb" and that it would not help students in high school. However, she also explained how the community ethos of not showing weakness deeply impacted students' experiences in and out of school. This was shown in one incident, where Rashanna recalled a "fight club" scene in the hallway.

> Nicole: You said, "I don't care. Like ask Mr. Dixon. He would say basically I don't care." What don't you care about?
>
> Rashanna: Anything really. He tries to give me that whole, I'm going to get out of here soon speech. I feel like most of the people who tell me that don't go to this school. They don't know how it actually is here and like not even the teachers understand. A few days ago or so they were having a full-blown fight club in the bathroom. And then me, Jalayla, Haliegh, and Bianca left off the floor and Ms. Johnson and them had all ran into the girls' bathroom.
>
> Nicole: The girls were doing this?
>
> Rashanna: Yeah. Like the whole hallway was *filled* with people. For some reason everybody was out in the hallway, like everybody.
>
> Nicole: No one was in class?
>
> Rashanna: No. We were all just walking around in the hallway and stuff. And they were like they are fighting in the bathroom. Ms. Johnson and them ran in there and everything got quiet 'cuz when they start fighting it got super quiet then it got super loud, like super, super loud. It was a lot of people screaming. Nobody in the hallway knew what was going on.
>
> Nicole: Why did they decide to do fight club?
>
> Rashanna: [Pause] To me, I think most of their maturity levels are just like down here. They consider me to be too mature, but

they didn't live the same way I did. I had no choice but to grow up. My nephew only had me at the end of the day, so I had to grow up. I feel as though there is nothing wrong with them still being kids and having fun, but they're still too old for that. They have to remember that they're on their way to high school, and high school's only four years. Middle school and elementary school is like nine, and most of them aren't going to college, so that's all they have.

Nicole: Why aren't they going to college?

Rashanna: They just don't think they can do it or [pause] they learn from most of the people on the streets that they don't have to.

Nicole: Do people get hurt? Sometimes I know there's been play fighting and then there's fighting. Sometimes play fighting turns into real fighting — like are people getting hurt?

Rashanna: No. They learn how to just walk away.

Nicole: So they might be hurt, but they wouldn't show it?

Rashanna: Yeah. Showing being hurt is not something that most of us want to do 'cuz showing weaknesses, people are just going to hold that against you [pause] like forever. And *everyone* thinks that they know you. Most people don't act like they know me because they know I'm going to get mad. (Interview, May 11, 2016)

Rashanna clearly explained that a habitus of fierceness was necessary because "showing weakness" would be "forever" held "against you." This underscores the way that students coped with and navigated their environments to their advantage. However, these strategies have been primarily considered negative because they do not conform to middle-class values and cultural capital (Lareau, 2011). In this regard, the students are blamed for not acting a certain way without recognizing the adaptive way in which students like Rashanna navigate their multiple worlds, largely by themselves, in order to survive (see Phelan et al., 1993; Phelan et al., 1994).

Rashanna frequently stated that she was ready to "get out of this school" and out of the neighborhood. She believed that the best scenario for her was to move out of Philadelphia or go to a boarding school. Both of which were not happening the next year, as Rashanna would be going to a charter high school in Philadelphia. It is also important to note that Rashanna was able to draw on *navigational capital*[1] to figure out the high school selection process and avoid going to the neighborhood high school. According to students, the neighborhood high school was a place "where you can say goodbye to your future" (Fieldnotes, March 9, 2016).

I argued earlier that when students make comments such as "I don't care," it is a form of resistance and protection. In chapter 5, Mr. Barnes described these kinds of comments as an illustration of students lacking "internal motivation." This mentality is an example of *symbolic violence* — in which students are blamed and their position in society is misrecognized as "natural" (Bourdieu, 2001). The power and consequences of symbolic violence in this example are that instead of recognizing the problems of the instruction, school, and broader system, students are positioned as needing to "care more" or "work harder." Thinking that students are the problem allows the nation to avoid considering the ways the education system has failed them.[2] Instead of recognizing these types of phrases as coping mechanisms and self-protection in an environment that punishes weakness, individuals and systems shift the blame to students for systemic problems.

Symbolic Violence and the Invisibility of Macro Structures

Jalayla: I just want a life that I always dreamed of. That I always wanted as a little kid. Basically a nice house, a family, a good career. Stuff I know my mom and dad would want me to have too. Things they probably didn't have when they were younger but want me to have. That's basically what I dream of, like better than my mom's, because I see the struggles my mom and my dad have with their careers, how they are always coming home tired. I just want to have a nice future. Something that [I] know that they [my parents] could be proud of me of doing and not being like some people uneducated, and not with a real bright future. Basically I just want to make my parents proud of me and what I do and the choices I make basically. That's mainly what my goals are and my future is.

Nicole: Do you feel like you know what to do in order to get that?

Jalayla: Yeah. Stay in school, don't drop out, control my anger, because I know how angry I can be when certain people say something. Just how to control my anger and everything basically. (Interview, May 4, 2016)

Teachers and students at Baker School were clearly struggling, and neither group was adequately supported. From the disproportionate lack of resources, test-based curricula, endless exams that many students did not pass, to the isolated teachers who lacked quality materials and professional development, it seems that an urban public school like Baker was designed to fail.

Students, especially those in middle school, were very aware of this. They recognize that they were given less, that the school was not "good," and that their chances for educational success were bleak. Yet many students, as evidenced in the conversation with Jalayla at the beginning of this section, still believed that if they stayed in school they would "make it." The daily affirmation that students recited every morning helping engrain this message is depicted here in verse form, which is how it was displayed in posters around the school.

> If it is to be
> It is up to me
> I can be anything
> I want to be
> I can decide to do
> I can do anything I want to
> As long as I listen to the people who care about me
> If I am weak
> I am beat
> If I am wise
> I will survive
> I will prepare myself
> So that when the doors of opportunity open
> I can just walk right in
> I can, I will, I believe
> It is done.

Students "can be anything" and "do anything" as long as they "listen" and are "wise," they "will survive." These messages focus on individual responsibility. This is articulated in the affirmation's first two lines: "If it is to be / It is up to me." Furthermore, ironically reinforcing the need for a habitus of fierceness, the affirmation states, "If I am weak / I am beat."

The Invisibility of Macro Structures

Students, parents, and teachers (especially in the media) are often blamed for the "failure" of public schools, despite the lack of resources and support described throughout the book and in chapter 6. The macro-structural processes, which are largely invisible, conspire against students such that students are blamed for their situation. Baker is filled with posters and murals containing aspirational messages. For example, in the auditorium, which many students are in daily as they wait for their bus, students see "Education = Opportunity" on the wall. While many students recognize that they are given less and that the school is not "good," they still believe that if they "stay in school" they will "make it." As a result, students end up blaming themselves if they are not successful despite the way that the system is rigged to not support them.

Symbolic Violence: Blaming Themselves

Symbolic violence is a misrecognition of inequality, hidden curricula, and the culture of power as "natural" (Bourdieu, 2001; Theoharis, 2009, 2020). Symbolic violence occurs when individuals are blamed and blame themselves for their social location (Bourgois & Schonberg, 2009; Ferguson, 2000). That is, individuals' place in society is misrecognized as natural and earned despite the broader macro, social, and political forces such as the specific disinvestment in urban public schools and their surrounding communities. Thus, students at Baker and schools like it are taught to believe that education equals opportunity, yet the education students receive is not equitable.

Students, like Jalayla, recognize how their education is inequitable, as she describes how other schools ("Jersey Schools" as she says) have "better stuff" and "nice[r] things" than their school. Jalayla states:

> Jersey people, Jersey people, Jersey people, some of them. I'm not going to say all of them, but some of them. Some teachers, they compare our school to schools in Jersey and all that stuff. Our school is different. Jersey kids are, [pause] they listen, they, you know, fold their hands and all that stuff. That's because they got better stuff than us. Well, not even [pause], that's because they got better stuff than us. How come [pause] I'm not explaining what I am trying to say [pause] they compare our school to a Jersey school, but they got better stuff than us. They have different things and they are trying to compare us to that and those schools are different. They have nice things. (Group Interview, June 15, 2016)

Despite recognizing how some schools have more resources, the internalization of meritocracy and individualism influences how students and the rest of society misrecognize social inequalities as natural, meaning that students are blamed and blame themselves if they do not achieve social mobility. Part of the transformative possibilities of teaching discussed in chapter 1 involves acknowledging this symbolic violence and the invisibility of structural processes. In addition, transformative teaching also includes recognizing the resilient way that teachers and students, like Rashanna, Jalaya, and Nyeisha, navigate the stressful environment of Baker School.

In the next section, I focus on Nyeisha, a bright fourth grader whose life at Baker School revolved around perceptions of her as "bad" and a "problem." Baker, in its attempts to control students and their behavior, did not foster an environment in which students were encouraged to learn. As the descriptions of Nyeisha's schooling experiences illustrate, the singular focus on controlling behavior does not equate with less chaos and more rule following. Bianca, Jalayla, Rashanna, and Renee frequently discuss how students might be more committed to following rules if they felt respected and if their input had been sought. Students' experiences are largely discounted at Baker, and one goal of this chapter is to bring their experiences to the forefront.

The Student Experience of a Culture of Control: Nyeisha

Nyeisha was a fourth grader with a great smile. The description of how I met Nyeisha for the first time is included in the following fieldnote when Ms. Smith introduced me to Nyeisha and negatively described Nyeisha to me while Nyeisha was standing there. This was a common experience for Nyeisha, in which adults spoke about her, in front of her, in largely negative terms.

> Ms. Smith says to me in front of Nyeisha: "This is Nyeisha. She has a lot of attention-seeking behaviors." Ms. Smith, Nyeisha, and I are standing at the back of the classroom by the door. Nyeisha has been standing here for about 30 minutes while Ms. Smith has been teaching and asking Nyeisha multiple times to sit down. I say hello to Nyeisha and ask her what is going on. She states, "Nothing. Everyone is messing with me." I ask if she did any anything, and Nyeisha smiles an impish grin and says, "No." She laughs a little as she says this. I ask her, "Ms. Smith just said you exhibit lot of attention-seeking behaviors. Do you want attention?" Nyeisha declares, "Yes." I ask, "Do you think you could get attention for positive behaviors instead of negative?" Again, she responds, "Yes!" I tell her, "I will be here first thing tomorrow morning. I will stop by and check on you, and I would like to hear from Ms. Smith that you had a good rest of the afternoon." Ms. Smith, who has been walking around but overheard some of our conversation, asks, "What time are you coming, Ms. Nicole?" I state, "About 9:30." Ms. Smith responds, "Well, that is when Nyeisha gets here. She arrives between 9:30 and 10 every day." I ask, "What time does school start?" Nyeisha says, "8?" Ms. Smith states, "School

> starts at 8:30." Nyeisha responds, "I thought it was 8:45." Ms.
> Smith: "She is never on time, never in uniform, never has home-
> work, and that is not all on you." She is referring to Nyeisha.
> Ms. Smith shakes her head in frustration and says directly to
> Nyeisha, "You didn't get to meet Ms. Nicole before because
> you didn't go on the fieldtrip. You probably won't get to go
> to the winter wonderland, and it was so nice last year." Ms.
> Smith smiles at me as she says this, like she really means it.
> "You need $50 in Baker Cash in order to participate. Do you
> have any Baker Cash?" Nyeisha responds, "I have about $10."
> (Fieldnotes, November 30, 2015)

Navigating Negative Labels

Not surprisingly, Nyeisha was angered and embarrassed by the exchange noted in the previous fieldnote, and classroom situations tended to escalate when Nyeisha talked back to Ms Smith and got into more trouble. Ms. Smith, as noted in earlier, had a habit of blaming parents, including Nyeisha's mother, for "not parenting." Yet Ms. Smith largely took out her frustration on students. As the fieldnote highlights, Ms. Smith demonstrated her low expectations of Nyeisha, including her expectation that Nyeisha would always arrive late to school. When Ms. Smith made these kinds of negative comments to Nyeisha, Nyeisha would shut down and characterize Ms. Smith and fellow students as "messing with" her.

The relationship between Ms. Smith and Nyeisha was clearly not positive. Ms. Smith always referred to Nyeisha in terms of what she did "wrong" (e.g., coming late to school, seeking attention) and what Nyeisha did not have (e.g., Baker Cash, uniform). Baker Cash was a part of a behavior incentive program at the school in which students earned slips of paper, called "Baker Cash," which students could use to "purchase" rewards, including school supplies or candy.

In the next fieldnote, which is one of the more positive classroom experiences that I observed, Nyeisha was having a "good week." Consistent with the hidden curriculum of control articulated earlier, a good week entailed that Nyeisha was not "acting out," that she was complying with what was asked of her, and she was listening to Ms. Smith. During this week, Ms. Smith and other adults acknowledged that there was "improvement in her behavior." Thus, a good week for Nyeisha meant that she did not disrupt class, argue with peers, or talk back to her teacher; it was not linked to what she learned or how she performed scholastically.

In the following fieldnote, Nyeisha is excited to get to work immediately on a math problem. However, Ms. Smith, who expects absolute compliance, demands that students follow certain procedures before they begin working on the problem. When the time comes that students are able to start answering the math problem, Nyeisha has lost interest and starts drawing on her paper. However, because Nyeisha is not disrupting class, this is not considered a problem. Nyeisha also talks about how she is proud and excited that she has gotten a lot of Baker Cash.

> The class is working on math, and there is a word problem on the dry erase easel in the front center of the classroom. I read the problem, and it takes me a few times to figure out exactly what it is asking. The problem is about eggs, cartons, and crates, and the question wants to know the total number of cartons of eggs that the woman sells. She sells them in a set of two. Ms. Smith gave each student a piece of white copy paper where there is a place for them to copy the problem in a box and then a place below the problem to show their work. Ms. Smith is repeatedly telling the students to copy the problem and this takes a while. Writing it, as much as I can gather from this lesson, is a part of the PSSA test, as Ms. Smith communicates to the students that writing the problem neatly is how they get one point out of a total of four points on these types of questions on the PSSA. She then states, "Put your pencils down. PUT YOUR PENCILS DOWN. Let's read the problem." Ms. Smith reads the word problem out loud.
>
> Nyeisha is excited about the problem as soon as she writes it down. After writing the word problem, Nyeisha started drawing boxes, I think to represent the cartons and then to ultimately count the number of cartons. Nyeisha lost her momentum when Ms. Smith yells out again, "PUT YOUR PENCILS DOWN. You can't pay attention if you are writing." They are not allowed to write until they have orally determined all of the key words in the question such as "each," "set," the "total number of things" while Ms. Smith puts boxes or underlines these words. Ms. Smith then starts hollering several times to the whole class, "Get out your notebooks. Get out your notebooks." She then asks, "Why do we need our notebooks?" No one answers. Ms. Smith states, "We did a problem very similar to this yesterday, and I want you to look back to see the steps we followed." Students look around to find their notebooks. While they are doing this, Ms. Smith makes comments about students that are organized and not organized. She now states, "OK. Now you can do this on your own. You should look back in your notebook to see how we did the last problem."
>
> Nyeisha has a hard time paying attention during the whole class activity of telling Ms. Smith what words to circle or underline. Now that the class is supposed to work independently,

> Nyeisha appears unable to focus and is no longer working on the problem. She is doodling in her notebook. Ms. Alexis, the ISS [In School Suspension] teacher, walks in and brings a black bag from the corner store and gives it to Nyeisha. Ms. Alexis says to Nyeisha, "This is your lunch. Your mom brought it, and there is a dollar in there for you. Are you doing good?" "Yes" Nyeisha responds. Ms. Alexis fills out a slip and gives it to Nyeisha. Nyeisha turns to me, "She gave me Baker Cash!" Ms. Alexis asks Ms. Smith in front of the entire class, "Improvement?" Ms. Smith responds, "Yes." Nyeisha starts to count her Baker Cash, which are slips of paper in different amounts that students can "spend" for rewards, such as ice cream. She pulls out a zip lock baggie, and unrolls and then counts all of her cash. Ms. Smith says to Nyeisha, "I'll put that away for you." She is referring to the black corner store bag that Ms. Alexis gave her with her lunch. Nyeisha says to Ms. Smith, "There is a dollar in there for me." Ms. Smith assures her, "I'll make sure it is in your backpack." Nyeisha is excited that her mother gave her a dollar. Nyeisha says to me, "I'm going to buy me some water and chips after school, wait I don't need chips, I am going to get some water and something else." I say, "It looks like you have had a good week." Nyeisha exclaims, "Yes! Look at all my Baker Cash! Plus, I'm not bad. There are no bad kids." This phrase is one I have heard from a couple of students, including Kiandra. Nyeisha continues, "Today my mom is going shopping. She is going to buy me a uniform." It is almost time for the fourth graders to go to lunch, and I am going to head upstairs to an eighth-grade class. I tell Nyeisha that I will come by at the end of the day to say goodbye to her. (Fieldnotes, December 4, 2015)

There Are Really No Bad Kids

As described in chapters 2 and 4, Ms. Smith did not have chaos in her class and was able to instruct largely because of her rigid control. At the end of the previous fieldnote, Nyeisha, who was not "on task" but was excited about all her Baker Cash, stated, "I'm not bad. There are no bad kids." Nyeisha internalized the idea that many adults in the school thought of her as bad and treated her as though she was bad. However, in this example, Nyeisha was pushing back against these deficit orientations that surrounded her. In many regards, Nyeisha was struggling to be considered good, but the perceptions of her as "bad" were difficult to overcome.

Days in which Nyeisha did not get in trouble were infrequent. In contrast to the previous fieldnote in which Nyeisha appeared happy, excited, and proud, Nyeisha often tended to appear upset or frustrated. She sat by herself and did not frequently engage with peers in positive ways. As the following fieldnote describes, Nyeisha was not allowed to sit with other students because Ms. Smith believed that Nyeisha would disrupt them and the rest of the class. Because order was the primary goal, Nyeisha had to be separated from her peers. Even though I spent many hours with Nyeisha at school and after school, I cannot name one student that she would consider a friend. As described in an earlier chapter, Mr. James believed that the rest of the students in Ms. Smith's class did not like Nyeisha because Ms. Smith did not like Nyeisha. Ms. Smith admitted being frustrated with Nyeisha, and a common refrain she made about her was "I have had enough." This kind of giving up on students, and then blaming them for the results of their abnegation of responsibility, was the norm and not the exception at Baker. The following fieldnote also illustrates the many complexities and challenges that students and teachers faced. For example, getting a substitute teacher to come to Baker was rare, and there were additional students in Ms. Smith's class because a teacher was absent.

> Marshall says, "Hi Ms. Nicole" as I walk into Ms. Smith's room. I smile and say hello to him. Marshall's desk, along with Ireena, Nyeisha, and Damien's desks, sits apart from the rest of the students whose desks are put together in groups of four. This is because, according to Ms. Smith, they cannot work well with others. Nyeisha smiles and waves at me as soon as I walk in. Someone whispers to Ms. Smith, whose back is turned, "Ms. Nicole is here." All of the fourth-grade students take turns saying, "Hi, Ms. Nicole." I say hello to Ms. Smith. She tells me that there are extra students in the class today because Ms. Glenn, one of the three fourth-grade teachers, is absent today. Sometimes when teachers are absent, their students will be divided up between other teachers for the day. These students are expected to work quietly on a packet of independent work. I ask Ms. Smith, "How are you feeling?" "Oh. I'm fine," she says. "That's not why I was absent on Friday afternoon." I state, "The students told me you were sick. Did you get our card?" Ms. Smith smiles and exclaims, "That was you! I do have a cold, but I am fine. How were the kids?" "They were really good," I say. Ms. Smith comments, "That is what I heard. I can't believe I got a sub. Everyone is like, 'who do you know downtown' that you got a sub."
>
> The class is a bit noisier than usual. Students are supposed to be copying their homework. It is close to the end of the day, and students seem excited. Students keep calling my name to show me scores they got on a recent quiz. There are a lot of 80s, 90s,

and 100s. The quiz was on fact and opinion. When they call me over, they show me their half sheet of notebook paper that lists eight questions. There is a capital "C" next to each correct answer. There is a "X" next to incorrect answers. I walk around from student to student as they are excited to show me their quizzes. Lashaya calls me over to show me her quiz. "I got a 10. I'm supposed to be one of the smart ones."

Lashaya says, "I have spelling problems." Ms. Smith responds, "It is not the spelling I am worried about. It is about the sentences. They don't make any sense, and it scares me. Take home these quizzes and show your parents. Everyone clear and clean your desks!" On the back of the half sheet of notebook paper are five sentences. Most of the grades that I see are much lower. Comments are written on the paper, including, "Read your work" or "Your sentences don't make any sense."

Nyeisha is crossing out the Xs and making them Cs. She turned her quiz into a 100. Ms. Smith yells, "Nyeisha. Stop banging your book on your desk." She says to me, "She is trying to get your attention." Ms. Smith then says to Nyeisha: "Nyeisha, Ms. Nicole doesn't want to see you banging your book on your desk. I'm so sick of you, Nyeisha. No home-work." Then to me, Ms. Smith says, "I gave her extra time, over the weekend, nothing." Ms. Smith now addresses the whole class: "I am so sick of her. Lashaya, you are taking too long [to clean her desk]." Nyeisha is visibly upset and says to Ms. Smith, "Leave me alone." I smile and say hello to Nyeisha and tell her that I will come sit with her in a minute.

Ms. Smith asks the class, "Who is my passer?" The students tell her who is the passer, and then Ms. Smith picks three students. Ms. Smith appears agitated. She is yelling at students who seem to not be doing anything wrong. She is saying things like, "Sit down." "Hurry up and pack your bag." "I told you to sit down." "I'm so sick of you." She gives the whole class a detention for tomorrow. A few minutes later, Ms. Smith states that the class now has two detentions. A few minutes later, the class now has three detentions. This means that the class will eat lunch in Ms. Smith's room for the next three days. There are a few groans, but it does not appear to change the students' behavior.

Ms. Smith asks, "Who didn't copy the words for home-work?" Most students raise their hands. Ms. Smith says, "OK. I will write them." I say, "Ms. Smith, do you want me to write them for you?" Ms. Smith, "Yes. Let me find them." She flips through a book. "OK. Here you are." I write eight words on the board. It is not exactly clear to me or to the students what they are supposed to do with these words, but I believe they are supposed to look up their definitions.

Ms. Smith yells, "Nyeisha. I have had enough. I'm going to call your mom." Ms. Smith takes out her personal cell phone while she keeps yelling at Nyeisha. Nyeisha responds adamantly, "NO!" "Yes. I have had enough. Your mom said if she had to come up here again, you were going to be in trouble." Nyeisha tells Ms. Smith, "I didn't do nothing." Ms. Smith says to me, "Ms. Nicole, you can tell Nyeisha's mom what she did." I don't say anything, and I hope she does not actually ask me to tell anything to Nyeisha's mother because I have no idea what Nyeisha did. Ms. Smith says into the phone, "Hello. This is Ms. Smith. I am calling to talk to you about Nyeisha's behavior. Please call me back."

Ms. Smith goes and sits down at the table at the front of the room where her laptop is. She starts filling out the students' behavior charts. These charts are a monthly calendar. At the top of the paper there are numbers, which list behaviors such as "Talking back. No homework. Disrupting class." On each day of the calendar, students either get a smiley face for good behavior or a number or numbers to signify what negative behaviors students exhibited that day. Ms. Smith calls students up for them to give her their chart to fill out. The class is still pretty noisy, and Ms. Smith occasionally looks up from the behavior charts and hollers at a student to sit down. She then says, "Girls at tables 1 and 2 get your things." No one moves. She then says, "Girls at table 4. That's you. Get your things." A student tells her, "We are table 3." Ms. Smith says, "Table 3."

Nyeisha is standing up making noises and is really angry because Ms. Smith called her mother. I whisper to Nyeisha that she should sit down because I don't want her to get in any more trouble. Nyeisha exclaims, "No. She shouldn't have called my mom. I didn't do nothing. She called my mom for nothing."

Ms. Smith calls Kristen up to her table and asks for her behavior chart. Kristen says, "I don't know where it is at." Ms. Smith corrects her, "I don't know where it is. Not where it is at. That is Philadelphia." Ms. Smith asks again, "Where is your behavior chart?" Kristen says, "I don't know where it is at." Ms. Smith says, "No at. I don't know where it is. Bring it tomorrow, OK?" Kristen says she will.

Nyeisha motions me to come over to her desk. I walk over to Nyeisha, who is now sitting at her desk. She shows me a paper that has 100% written on the top. I then look closely, and I see that the paper said, "0/12." Nyeisha changed all of the Xs to Cs, and she scribbled out the "0/12" and wrote "100%."

> Nyeisha asks, "What does 0/12 mean?" She laughs before I have a chance to answer. I ask her, "Why did you change it?" Nyeisha just smiles and laughs. I ask, "Don't you want to learn from the problems that you got wrong so that you can do better next time?" Nyeisha nods and returns to her paper and begins erasing all of the scribbles that she made on her paper. Nyeisha and I talk quietly for a few minutes, but since Nyeisha keeps getting yelled at, I don't want her to get in more trouble, so I tell her that we should both probably be quiet. (Fieldnotes, December 14, 2015)

Ms. Smith tells Nyeisha in front of the class that she is "sick of her." Ms. Smith frequently made these kinds of comments to and about Nyeisha, and Nyeisha tended to respond with a shoulder shrug followed by commenting, "I don't care." However, it is clear that these comments upset and hurt Nyeisha, and in turn, Nyeisha started to act out her anger. At the end of this day, Ms. Smith called Nyeisha's mother, which made Nyeisha even more angry. As this fieldnote highlights, Ms. Smith's perception of Nyeisha as a "problem student" influenced how Nyeisha appeared to get in trouble no matter what she did. Nyeisha does not embody a habitus of fierceness in the same way Rashanna does; however, Nyeisha talks back to Ms. Smith, bangs on her desk, and disregards Ms. Smith's directions as a means of pushing back when she believes Ms. Smith is "messing with her." These particular actions are examples of the micro-resistance strategies that students often employed at Baker. To counter the curriculum of control and compliance, Nyeesha looks for ways to resist and push back against Ms. Smith and the school.

Self-Fulfilling Prophecies

The previous fieldnote illustrates how Nyeisha's reputation and Ms. Smith's perception of Nyeisha as a "problem student" made it difficult for Nyeisha to avoid getting into trouble no matter what she did. The fieldnote is yet another example of the disparaging ways that Ms. Smith talked to and about students and parents. Ms. Smith had a deep-rooted negative understanding of the community (Gorski, 2011, 2018; Valencia, 2010, 2019). The way that Ms. Smith corrected Kristen's speech can be seen as an example of her trying to educate students about the *culture of power*.[3] She knows that changing the students' speech patterns can help them to be more accepted in the larger community. However, Ms. Smith appears to lack a *funds of knowledge* approach about her students and the community, meaning that she does not celebrate their strengths and their different forms of capital and is thus not able to be as transformative as she would like (see González et al., 2005; Moll, 2000).

Ms. Smith, as described earlier, expected complete deference from her students; so students like Ireena, who Ms. Smith believed was smart, got into trouble because she pushed back against Ms. Smith's authority. Ms. Smith also thought that Nyeisha was smart, but she believed that Nyeisha was "too far gone" primarily because of what Ms. Smith considered her lack of parenting.

Navigating Complex Challenges

I became an unofficial mentor to Nyeisha. Her mother, Ms. Crawford, often asked me about how things were going for Nyeisha. For example, Ms. Crawford would ask, "Do you be checking up on her [Nyeisha] when she is in the classroom?" I tell her, "Yes. I check in on her." She states, "OK. Good. Because her and her teacher don't see eye to eye. I don't know what the problem is, but they don't get along" (Fieldnotes, January 12, 2016).

A few weeks after this conversation, I saw Ms. Smith and Nyeisha in the behavior support room (BSR) with Ms. Johnson along with the director of the BSR program, Ms. Hill. They were having a conference because Ms. Crawford filed a report stating that Ms. Smith "gripped up" Nyeisha. Ms. Smith said, "You're lying." Nyeisha insisted, "You gripped me." Ms. Smith again said, "You're lying." Then, Ms. Hill leaned in and told Nyeisha, "Well, if we go — if you go where we're sending you, they're going to do a lot more than just grip you up." Ms. Smith said, "I'm sick of it" (Fieldnotes, January 29, 2016).

Ms. Crawford asked me to help Nyeisha get into the after-school program, and I told her I would do what I could. I asked Mr. James, the director of the after-school program, if Nyeisha could participate, and he was wary because of her reputation as a "problem student." I encouraged Mr. James to give Nyeisha a chance. I told him that Nyeisha frequently pushed the limits, but I believed that all the children did this. I said that Nyeisha just gets into more trouble somehow, but not because I thought her behavior was especially bad. When a spot opened up for Nyeisha in the after-school program, Mr. James asked me jokingly if he should list me as her guardian.

Ms. Smith tried to lobby Mr. James to not allow Nyeisha to participate because she insisted that "she can't act right." This was an example of how Ms. Smith had such a negative opinion of Nyeisha that she did not think that Nyeisha "deserved" to participate in anything remotely positive. Ms. Crawford knew that Ms. Smith would not help to get Nyeisha into the after-school program; so Ms. Crawford activated her *social capital*[4] through her relationship with me to try and get Nyeisha into the program.

As described in chapter 4, Nyeisha and her siblings were frequently late to school. Nyeisha was one of six and soon to be seven children. During one parent-teacher conference, Ms. Smith told Ms. Crawford that Nyeisha's lateness was a problem. Ms. Crawford responded by saying, "I am so sick of hearing about how they are late. I wash my hands. I wash my hands. This is enough." Ms. Crawford then asked Nyeisha, "Do you make yourself late, or do I make you late?" Nyeisha responded, "I make myself late." Ms. Crawford continued, "I might get up at 7:45 or 8:00, and I might roll back asleep, but they need to get their things ready. She and her sister stay up until 10:00 or 11:00 playing" (Fieldnotes, February 24, 2016).

Ms. Crawford *parentified* her children by expecting Nyeisha, age 10, and Nadira, age 8, to assume the responsibility for getting themselves and their younger brother, age 6, to school.[5] Ms. Crawford reached out to the school for help on multiple occasions, and many adults at the school acknowledged that Nyeisha needed additional support, resources, and attention. However, the school and the broader social sectors were not able to support the Crawford family. Instead, the family was looked down upon. Furthermore, teachers, as discussed in the previous chapter, were exhausted and faced many competing priorities. In the following fieldnote, the two administrators of the after-school program talk about how Nyeisha's issues can be challenging for an after-school program with limited resources and that staff do not have enough training to support students with complex challenges.

> I ask Mr. James how Nyeisha is doing. He states, "She is OK. She has been picking on a second grader, and I mean really picking on her. The second grader came to me again and told me she was really scared. Nyeisha was getting in her face and yelling at her. And making her really scared." I ask, "Why is she doing that?" Mr. James says, "I don't know. Nyeisha has a life of instability, and it has impacted the way she operates in school. You can just look at her and tell that she is less groomed than the other kids. She doesn't look well taken care of. There are little signs of trauma." I ask, "What are those?" Another after-school administrator states, "She doesn't look you in the eyes, for example. She also appears to be in a flight-or-fight mode all the time." James tells me, "I'm not going to kick her out, but after-school can't handle 20 kids with issues. One or two. The staff don't have enough training. Nyeisha needs lots of one-on-one." (Fieldnotes, March 21, 2016)

Teachers and other staff at the school tended to focus on putting out fires and dealing with day-to-day issues. They acknowledged that Nyeisha needed support, yet they had a hard time giving her that support. A lack of resources for the school is also important to note here, as there is one counselor for the entire school who, as described previously, is burned out and overwhelmed given her unrealistic and unsustainable workload. This is an example of how opportunity gaps manifest in schools in the lack of school support services such as counselors or nurses to address these student support issues (Gorski, 2018). Teachers often dealt with Nyeisha and other students by sending them out of the classroom. This was perhaps a way of deescalating a potentially problematic situation; however, it also reinforced the hidden curriculum of control at Baker, which prioritized controlling behavior.

The following fieldnote highlights the rhythm of school life for Nyeisha, which includes coming late to school, getting removed from class, coming back to class, getting yelled at, and then getting removed from class again.

As I approach Ms. Smith's classroom, I hear her shouting, "I am tired. I am sick of it." Her door is open, which is not typical. I walk in. The class says, "Hello, Ms. Nicole." I smile and say hello. I immediately look around for Nyeisha because she was not at school yesterday. I see her standing in front of her desk, which is at the front of the classroom by Ms. Smith's desk. Ms. Smith gives me a small smile and asks, "Can you do me a big favor?" I say, "Sure." She asks, "Can you take Nyeisha and walk with her and talk to her?" "Of course," I say. "She was late. She missed theme. I don't have time for this. She is disrupting the class. Can you take her and talk to her?" "No problem," I tell Ms. Smith. Nyeisha walks into the hallway with me, she has a stack of papers in one hand and what she calls a pencil case, which looks like a glasses case, in the other hand.

I ask Nyeisha, "What's going on?" Nyeisha says, "She is steaming on me the minute I walk in. I was organizing my desk, and she doesn't want us to have messy desks, and she kept yelling at me and telling me to sit down and then she told me to get out that she needed a break from me." Nyeisha is playing with her pencil case. There is a pair of glasses in there, lipstick, lip gloss, and mascara. Nyeisha's hair is done, and she is dressed nicely in a clean white button-down shirt with a scalloped collar and light denim jeans. I say, "Let's take a walk."

I ask her, "Why weren't you at school yesterday?" "I was at the dentist." I look at her slightly skeptically. She laughs a little bit. Nyeisha says, "Really I was. I have a cavity. My note is at home. I forgot to bring it." I ask, "How come someone saw you walking in the street?" Nyeisha says, "I was taking my little brother to school because my sister couldn't take him." "Why not?" I ask. "She is suspended." "Why? What grade is she in?" Nyeisha says, "second grade. She is always acting bad and getting in trouble."

Nyeisha and I are now standing in front of an open classroom. Nyeisha starts to walk in because this is where she says she goes sometimes to take a break from Ms. Smith. Nyeisha says, "I need to go in here because Ms. Smith said I need to take a break." There are two Black men, one larger set, and one Black female, Ms. Hill, who is the director of the support team. Nyeisha and I walk in. The adults look at us skeptically, and I say, "Nyeisha said she is supposed to come in here to take a break."

Nyeisha says, "Ms. Smith was yelling at me and telling me she is tired of me and that I need to leave." The young, heavy-set Black man says to me, with a smile of disbelief, "She is not lying." Ms. Hill, the director of the behavior support team at the school, says, "Why? You should not be missing instruction Nyeisha." We walk over to her desk, and I briefly introduce myself to her, "Hello. I'm Nicole. I'm a graduate student researching for my dissertation. I am often in Ms. Smith's classroom, and I have worked with Nyeisha before, and Ms. Smith asked if I would take her out. She said that she was late and that she was disrupting class." Ms. Hill says, "It is nice to meet you Nicole. I am a [name of university] alumna, from the school of social work, many years ago." She then asks Nyeisha, "Were you late?" Nyeisha says she was, and Ms. Hill tells her, "Your hair looks nice." I also say that Nyeisha's hair looks nice. Nyeisha smiles. Ms. Hill says to me, "She is late a lot, and as a child, that is not her fault." She asks Nyeisha, "Can I tell her?" Nyeisha nods affirmatively. Ms. Hill says, "Sometimes they are late because they have to wash things out in the morning and wait for them to dry. It takes a long time to get all of the children ready. Sometimes Nyeisha leaves without them so that she can get here on time, don't you?" Nyeisha nods and says, "She just starts yelling at me and telling me to hurry up and that she is sick of it. And I didn't want my desk to be messy, and she always tells us to not have messy desks." Ms. Hill says to me, "The problem is, and I have talked to Ms. Smith about this, it is not that Nyeisha is late. It is that Ms. Smith yells this in front of the whole class, who is there on time, and they turn to look at Nyeisha, and she gets embarrassed. Then that embarrassment turns to anger. Ms. Smith goes on and on about how she is always late and how she disrupts the class. I think we need to get the mother in here. Maybe since your sister is suspended, your mother will come up and we can talk to her. Nyeisha is a good kid and a smart kid, and she has to overcome people telling her that she is bad." I say, "I know that she is a good kid. She is very smart. That is why I am working with her. I also know what it is like to have negative expectations about you, and it is hard." Nyeisha looks at me and smiles. "I know that you can show people that you are good because you are." Ms. Hill says, "I don't want you in here long, Nyeisha. You need to be in class." Nyeisha is putting on lip gloss and playing with her pencil case.

I suggest, "Why don't we take a few minutes and read the passage Ms. Smith gave you and then we will go back to class?" Nyeisha smiles and says, "OK." Ms. Hill says, "I think this" pointing to the pencil case "is going to cause distractions. Why don't I keep it until after lunch?" Nyeisha takes her glasses out of the case, and we head to a table to sit down. She keeps trying to clean her glasses by wiping them with her fingers, and then I get a cloth and ask, "Can I try?" She hands them to me. I wipe them off with a cloth, and say, "Sometimes when you use your fingers it can make more smudge marks on them." I try on the glasses, and they look clear to me. Nyeisha puts them on, "Thank you!" She smiles a really big smile.

We start reading a story together. It is a test prep worksheet that says "4th grade ELA [English Language Arts]" at the bottom. Nyeisha wants to take turns reading. She reads a sentence and then I read a sentence. We read the passage, and then it says to answer the questions, but there are no questions. I say, "Now is probably a good time to head back to class so that we can get the questions." Nyeisha agrees, "OK. I need my glasses case." I remind her, "Ms. Hill said she is going to keep it until after lunch." Nyeisha responds, "But I need to put my glasses in it." "Maybe you can take the makeup out and put the glasses in," I suggest. Ms. Hill walks back in, and I ask her if Nyeisha can have her case. Ms. Hill says to Nyeisha, "I told you I am keeping it until after lunch." Nyeisha protests, "I need it." Ms. Hill takes out the makeup and hands the empty case to Nyeisha. Nyeisha asks, "Can I at least have my clear lip gloss? It is clear." Ms. Hill hands Nyeisha only the empty glasses case, and Nyeisha and I walk back toward her classroom. It is just around the corner. When we get to the classroom, Nyeisha starts stalling. She says, "I don't want to go in. Will you sit next to me?" I tell her, "Yes. I can't stay that long because I have to go to work." "Don't you work here?" Nyeisha asks. "Yes. I do research here, but I have other work too." Nyeisha and I walk in, and Ms. Smith is sitting on Nyeisha's desk. We have to walk around the room because Nyeisha wants to walk a certain way. I sit down next to Nyeisha, and the class is answering oral questions that Ms. Smith is asking about the passage Nyeisha and I just read. I whisper to her, "You know the answer to these. You should raise your hand." Ms. Smith calls on Nyeisha to answer a few questions, and Nyeisha has a huge smile on her face and appears very excited when she gets the correct answer. Ms. Smith yells at one student, "What are you doing? Why are you doing that? I am so sick of it!" The student is reaching in his desk.

Ms. Smith then pulls up a few of the questions onto the projector. It is the teachers' edition because the answer is marked next to the question with an asterisk. The students start telling Ms. Smith this, but she doesn't realize it quite yet. They are going over the question verbally, and she says, "This is really deep stuff. The goal of the PSSA is to trick you. It is really hard." The reason why she explains the answer to the class doesn't make sense. I chime in, in a casual way, and say, "It is confusing. I think it is B because A is only about one part of the sentence, C is only about one part of the sentence, and B is about all three aspects so that must be why it is the correct answer." Ms. Smith states, "Oh you are right." I say, "It is confusing." Ms. Smith says, "Yes. It is very confusing. Now we are going to read the textual evidence question." She says to me, "They aren't going to do well on this because this is their first time taking it." Ms. Smith reads the question aloud. "We are going to answer it, but not today. I hope it is better than the last one we did because that was a hot mess." They read the question and then Ms. Smith says, "OK. Because we didn't have a prep today, we are going to play some games." "YAY!" The students respond.

Ms. Smith gets out fact and opinion, main idea, and other bingo games. While the students are arranging their desks into groups, she says to me, "Nyeisha missed theme. Am I supposed to reteach it to her? I didn't sign up for this. It is so sad. She just needs so much help and attention. I didn't sign up for that. I signed up to teach not be a mother and a social worker. In my charter school, it wasn't like that. I don't think I am going to be doing this much longer." I tell Ms. Smith that Ms. Hill said that she is going to try to bring in Nyeisha's mother. Ms. Smith shakes her head: "We have talked to her 10 times. You know what she says. She says, 'I'm pregnant. I have six kids." I just didn't sign up for this. Thank you, though. She needs a lot of attention." I say, "Anytime. I am happy to work with Nyeisha. I will be back on Friday."

I bend down and talk to Nyeisha. Nyeisha says, "Don't leave." I tell her that I'll be back on Friday. "I wish you worked here. You told Ms. Hill that you come three days a week." I say, "I was here yesterday, today, and then I will be back on Friday." Nyeisha counts on her fingers and says, "Oh." I ask her if she is excited to play bingo, and she says that she is. I state, "I will see you on Friday. I hope you have a great day!" Ms. Smith is hollering at the class about how they are getting into groups. "Who wants to start with main idea? You will all rotate to main idea." I wave goodbye. The class says, "Goodbye, Ms. Nicole."

(Fieldnotes, January 6, 2016)

In a previous fieldnote, I documented how Nyeisha said, "There are no bad kids." Nyeisha was trying to resist the negative way in which a majority of the adults at the school characterize her. Ms. Hill understood the struggle it took for Nyeisha to get to school in the morning; she celebrated the child's efforts as a positive, something that very few other adults did. Ms. Smith considered Nyeisha just one of "these kids" — ones who "need discipline" and are generally "deficient, deviant, and difficult" (Nygreen, 2013, p. 27).

Consequences of Parentification in the Curriculum of Control

Nyeisha, like all students, wanted to be recognized and considered "good." She was so proud and excited when she was called on to answer a question to which she knew the answer. Ms. Smith, who was clearly struggling and exhausted, considered any student misbehavior a personal affront and did not consider how her comments might hurt students. She was able to show empathy for some students, like when she told me that Rashed's mother "is a junkie," and she seemed very concerned for Rashed. However, Ms. Smith did not consider Rashed a behavior problem.

Because Ms. Smith, and the school, focused so much on controlling behavior, it appeared that there was nothing Nyeisha could do to get rid of her label as "bad" and "disruptive." Ms. Smith had little regard for what Nyeisha experienced at home even though Ms. Smith repeatedly discussed Nyeisha's home life as "so sad." She was one of "those" kids (Nygreen, 2013; Rist, 2017). Nyeisha was struggling for her humanity in and out of Baker, and she was also struggling for a childhood (Borchet et al., 2018). Because of her parentlike responsibilities at home and the joyless schooling experiences, Nyeisha had not really been able to simply be a child.

According to Nyeisha, she was often "kicked out" of Ms. Smith's class. Ms. Smith would describe the situation as Nyeisha needing to leave or to take a break in another classroom. Gwen, Nyeisha's school-based behavior support caseworker, believed that Nyeisha was removed from class too frequently. In the subsequent fieldnote, Nyeisha is taking a break in another teacher's class. Again, the rhythms of schooling for Nyeisha involve a cycle of being yelled at, "kicked out," and yelled at again.

> I walk up to the second floor, and I see Gwen, Nyeisha's behavior support caseworker. She tells me that Nyeisha was kicked out of Ms. Smith's room three times yesterday. Gwen says, "She is across the hallway in Ms. Myers's room now." "What happened?" "Same thing as usual. I don't think she should be in there. That is sixth grade." I tell her, "I'm going to go and say

hello to her."

I walk across the room to Ms. Myers's class. She is the math prep teacher. I recognize a few of the sixth-grade girls, who are in lacrosse. They smile and wave at me and ask, "Are you coming to lacrosse today?" I tell them that I am. One student says, "I'm not, I can't stand coach Lewis." Another girl says, "I'll be there." After a few minutes, Ms. Myers notices that I am there, and I ask if it is OK if I say hello to Nyeisha. She says, "She is over there in the corner. You can sit on the chair, and Nyeisha can sit on the stool." "Thanks." I walk over to Nyeisha, and she is quietly reading a book in a light beige arm-chair. It is soft and clean, but old. Nyeisha is in the reading corner. There is a magazine rack with *Oprah*, *Woman's Day*, *Country Living*, and a few other magazines on it. There are two windows and books displayed on the window ledges. There are also two bar stools in the reading corner. I kneel down so that I am eye level with Nyeisha and say hello. She smiles a really big smile. I ask, "How are you?" Nyeisha says, "Good." "Why are you in here?" Nyeisha tell me, "She kicked me out." I ask why, and Nyeisha says, "Because I wasn't paying attention." I ask, "Why?" Nyeisha, "Because I was mad." "At her?" "No." I ask Nyeisha, "What made you mad?" She states, "I don't know. I was just mad in general." I also ask, "Did you get kicked out yesterday too?" Nyeisha says, "Yes. I was being disruptive." She says it like destructive, so I ask her, "Were you being disruptive or destructive? Nyeisha is not sure what I mean. I ask, "Were you making noise and not paying attention, which is disruptive, or were you destroying things, which is destructive?" Nyeisha answers, "Disruptive." She still says it like destructive. "I was making noises and calling out to people." I ask her why, and Nyeisha tells me, "I be getting mad."

As we are talking, Nyeisha has started taking all of the books out of a crate on the floor and is organizing them to put them in order of height and making sure that they all face the same way. Nyeisha explains, "I am going to go to a partial placement." I inquire, "What does that mean?" Nyeisha says, "It means I am going to go somewhere where they give you help." "What kind of help?" Nyeisha responds, "I don't know, but they help you with your behavior." I can tell that Nyeisha does not want to talk anymore, so I ask her, "Would you like to read a book with me?" She smiles and says, "Yes. Which one?" I tell her, "Up to you." Nyeisha looks through the books, and picks one. I forget the title, as I was not familiar with it, but it was something about "Two bedtime stories." We take turns reading a page. We were

> about halfway through the book, and the class starts to dismiss,
> and I get called away. I suggest that she finish the book, and that
> she can fill me in on the ending later today. She nods and keeps
> reading. (Fieldnotes, March 9, 2016)

As Nyeisha stated, she was angry. Taking a close look at Nyeisha's daily experiences, it is not hard to understand why she felt that way. It is important to remember that Nyeisha was 10 years old. She was responsible for getting four younger siblings dressed in the morning and taking two of them to school. In addition, she had to wash her and their clothes in the sink, and was often late waiting for the clothing to dry. As soon as she got to school, she was yelled at, and as the day went on, Nyeisha often got into more and more trouble. Schooling for Nyeisha often turned into a series of frustrating, embarrassing, and dehumanizing events. However, Nyeisha navigated her daily schooling experiences with resiliency, which I discuss in the next section.

Navigating a Deficit Default with Resiliency

Outside forces clearly impacted Baker School. Similar to the way Rashanna describes the local community, Officer Perry, the security guard, once stated, "The power and prestige of this neighborhood is drugs and violence" (Fieldnotes, April 28, 2016). Officer Perry and Ms. Johnson, the counselor, stated that young men in the community were allured by the instant gratification and quick money of selling drugs (Fieldnotes, April 22, 2016). As early as fifth or sixth grade, according to Rashanna, some students get pulled into gangs and life on the streets. Danielle, a grandparent and longtime community resident, talked about students who come to school "smelling like a weed factory" (Interview, June 21, 2016). Without realistic job prospects, selling drugs often becomes a viable option for many students. Some seventh and eighth graders at Baker were already involved in selling drugs.

The Drug Community

Most students and adults knew which students were selling drugs and those who were on drugs. Students, even those in the younger grades, were aware of the prevalence of violence and drugs in their community. Lashaya, a fourth grader, casually told me, "My uncle was flinging his money around thinking he all that. He got shot. In the head. He flung his money around. He just got shot two weeks ago. They found him in a dumpster by the rec center. It was on the news" (Fieldnotes, May 27, 2016). Two of Lashaya's fourth-grade classmates told me that people "be selling drugs and other bad things at the Chinese store" near their housing complex (Fieldnotes, June 7, 2016). As Renee said in a previous chapter, she and other students wanted teachers to understand their life "is hard."

It was common knowledge among students that life in the local community was "hard." Two sisters, a third grader and a fourth grader, talked about how they were ready to move out of the housing complex they lived in. The fourth grader, Aleah, stated, "There is, smoking, shooting, and stabbing. Someone tried to shoot my mom because they got into an argument." Her sister chimed in, "There is a park and we can't even play there because people are smoking, drinking, and playing cards, and I have asthma so I can't be there." Aleah added, "I have allergies. We are moving out of [name of the housing complex]. There is too much drama there. We have lived there for six years. We are leaving because we don't have a bed because we were getting bit [by bugs] up so we had to throw it away" (Fieldnotes, June 14, 2016). In the same way that Nyeisha navigates many challenges before she gets to school, other students at Baker experience challenges in the community that impact their psychological and physical safety.

Dehumanizing Conditions

In addition to issues present in the community, students, as previous chapters describe, had challenging and often dehumanizing conditions at Baker School. As Aleah mentions, there was a large bed bug problem in the community and at the school, and many classrooms had bed bugs, including Ms. Smith's and Mr. Crowley's rooms. Students frequently received letters addressed to their parents stating that "a bed bug was found in your child's classroom." These letters provided a website for parents to refer to for how to eliminate bed bugs. Renee, Bianca, and Jalayla rushed to find me as soon as they got their first letter. They were outraged and brought an extra copy of the letter for me. Ms. Smith described bringing her own bug spray and spraying the room herself after school on a weekly basis.

Students and teachers were clearly operating in a survival mode. Rashanna explained why she said she didn't care, "I feel like most of the people who tell me that, 'don't go to this school,' they don't know how it actually is here and, like, not even the teachers understand." Part of students' survival included the micro-resistance strategies of cutting class and stating that they did not care. Nyeisha, like Rashanna, had also adopted the coping strategy of stating that she did not care. However, students like Nyeisha and Rashanna were primarily waiting for adults to show them that they cared, as positive relationships between students and teachers are one of the most important aspects of student achievement and well-being (Ansari et al., 2020; Kuriloff et al., 2017; Raider-Roth, 2005; Stevenson, 2014, p. 122).

Students believed that many teachers did not understand what life was like for them, but they acknowledged that some teachers did, including Ms. Jenkins and Ms. Johnson. Ms. Johnson, reflecting on the school and students' experiences stated, "School is the best part of the day for kids. They get two full meals. They have friends, and teachers who supposedly care" (Fieldnotes, June 14, 2016).

However, instead of being transformative and nurturing, school was often an additional place of stress. Although many teachers stated that school was the best part of the day for many students, it is important to note that many teachers were in survival mode. They either were unaware or forgot the way that students internalized and navigate the deficit default of the school as well as the stressful and toxic environment (e.g., Bottiani et al., 2019; Madigan & Kim; 2021; Paulle, 2013). The physical environment of the school was dirty and falling apart, as the eighth graders described earlier. Basic tasks that should have been taken care of immediately were often ignored. For example, as the following fieldnote describes, Ms. Smith and her students had been waiting for vomit to be cleaned up for over an hour.

> Today when I walk in, Ms. Smith tells me to be careful. There is throw-up on the floor. She asks a student to go to the office to tell them there is still throw-up on the floor. Ms. Smith states, "Jasmine was so sick. She just had her head down. I knew something was wrong." Ms. Smith states that Jasmine threw up as soon as school started, and the throw-up has been there for over an hour. Jasmine is in the classroom with her head down waiting for her mother to come and pick her up. (Fieldnotes, February 16, 2016)

Both students and teachers contend with these dehumanizing conditions that physically include vomit and vermin as well as significant physiological stress, yet students and teachers come back daily. Rashanna would not be considered successful by middle-class standards of working toward social mobility. However, Rashanna is certainly resilient. So is Nyeisha. At age 10, Nyeisha takes care of herself and four younger siblings. Her resiliency, however, is not acknowledged. She is labeled as "difficult" and "a problem."

Students and teachers coped with their environment at Baker School, but some of their coping mechanisms had negative unintended consequences. When teachers blame students and parents, or when students engage in micro-resistance strategies such as cutting class that could ultimately hurt their chances of getting into a "better" high school, these actions became a self-defeating prophecy. It is important to situate these coping mechanisms within the systemic racism and disinvestment of such schools (see Anyon, 1997, 2005; Royal & Cothorne, 2021). Furthermore, acknowledging the daily struggle for humanity that both teachers and students at Baker and similar schools experience is a part of humanizing the individuals who attend and work at Baker School.

The Importance of Shifting the Narrative

Focusing on the contextual, lived experiences of individuals can help to shift the narrative from deficit-focused to more asset-focused. Students and teachers are resilient. John, a former colleague who was the counselor at the school where I taught for many years, told me, "Every child that goes to school here is resilient. To come back to this place day after day, to go through what many of them go through before they even get here is resilient. These are the most resilient kids I have ever met." I always thought about John's comment as a teacher, although I do not think I could fully understand it when I was a new teacher struggling and in survival mode myself.

It is now, in my role as a researcher, that I can better appreciate what John meant. What helps me to see the resiliency of students is that I have spent hundreds of hours listening to them, sitting in class with them, having lunch with them, and going on trips with them without having the pressures of being a teacher. I have also developed an understanding of the many external pressures in the community and how these directly impact schooling experiences. Teachers, too, are resilient. They are physically and emotionally exhausted and face many challenging situations with limited pay, recognition, and support. Instead of creating an environment in which teachers and students are poised against each other in a culture of control, it is important to recognize how both teachers and students are dehumanized in this schooling context.

Summary

This chapter underscores the symbolic violence that occurs as students internalize the deficit default that surrounds individuals connected to Baker School and the local community. Despite the systemic lack of resources and disinvestment in inner-city public schools like Baker, the individuals within them are blamed and thought about as "unmotivated" and "undeserving" of a better, more equitable education. Rashanna is considered by most school staff to be a "bad" student, and she describes raising her nephew and the many encounters her family had with the justice system. Rashanna embodies the habitus of fierceness and claims that she does not care, but from my relationship with her she is doing this to protect herself from being further hurt by adults. Nyeisha is also labeled as a "bad" student, and the challenges she experiences at home and school often result in Nyeisha being angry and upset, which further contributes to the difficult relationship she has with adults at the school. Nyeisha is parentified by her mother and teachers at the school and is not allowed the opportunity to be a child.

Teachers want to do a good job, and students want adults to consider them "good." However, at Baker, teachers and students are often positioned against each other and dehumanized. Teachers and students at Baker are struggling for their humanity. The stories of Rashanna and Nyeisha illustrate how multiple factors from students' home and community life influence their experiences and how the culture of control, parentification, and infantilization compound already challenging situations so that attending Baker School is about survival, and the individuals connected to it are often dehumanized and left behind.

Conclusion

Schooling at Baker was often dehumanizing and demoralizing for students, teachers, staff, and parents / family members. Many individuals connected to the school were struggling for their humanity, especially the students and teachers. If the United States is committed to educational equity, policymakers, scholars, and citizens should be concerned about the inequities and intergenerational harm being enacted upon students, families, and teachers at schools like Baker. In this concluding chapter, I describe potential recommendations and implications for theory, future research, and practice based on this research.

This research suggests a need for a continued reexamination of social reproduction and resistance theories in education, as social mobility and the myth of meritocracy remain embedded in the consciousness of the United States. Students at schools like Baker, which involves instruction that directly contributes to social reproduction, experience symbolic violence when they internalize deficit ideologies about themselves that if they only worked harder, they would be "successful." For this reason, it becomes important to state that education does not equal opportunity at Baker. Future research studies should contextually examine the social reproduction of schooling and recognize the necessity for scholars, practitioners, and citizens to acknowledge that the education at schools like Baker is neither equitable, nor does it provide students with opportunities for social mobility. Additional implications discussed in this chapter include how schools like Baker should be funded equitably so that they can provide students with an equitable education. This research also suggests implications for practitioners, including that they reframe and learn from student resistance and behavior as well as how to design curricula and lessons that engage students and respect their experiences as whole people. Related to that, teachers should be given the ongoing learning and professional development needed so that they can engage in these transformative pedagogies. Additional recommendations include ways to dismantle the curriculum of control by democratizing schooling by providing opportunities to genuinely include student voices as well as the voices of the local community and parents. Finally, I close this chapter by suggesting ways practitioners can adopt a resource orientation toward students and communities.

Education Does Not Equal Opportunity

As the data describe, Baker School is chaotic. Teachers' and school staff's attempts to lessen the chaos result in blaming students and their families. Narratives of students as "out of control" and "unmotivated" and parents as "uninvolved and apathetic" are pervasive. The didactic pedagogical practices of having students copy off the board or complete worksheets further contributes to the controlling environment and social reproduction (Anyon, 1980). The ideology evolves that students do not have structure and consequences at home, and thus the school must provide the lacking discipline and then some. However, despite what I have described as the culture of control at Baker, it is still a chaotic environment in which compliance becomes a proxy for being a good student and ultimately for success.

This is another example of the hidden curriculum of social reproduction (e.g., Anyon, 1980; Bowles & Gintis, 1976, McFadden, 2023) because the type of schooling that students experience at Baker prepares them to follow rules, obey commands, and complete mundane tasks, and this research shows how these processes of control begin as early as elementary school. However, the political economy has changed, and the manual labor and factory jobs that schools socialize low-income students to be prepared for no longer exist. Thus, students at Baker are exposed to low-quality instruction in a dehumanizing environment that prepares them for jobs that do not exist. Consequences of this system are, among others, perpetuating the school-to-prison pipeline (Kennedy & Marsano, 2024) as well as subjecting students to dehumanizing and carceral practices.

This study suggests future empirical and theoretical research that specifically examines the social reproduction of elementary schools contextually with a focus on potential changes. Understandably, scholars and educators want to make room for individual agency. However, not examining the impact of structural forces only further contributes to the arguments that blame students for not "working hard enough." Although this may be a hard message for individualistic Americans to believe, education, in the way that it is currently enacted, does not equal opportunity for the vast majority of students at schools like Baker School. Acknowledging this, both theoretically and in practice, can potentially help to improve schools like Baker to chart a path for students that does provide opportunity.

In addition to the theoretical and scholarly implications related to the social reproductive nature of schooling at Baker, there are also important implications for practitioners. School leaders, district officials, and teachers should think about the messages they are sending students through curricula and school resources. Districts often have high-quality curricula created by curriculum specialists, but schools like Baker do not have the books and supplies needed to use these materials. Examples such as these begin to compound especially in schools located in high-poverty areas in which students and communities have been historically underserved by public institutions. Thus, it becomes even more important to equitably fund such schools and properly support and compensate the educators who work in them.

Reconceptualizing Resistance

Many teachers might consider changing the ways in which they engage with and conceptualize student behavior and resistance as well as the pedagogical practices they employ. Teachers tend to rely on behaviorist approaches to schooling, which contributes to the curriculum of control, reinforces social reproduction, and creates micro-power struggles between teachers and their students. Students at Baker resist the dehumanizing schooling environment in which learning is forfeited for behavioral control.

The students, through what I have termed micro-resistance strategies, push back against the culture of control and dominance. Rather than attend classes that primarily consist of "copying of notes," students cut class, volunteer to help in the main office, see if any of their former teachers need help, or play games in the hallway with their peers. Students also resist, respond to, and navigate the environment of Baker by cultivating a habitus of fierceness. Students do not believe that the school and/or the teachers will protect them, and they demonstrate a habitus of fierceness so that other people (peers and/or teachers) will not "mess" with them and so that they are not perceived as weak. While this habitus sometimes involves violence, it also demonstrates resilient and adaptive problem-solving, which are necessary skills for their environment in and out of school. It is also a way in which students cope with and protect themselves when they feel threatened. Reframing these types of behaviors is an important implication for practitioners at Baker and schools like it. This is part of adopting a resource orientation toward students, and additional staff training is necessary to help practitioners cultivate this stance.

It is important to note that student resistance strategies at Baker also contribute to social reproduction. For example, a habitus of fierceness does not align with the middle-class values that schools reinforce, so it is therefore rejected and punished. In extreme situations, students are suspended or expelled from school. In other situations, younger students are often sent to another classroom, as the example of Nyeisha illustrates. Many older students cut class, as Rashanna's example describes. In all these scenarios, student behavior is being controlled. Despite the boring instruction and dehumanizing environment, students are continuously blamed and looked down upon, creating a culture of symbolic violence. Again, it becomes crucial to learn from student resistance rather than continuously punish it.

An example of learning from student resistance starts with listening to students. When I shared that the goal of my research was to learn about the student experience of schooling from students, most people I encountered — colleagues, teachers, and other staff members — reacted in disbelief. Why don't you talk to the teachers? Are you really going into the student lunchroom? Talking to students about their experience and going through the schooling experience with students from one class to the next is a fundamental way to understand how students think about themselves, schooling, and the messages schools and school officials communicate to them. Students are the experts of their experiences, yet they are rarely included in the conversation. Learning from student resistance begins with asking students why they are not going to class. When they tell you it is because they don't learn anything in that class, it involves going to that class to see what is happening. Rather than punishing that student for skipping class or the teacher who is not teaching, it involves talking to the student and supporting the teacher to improve their practice. These things can't happen at once and they can't happen when schools like Baker are under-funded, understaffed, and in survival mode. Funding will not solve all the problems, but it will help to provide necessary professional development to teachers who teach in urban schools, help to repair physical building structures, and help to increase the pay of teachers so that teacher turnover is not as high.

Equitable Funding

An additional implication related to the ways that schools like Baker reproduce social inequity is related to issues of systemic inequality. Policymakers at local, state, and national levels should give schools such as Baker *more, not less, funding*. The requirements of the fair funding lawsuit in Pennsylvania may be a step in the right direction, as research (e.g., Martin et al., 2022) has found that equitable funding can decrease the opportunity gap in urban public schools. The lack of basic educational resources such as personnel and instructional materials impacts everyone at Baker. When educators take on multiple roles because of insufficient personnel, they become increasingly stressed and overwhelmed. This stress contributes to the survival mode mentality that many educators at Baker experience. It also perpetuates the deficit default ideology toward and within students and parents.

The deficit default perspective has significant implications for students at Baker, especially as students internalize these negative descriptions of themselves. It is important to note that these types of issues are systemic and reflect the disinvestment of high-poverty schools and communities (Anyon, 1997, 2005; Owens & Candipan, 2019). As such, a crucial component to addressing these systemic inequalities is funding schools like Baker equitably. A part of funding schools more equitably involves paying teachers more and improving working conditions, as dissatisfaction with the hours worked, base salary, and conditions contribute to teachers' decisions about remaining in the classroom (Steiner et al., 2023).

Opponents to funding increases state that education funding has increased in the United States without a parallel increase in student achievement (Hanushek & Lindseth, 2009). However, the facts shown here clearly show the ways in which education funding is not distributed equitably. Not only is it not distributed equitably; it is not distributed equally. Reforming the ways that education is funded in this country is a crucial step toward improving public education in urban, high-poverty schools and can have a direct impact on students' opportunities and experiences.

Democratizing Schools

Students and teachers engage in power struggles for control at Baker. Ultimately, the teacher tends to retain power in these situations, and these power struggles foster strained relationships between students and teachers. However, the relationships between students and teachers are generally acknowledged as especially important in students' experiences of schooling and achievement (e.g., Kuriloff et al., 2017; Raider-Roth, 2005; Sethi & Scales, 2020; Stevenson, 2014; Walker & Graham, 2021). A way to make schools more humanizing for both students and teachers is to democratize them. Teachers can share power with students by incorporating students' opinions, providing genuine opportunities for student decision-making about norms and curricula, and developing lessons that reflect an understanding of students' experiences (see, e.g., Bounous, 2001; Cook-Sather, 2020; Johnson, 1995).[1]

In a school dominated by a culture of control, it can be challenging for teachers and leaders to engage in more democratic processes. Mr. Barnes, like other new teachers, was put off by what he perceived as less progressive teaching practices. However, it is important for all teachers, and especially new teachers, to think about the role of structure and classroom community. Everyone wants to feel safe, and thinking about ways to create positive structures that are co-created with students is a powerful way to engage students and provide structures that foster a positive classroom community.

At the heart of attempts to democratize schooling practices is a mindset shift in which students, parents, and community members' values, opinions, and experiences are valued and engaged.

Engaging Students

During my fieldwork at Baker, students frequently told me that I was the only person who asked what they thought. I saw this reflected in the teachers' and staff's reactions when I ate lunch with students or described my research to them. Shifting the paradigm from hierarchical to collaborative may seem like a leap for a school like Baker because of the chaotic environment. However, the culture of control is not working. Thus, I suggest systematically involving student voices in school decisions in authentic ways. For example, having students vote on the school colors, which happened at Baker, is not what I am referring to as ways to engage students. Democratizing schooling practices means to genuinely include students in school reform. This type of student voice shifts the paradigm so that student voices are respected and appreciated. There are ways for teachers to do this in their individual classrooms, but systemwide (or at least schoolwide) paradigm shifts are necessary to think about how students can be seen as partners instead of problems. Additional research would then be necessary to determine the extent to which these types of initiatives influence the curriculum and culture of control at Baker and schools like it.

Another way to engage students is related to the previous section about how practitioners can reconceptualize student resistance and then to engage students in conversations about their responses. In addition to training about alternative conceptions of student resistance, practitioners may need explicit professional development for how to understand students' experiences and learn from, instead of control, their behavior. This could also address the deficit ways that teachers view students and help students to feel cared about at school. Furthermore, initiating dialogue between students and teachers is a way for schools to let students know that they value students' perspective and is a way for students and teachers to develop more positive relationships. One potential way to begin this type of work is by thinking holistically about relationships with students related to teaching and modeling social emotional skills in all content areas (see, e.g., Ferreira et al., 2020). A social-emotional skill that adults can model is listening to students. This involves the premise throughout this book based on an acknowledgment that students have important insights about schooling and how it could be improved. The students, for example, clearly described how schooling at Baker is about making the school "look" like a good school by having murals and paintings on the walls rather than engaging students in genuine learning processes. Asking students what they think and listening to their responses and feedback is an important first step to improve students' experiences at Baker School.

Engaging the Community

Another aspect of democratizing schools involves thinking differently about ways to engage the community. At Baker, there is little to no authentic interaction occurring with the community. When interactions do occur, such as when local university students volunteer at Baker, these exchanges primarily benefit the individual university student and their institution. It is also important to note that this type of engagement does not involve the *local* community surrounding Baker.

As discussed earlier, Danielle stated, "Maybe we have to get more community things going on here at the school, where the community is." Some ideas that Danielle mentioned in our conversations include ways to make the school more of a hub for resources that members of the community might need such as access to internet and computers, training for jobs, mental and physical health services, and so forth. The first step in truly engaging in the community is shifting the mindset of staff members at Baker to view the community, and parents in particular, as partners and not problems. To achieve the first step, ongoing professional development and reinforcement from leadership is needed for school personnel. Once school personnel recognize the value and resources of the parents and community, next steps could follow to determine how, if at all, the community could become more connected to the school. Community-informed participatory research is one way that efforts such as these could be undertaken at Baker and other schools to develop and then implement a plan for more genuine community involvement.

Engaging Parents

Related to engaging with and reconceptualizing the local community as partners, Baker and other schools should think about how to more authentically engage parents and families. Instead of blaming parents when they do not behave like middle-class suburban parents, schools and districts should rethink what parental involvement could look like. Most importantly, parents should be involved in the reform and design processes.

Parents at Baker contend with multiple, complex issues. Ms. Crawford, for example, stated on multiple occasions that she was struggling and needed help. However, the school environment disparaged and blamed Ms. Crawford and expressly situated her as "the problem." When the education system has been unsuccessful for parents like Ms. Crawford, who tells her daughter, "I want more for you, Ny Ny," a new set of questions regarding engaging parents at Baker emerges. What does it mean to involve parents in this school environment, and what would parental involvement ideally look like at Baker? When I taught at a school like Baker, I called the families of all 90 of my students during the first few weeks of school. I set the tone as a partner and asked what I should know about their child so that I could be the best teacher for them. These questions are similar to the ones Danielle mentioned as important to ask parents: "What would help you to help your child?" or "What would help you?" Asking these questions is a preliminary first step in demonstrating to parents that the teacher and the school care about them and are invested in building a non-deficit-oriented relationship. This also shifts the relationship to be more collaborative and participatory so that a relationship of productive dialogue and mutual understanding can be fostered.

If increased parental involvement is the goal, the negative ways in which parents are blamed at Baker does not appear to be making strides toward achieving that end. Humanizing parents and recognizing the way that the system has failed them is an important part of stopping the cycle of the deficit default at Baker. It will also help develop a relationship between the school and the parents that situates parents as a resource and a partner instead of a problem. By taking the time to listen to parents without judgment, schools can learn what students and families might need. For example, Nyeisha was often late because she was washing her uniform in the sink and waiting for it to dry in the morning. Knowing this could help Nyeisha and her mother access laundry facilities — potentially in the school — and subsequently help Nyeisha arrive on time to school and support parents like Ms. Crawford. This would involve locating more social services personnel in schools to help address systemic issues that teachers like Ms. Smith declare are not their jobs to address. However, learning this information involves listening to Nyeisha and Ms. Crawford in the way that Ms. Hill took the time to understand the underlying reasons Nyeisha was late to school every day. Ms. Smith would argue that this is not her job, and in some respects it is not. However, the status quo of compliant classrooms in a culture of disrespect and deficit ideologies is not working for most students at

Baker. This is an example of how addressing the many problems facing Baker is complex and involves multiple actors and systems. However, we owe it to Nyeisha and Rashanna and the many other students at Baker that schools are a place of opportunity instead of oppression.

Students' Resiliency and Resources

This text centralizes students' experiences of schooling, and by doing so it makes way for a new way of understanding schooling that places student voice and perspective at the forefront. The rhythms of schooling at Baker revolve around control and behavior instead of learning and engagement. Contextualizing these experiences in the examples of Nyeisha and Rashanna, as well as Renee, Bianca, and Jalayla, humanize these students' experiences and force adults to ask questions related to the underlying assumptions about the purpose of schooling and the related outcomes at Baker and similar schools. In addition, it also points out the many resilient ways that students adapt to the schooling environment.

The rhythms of schooling for Nyeisha involved being responsible for getting herself and her younger siblings to school, getting yelled at for being late, arguing with her teacher, being "kicked out" of class, coming back to class, and getting yelled at again. This cycle of schooling for Nyeisha, while demoralizing, also highlights Nyeisha's amazing resiliency. Despite all this, Nyeisha returned to school every day. In addition, Nyeisha resiliently navigated her home life and took on additional responsibilities at a young age. Despite the parentification and infantilization at the school, students like Nyeisha and Rashanna creatively adapted to the stressful and often dehumanizing environment in ways to protect themselves through micro-resistance strategies as well as cultivating a habitus of fierceness. Recognizing these qualities as a resource, instead of a deficit, perspective is part of how teachers can take a funds of knowledge approach (González et al., 2005; Moll, 2000) toward students, families, and communities, which is discussed in the next section.

Having a Funds of Knowledge Approach

One example of the funds of knowledge that many students at Baker have is how they, like Nyeisha and Rashanna, take on additional responsibilities at home by caring for younger siblings or fending for themselves. Thus, instead of infantilizing and looking down on students, schools like Baker could solicit their opinions and provide them opportunities to take on leadership and make important decisions in the school. In this way, it is possible that the power struggles between students and teachers would become less frequent and could pave the way for better, potentially transformative relationships between students and teachers. To this end, professional development for teachers and other staff members about ways to do this would be a necessary first step for practitioners to avoid the mechanisms of a controlling curriculum based on behaviorist notions of consequences and punishments. In addition to professional development for teachers like Mr. Barnes, changes are also needed to address structural and systemic conditions that contribute to the curriculum of control at schools like Baker that make teaching and learning challenging for students and teachers.

This research presents an asset-based way of viewing the students' enhanced responsibilities at home as building their resilience that also disrupts the deficit notion that the students don't care or try and instead highlights that their focus is on other, bigger responsibilities. The paradoxical tension between the concepts of parentification and infantilization of students adds to the complexity of the hidden curriculum and all the players' roles in it. Clearly, the students' reactions and responses to the curriculum of control perpetuates educators' deficit thinking and thus their inhumane treatment of the students. Stopping this cycle and recognizing the tensions as well as the multiple and varied assets that students bring are central to creating more humanizing schools that could offer places of educational opportunity for students.

Another component of a resource orientation that does not blame and look down upon students and families includes researchers and practitioners acknowledging the invisible macro forces that impact schools like Baker. One of these forces is systemic racism and the ways that individuals at Baker respond to racial stress (Stevenson, 2014). Schools are designed by and for middle-class White people, and when Black students, parents, and teachers navigate these institutions, they experience institutionalized racial stress. At racially homogeneous schools like Baker, issues of racism are often dismissed or ignored because the student body and majority of the staff are Black. However, racial interactions and racial stress are enacted and experienced constantly at Baker when adults and students internalize the curriculum of control that messages that Black, Brown, and poor students need to be controlled.

In addition, Ms. Smith's behavior toward her students, her insistence that they "get it," and the comments she makes revolve around issues of racialized stress. For example, Ms. Smith stated, "I just don't know what to do about the lack of achievement. I don't know if it is us," Ms. Smith points to her skin as she says this, "or economics. I'm thinking it is economics. I just don't know." It's clear that additional research in racially homogeneous environments is necessary to better understand this stress and how it impacts individuals, such as Ms. Smith and her students, and the entire institution of schooling. In addition to research, training for staff in the concepts of racial literacy and racial stress could help teachers like Ms. Smith better cope with racial stress and think about more positive, resource-oriented ways to engage with students, parents, and fellow teachers (see Stevenson, 2014). Professional development related to culturally responsive/sustaining pedagogy is another way to incorporate some of these concepts in ways designed to influence teachers' practices and improve the relationships between teachers, students, and families (Hewko, 2024). Having a funds of knowledge approach is central to culturally sustaining pedagogies, and such an approach has the potential to greatly influence how students, families, and the local community experience the school.

Summary

Efforts to control students as opposed to teaching them have not been successful at Baker School. Much work needs to be done so that schools can reframe student behavior and learn from their resistance rather than punish it, and learn with and from students by listening to them and including them in decision-making. These efforts could help to challenge the deficit mindsets to make schools more humanizing places for students, teachers, and families. Challenging deficit mindsets involves valuing the local community and parents by creating opportunities for more genuine engagement.

Ignoring the ways that schools contribute to social reproduction gives power to the deficit default ideology that occurs at Baker and schools like it. Believing that students are not motivated and do not care makes students, instead of society, responsible for their social location (Theoharis, 2009). Thus, it is necessary to flip that narrative so that the blame and responsibility are not focused on students. In addition to reframing the narrative, it is our responsibility to improve schools like Baker. Students and parents have faith in schooling, even though it has not yet proven worthy of that faith. For example, in the following excerpt, Bianca discussed her future dreams: "I had a dream that I finished school, and I went to college and my mom was proud of me, but I didn't stay at college, I didn't live there. I just went there and came home. And I had a dream that I had got myself a car, a job, and I was successful and I had this big house. I bought my mom all this stuff. I had a dream" (Interview, May 11, 2016). To make these dreams a reality, we owe students like Bianca, Rashanna, Jalayla, Renee, and Nyeisha an opportunity for an equitable education. Otherwise, the narrative will fall back to blaming students for "not making it." Even in this dehumanizing place, it is a testament to student resiliency that they maintain aspirations to what they believe that school can do for them. It is my sincere hope that this book can help make schools like Baker more equitable and humane places for students, teachers, and parents.

A few months ago, I described parts of this book to my aunt, a special education preschool teacher. She asked me what happened to Nyeisha. I told her the point of the book is not specifically the resolution of Nyeisha's story but that there are many students like Nyeisha. What happens to the many students, who like Bianca believe that education will help them to achieve their dreams and trust in our education system? Listening to and learning from Nyeisha, Bianca, and Rashanna's perspectives and understandings of schooling are important for all educators at schools like Baker and throughout the country.

Appendix

Research Methodology and Design

The Baker School study employed *ethnographic* (participant observation) methods to explore, engage with, and better understand students' experiences and perspectives about schooling as well as socialization processes and the opportunities they do or do not foster. Participant observation and interviews were well suited to this research because they emphasized in-person field study and immersion to understand cultural meaning, while acknowledging that culture is historically constructed (Bourgois & Schonberg, 2009; Ravitch & Carl, 2021). The study's epistemological standpoint was that students were important knowledge generators from whom practitioners and scholars had much to learn.

The following research questions guided this study: How did students experience schooling at an underserved, urban, public school in a high-poverty neighborhood? How did direct and indirect messages of possibility at the school influence students and teachers? The concept of *possibility* refers to how teachers and students conceptualize the opportunities available to them as well as their conceptions of themselves. Additional questions that emerged through the research included the following: What were the subtle and overt messages that students received about themselves, their abilities, their preferences, and how they were expected to act in certain spaces? How and what did teachers teach, what were the activities and assignments? How did the school broadly, and teachers specifically, engage families? In what ways were students disciplined, which behaviors were privileged, and which behaviors were punished?

Site and Participant Selection

I engaged with participants, including students, teachers, and parents, in all grades and classes of the school. However, I conducted extensive fieldwork in two classrooms, a fourth-grade class taught by Ms. Smith, a middle-aged Black woman, and an eighth-grade class taught by Mr. Barnes, a twenty-two-year-old White man. I spent significant time with many students in these two classes, but my focal group of students included four eighth-grade girls: Bianca, Jalayla, Rashanna, and Renee. In addition, there were other eighth-grade students, who were not as focal to the study but that I observed and engaged with frequently, including Haleigh, Talik, Khalil, Kiandra, and Melvan. In addition to the eighth-grade students, four fourth-grade students were also focal participants in my study, including Nyeisha, Lashaya, Ireena, and Stefon. Many other students, in a variety of grades, were included in fieldnotes. As described previously, the students at Baker School were predominantly African American, and all the students in this study identified as Black.

In addition to Mr. Barnes and Ms. Smith, other focal adult participants include the counselor, Ms. Johnson, a middle-aged Black woman; a grandparent volunteer, Ms. Carol, an older Black woman; the disciplinarian, Mr. Dixon, a forty-year-old Black male; and Ms. Crawford, a parent of six who is a twenty-nine-year-old Black woman. Additional adult participants include, for example, the lunchroom supervisor, Mr. Kelly, a middle-aged Black man; the principal, Ms. Washington, a middle-aged Black woman; Ms. Redmond, a Black woman in her 30s, mother of eight, and parent volunteer; and the director of after-school programs, Mr. James, a thirty-year-old Black man.

Although I observed schoolwide events and activities, I primarily focused on students in grades 4 through 8 for a variety of reasons, including my familiarity with this age range as a former middle school teacher. Middle school is also a time when students often begin to struggle with academic motivation and self-esteem and consider dropping out of school (Szabó et al., 2024). These factors shaped the important perspectives that students had to share about their thoughts and experiences of socialization processes in school.

Data Collection Methods

Primary data collection methods included observation, fieldnotes, and in-depth interviews. Secondary data sources included researcher memos and archival data. Consistent with a qualitative approach, the research design emerged and evolved based on learnings (Ravitch & Carl, 2021). The methods of data collection are described in the following subsections.

Participant Observation and Fieldnotes

To fully understand the ways that students in an underserved school experience schooling, including practices of the school and those working within it, participant observation and fieldnotes that occur in the school environment are an important source of data. Observations enable researchers to experience and document, through the taking of careful, detailed fieldnotes, the activities in which participants are engaged so as to get a firsthand account of participants' behaviors and experiences (Emerson et al., 2011).

Consistent with the importance in ethnographic methods of building relationships, I spent the 2014–2015 school year conducting exploratory observations and developing relationships with participants, including the principal, the counselor, a grandparent volunteer, and the director of after-school programming. Observations occurred in classrooms, at school-related activities and events, during arrival and dismissal, at lunch, during after-school programs and activities, at fieldtrips, school dances, report card conferences, in the hallways, and the like. During the 2015–2016 school year, observations became more focused in specific locations and classrooms based on participants who had consented and/or assented (for minors) to participate in the study.

Observing the school in a variety of settings and contexts helped contribute to a more detailed understanding of students' behaviors and experiences. As focal student participants were determined and the observational focus began to narrow, I primarily conducted observations in the settings and contexts of the students in Ms. Smith and Mr. Barnes's classes. I attended multiple fieldtrips as a chaperone with the fourth graders, and I attended one field trip, dance, and graduation with the eighth graders. I also observed report card conferences with families with Ms. Smith, Mr. Barnes, and other middle school teachers. I got to know the families associated with the fourth-grade students, especially Nyeisha and her mother, Ms. Crawford, and jottings were taken in the field and developed into fieldnotes as close to the actual time of the observation as possible (Emerson et al., 2011).

Participation in research settings often operates on a continuum, so my presence as a researcher working with the school community was established during my first-year at the school. As a means of developing reciprocal research relationships, I was involved in supporting other efforts at the school that were distinct from this research, including supporting the school in development, implementation, and evaluation of a service-learning curriculum.

In-Depth, Group, and Informal Interviews

Qualitative interviewing helps researchers develop contextualized perspectives and determine the range and variation of participants' experiences to foster a holistic understanding of a phenomenon. In this regard, interviews provide necessary insights about students' schooling perspectives. I employed in-depth interviews, which are also referred to as unstructured interviews. This type of interviewing, common to ethnographic studies, allows for interviews to be inductive and relevant to each participant's experiences. Thus, a prespecified list of questions was not used.

However, I often made notes of ideas I wanted to address at subsequent interviews, as many individuals participated in multiple interviews. These notes and ideas were based primarily on observational fieldnote data. Broadly, participants were asked about their thoughts, opinions, and understandings about Baker School and the surrounding community. Furthermore, participants were asked for specific examples that contextualized and described their responses in detail. Interviews were based on emergent field-based data and included conversations about events that occurred in and out of school, interactions with other participants, how individuals characterized themselves, and how they were characterized by others.

The goals of the interviews were to develop a holistic understanding of schooling at Baker, and this included getting the in-depth perspectives of multiple stakeholders, including students, parents, teachers, administrators, and other staff members. Some of the in-depth interviews occurred in a one-on-one setting. However, some of the interviews took place in a group format, which the middle school students enjoyed and requested. There were never more than four students in a group, and I followed up with individual participants to address aspects that they appeared to not want to discuss in the group setting.

All in-depth interviews were audio-recorded, with permission, and professionally transcribed. I then reviewed each transcript while listening to the audio recording to make sure transcripts were as accurate and verbatim as possible. This combination of group and individual interviews with the students worked well as a means of data and perspectival triangulation, which I discuss in subsequent sections.

In addition to the in-depth one-on-one and group interviews, many individuals at the school participated in informal interviews. These informal interviews, which are common in ethnographic research, tended to occur spontaneously during fieldwork and resembled casual conversations with participants. The informal interviews were recorded as jottings and then developed into field-notes as close to the time of the conversation as possible. I conducted over 50 informal interviews and 33 recorded and transcribed in-depth interviews. The focal student participants participated in multiple and frequent interviews, which the students referred to as "group."

Researcher Memos

Before, during, and after data collection, I composed multiple memos to reflect on and document research processes, capture emergent learnings, and discuss my positionality. In these memos, I closely examined how aspects of fieldwork, emerging themes, and my social location and positionality impact data and ultimately findings. Memos were composed ongoingly as a part of the data collection and analysis processes as well as at strategically selected points. For example, after conducting a few interviews with students, I wrote a memo that reflected on the type of data I was generating, how it aligned or differed from observational data, what follow-up themes I should discuss in subsequent interviews, who else I needed to interview, and what I was learning about students and their experiences.

The structure of these memos was informal; they were written in prose form and included bullet points of next steps. While many memos were written as internal sense-making documents, I also shared these with critical friends and colleagues to initiate dialogic engagement (Ravitch & Carl, 2021). These individuals included my colleagues and members of a research inquiry group, and groups of current and former teachers.

Description of Researcher Memos

The following memos are examples of the types of memos composed throughout the data collection and analysis processes. These memos were written as internal sense-making documents and shared with critical friends to initiate dialogic engagement (Ravitch & Carl, 2021). These individuals included my advisor and dissertation chair, other members of my dissertation committee, members of a research inquiry group, and fellow doctoral students.

- Researcher identity / positionality memos, as discussed by Maxwell (2013) and Ravitch and Carl (2021), were used to document specific aspects of my identity and positionality in relation to the research. Aspects I focused on included my experiences as a teacher, as a researcher, my own socializing experiences as a student and child, and site-based relationships. I discussed how these were related to research processes and learnings.
- Fieldwork and data collection memos, such as discussed by Ravitch and Carl (2021), were used to reflect on my experiences in the field, impressions about the research setting, any changes to the research design and research questions, preliminary codes and themes, and other site-based learnings.
- I again followed the recommendations of Ravitch and Carl (2021) to create vignette memos based on fieldnotes and interview data and that reflected on various facets of my design and analysis.
- Formative data analysis memos that documented initial understandings and solicited feedback from inquiry group members.
- Precoding and coding memos, as described by Ravitch & Carl (2021), documented the analytical coding processes. Topics addressed include reactivity; whether codes are emic, etic, or a combination; how theory does or does not align with codes; next steps; and lingering questions.
- Thematic memos, as described by Maxwell (2013), helped me to explain emerging themes throughout the research process, excerpts of data that supported these themes, data that served as disconfirming evidence, and my reflections about the data and themes.
- Theoretical analysis memos that reflect on my arguments in relationship to existing theory. These memos also included emblematic data excerpts and discussed them in relationship to theory.

Archival Data

Pertinent internal and publicly available documents specifically pertaining to the research setting and to schooling in Philadelphia were reviewed. These documents helped to develop my understanding of schooling in Philadelphia as well as specific processes at the research site. Examples of such archival documents included personal, official, and popular culture documents (Bogdan & Biklen, 2006). For example, personal documents included student work, teacher-created correspondence with parents, lesson plans, and student assignments. Official documents entailed, among others, school mission statements, posters, letters to parents, rules posted in classrooms and hallways, handbooks, and publicly available data from the city. Popular culture documents primarily included newspaper articles.

Sequencing of Data Collection Methods

The methods previously described were employed concurrently throughout the data collection process. However, I spent considerable time immersing myself in setting and taking fieldnotes and recording informal conversations before conducting in-depth interviews to help me develop a more complex understanding of the site and before asking more specific questions in interviews. After initial observations and conversations, all the data collection methods, including observation and fieldnotes, interviews, researcher memos, and review of archival data, occurred concurrently. For example, if participants mentioned a specific event or school program, I asked the participant or other participants for the relevant documents related to the event or program so that I could examine how what was presented in the documents compared with the interview data and fieldnotes. The triangulation of these multiple sources of data helped to develop a more rigorous and complex study.

Data Analysis

Qualitative data analysis took place formatively to help develop more nuanced and complex interpretations. During formative analysis, I composed analytical memos that reflected potential themes, contradictions in the data, commented on fieldnote vignettes, and documented difficulties and learnings. I paid specific attention to three important aspects of data analysis, including data organization and management, immersive engagement, and writing and representation (Ravitch & Carl, 2021).

Data was also analyzed and summarized after it was collected. I conducted multiple readings of my data corpus and employed open and axial coding processes (Miles et al., 2014; Ravitch & Carl, 2021). Open coding processes were as inductive as possible to develop emic understandings of the data (Maxwell, 2013), and axial coding combined inductive and deductive processes. I developed a code set that included both descriptive and theoretical categories (Maxwell, 2013). For example, one emic code that recurred frequently was *they listen when we yell*. Examples of other preliminary codes include *teachers in survival mode, students raising themselves, perceptions of motivation, teachers don't understand us*, and so on. Once all data were coded, codes were analyzed to determine key themes and develop thematically based findings (Gibson & Brown, 2009).

While developing codes, code definitions, and themes, I deliberately looked for disconfirming evidence and alternative examples and explanations. I also systematically engaged with others to elicit feedback, challenge my interpretations, and scrutinize codes, themes, and findings throughout formative and summative data analysis. In addition to thematic coding, I employed connecting strategies to holistically look at data in their entirely rather than solely pulling coded excerpts with the goal of seeing relationships to broader contexts and the entire "story" of the data (Maxwell, 2013; Maxwell & Chmiel, 2014; Maxwell & Miller, 2008). Developing holistic stories of the data helped to keep the findings as contextualized as possible.

Writing was integral to my analysis, and throughout the data analysis process, I composed multiple analytical memos that reflected on processes, codes, and themes to document and further my thinking. To resist interpretative authority in analysis and in my writing, I engaged in the validity strategies described in the next section as well as the dialogic engagement strategies described previously.

Validity

Consistent with many qualitative approaches and with ethnographic methods, I maintained a fidelity to participants' experiences rather than to specific methods (see Hammersley & Atkinson, 2007). While acknowledging that validity can never be entirely ensured, I was mindful of transactional processes as well as transformational approaches to achieving qualitative rigor and ultimately conducting a trustworthy study (Cho & Trent, 2006). To have a study that was credible, transferable, dependable, and confirmable, I employed multiple strategies to help establish the validity of my data and rigor of my study (see Guba, 1981; Toma, 2011). Specifically, I incorporated the validity strategies of triangulation, participant validation, thick description, and structured reflexivity processes to enhance the study's validity, rigor, and complexity. These validity strategies are described in the following subsections.

Triangulation

I specifically considered methodological, data, theoretical, and perspectival triangulation. Methodological triangulation consisted of between-methods triangulation by looking across data sources (observations, interviews, memos, and archival data) to see how, if, and to what degree data are consistent across different methods (Denzin, 2009). Data triangulation entailed that data sources were compared according to time, space, and person. For example, when conducting classroom observations, I noted if students were responding and interacting differently according to the time of day, the location (e.g., classroom, hallway), or the person (e.g., science teacher versus math teacher). I also incorporated theoretical triangulation so that my findings, while as inductive as possible, could be analyzed by considering contrasting theories.

Because a social reproduction and cultural capital argument heavily influenced my theoretical framework, I reviewed and considered literature that refuted this argument. Finally, I also incorporated a range of perspectives and stakeholders so as to achieve perspectival triangulation and develop a more complex and nuanced data set (Ravitch & Carl, 2021). In addition to these processes of triangulation related to data collection, I also analyzed data by paying attention to connections and contradictions within and between different data sources, methods, participants, and theories; these processes are known as analytical triangulation.

Participant Validation Strategies

I "checked in" with participants (often called member checks or participant validation strategies) throughout the study to share emerging learnings and interpretations and to see how my interpretations did or did not align with participants' understandings. Specifically, I had many informal conversations with Mr. Barnes, Ms. Smith, Ms. Johnson, and Ms. Carol in which I mentioned ideas and potential themes and solicited their thoughts. I also did this with my group of four eighth-grade girls during our conversations and "tested" emerging hypotheses to elicit their reactions.

The specific processes of participant validation varied depending on the participant. With students, I asked questions that were related to a particular concept, theme, or finding. I asked these questions in a variety of ways to determine if and how their understandings changed and how that aligned with or contradicted the data. With adult participants, I engaged in conversations about my emerging findings to determine if and how they resonated with their experiences. Because participant validation processes are considered crucial to having credible findings, I engaged these participants throughout the study so that I could focus my data collection and analysis throughout my research and not just at the end (Lincoln & Guba, 1985; Maxwell, 2013).

Thick Description

Consistent with the ethnographic methods, I employed the validity strategy of thick description, which refers to how researchers write about and describe a research setting and participants, to enhance the credibility, transferability, and complexity of a study (see Guba, 1981; Ravitch & Carl, 2021). Thick description includes providing accurate and thorough contextual information so that readers of the study will be able to understand processes as well as transfer and apply findings to different contexts.

Thick description, as opposed to thin description, includes commentary and interpretations of participants and events within the research context (Denzin, 2009). This includes making sure the study's contextual factors, participants, events, and experiences are described clearly, with sufficient detail, and situated in contextual understandings so that research audiences and participants can develop more complex interpretations of the study and develop mental pictures of the research setting (Ponterotto, 2006).

Structured Reflexivity Processes

As previously described, I employed structured reflexivity processes in the form of memos as well as engaged in dialogic engagement exercises with colleagues and advisors. Both activities helped me to monitor, analyze, and question ways that my interpretations are shaped by my understandings and experiences. Examining and monitoring the ways that my biases may have impacted the data and findings was crucial to having a valid and rigorous qualitative research study (Ravitch & Carl, 2021).

Researcher Roles and Positionality

As a former Philadelphia middle school English teacher and lead teacher for five years and mentor to first-year teachers in multiple schools throughout the city, I had conceptions of what "good" teaching looked like. I care deeply and am passionate about education in Philadelphia. I acknowledge that my "wisdom of practice" (Shulman, 1987) influences how I understand the world. However, as with all qualitative research, there is no universal truth, and my biases and understandings cannot be separated from my interpretations (Scheper-Hughes, 1992; Ravitch & Carl, 2021). It was my goal to conduct "good-enough ethnography" in which I did my best "to listen and observe carefully, empathically, and compassionately" (Scheper-Hughes 1992, p. 28). In addition, I built into my processes deliberate ways for me to subject my interpretations to scrutiny to resist interpretative authority.

In my role as researcher, I also acknowledged that additional power asymmetries exist. This was part of the reason why I employed ethnographic methods because, "although it is framed by the unequal relationship of 'investigator' and 'informant,' ethnography renders its practitioners vulnerable to the blood, sweat, tears, and violence of the people being studied and requires ethical reflection and solidary engagement" (Bourgois & Schonberg, 2009, p. 14). There are both strengths and limitations to ethnographic methods. While I attempted to conduct a valid and rigorous study that placed a primacy on participants' experiences, I acknowledge that my understandings and biases influenced what I saw in observations, the participants I included and did not include in interviews, and the way I analyzed my data. I worked to subject my interpretations to scrutiny, and I have been as explicit and transparent as possible about potential biases and assumptions that informed my understanding.

Furthermore, an additional aspect of my positionality is my race, age, and social class. As a young White woman, among a largely Black staff, racial dynamics were clearly at play. Furthermore, as I noted, my role as an educator and a doctoral student at an Ivy League university further complicated certain relationships. Developing a presence as a trusted and respected member of the community took time, and it was not without frustration on either side. Although I grew up poor, my current social location at an Ivy League university and living in a more economically resourced neighborhood highlighted and served as a continual reminder of important aspects of privilege and resource that I could not deny — and that I remained actively aware of throughout my engagement.

One of the biggest challenges I faced was how I decided to write about the teachers at Baker. I spent countless hours with them, and I understand how challenging and grueling their job can be daily. Yet, I was often frustrated with either their pedagogy or the way they interacted with children. I've provided a fieldnote that illustrates some of the tensions and frustrations that surround my positionality at Baker.

> Lamar keeps getting in trouble today. I have been in the class for a few minutes, and Ms. Smith keeps hollering at him: "Sit down, do your work, I have had it!" Ms. Smith walks over to the back of the classroom by the door to greet me. Lamar gets up to throw something away. She elbows me and says, "Follow my lead."
>
> Then to Lamar, Ms. Smith yells: "Come here. Come here." Lamar says, "I didn't do nothing." Ms. Smith hollers, "What did you say?" Lamar responds, "What?" Ms. Smith screams again, "Get over here."
>
> Ms. Smith asks me in front of Lamar: "Ms. Nicole, why don't you tell Lamar what White people expect of them?" I don't say anything.
>
> She gets in Lamar's face and says, "They are building more and more prisons because they think that is where you are going to end up. They expect that of you."
>
> She continues, "You need to get a good job so you can afford things. You need to work hard. Minimum wage isn't going to cut it. You are going to end up poor. Lamar, don't you have a lot of little brothers and sisters?" "Yes," he says.
>
> Ms. Smith asks, "How many?" Lamar answers, "Eight." She is surprised and asks, "Eight. Are you sure?" Lamar states,

"Yes, counting my stepbrothers."

Ms. Smith asks, "And they all live with you?" Lamar says, "Yes."

Ms. Smith says to me in front of Lamar, "His mom is pregnant so it is about to be nine." She then asks Lamar, "Don't you want to set a good example for them?" He nods.

I say to Lamar, "Hi, Lamar. I'm Nicole. You seem like a nice kid. I hope that the next time I talk to you, you are not in trouble. I know that it is hard to sit still all day."

Ms. Smith says, "He doesn't sit still all day. He doesn't listen and just shrugs his shoulders." (Fieldnote, March 2, 2016)

This fieldnote provides one example of many in which I was frustrated with Ms. Smith. Many factors were at play, including my race. I was upset with how she was treating the students, and I was angry that she tried to make me a part of that. However, as I articulate in other chapters, Ms. Smith, Lamar, and I were experiencing racialized stress, which is often not considered in largely homogeneous populations (Stevenson, 2014).

I suggest in the concluding chapter that schools such as Baker take steps to address these instances with their staff and students. I was conflicted about representing teachers negatively, as they are all too often blamed for educational failure without recognition of broader systemic issues; I address these issues in chapter 6. What I have attempted to do is represent what happened at Baker faithfully to my data, and this means that I do not shy away from describing situations such as the previous fieldnote. However, I also show the complexities and nuances that surround daily life in this school for students and teachers.

Credibility and Transferability

The validity strategies described earlier were employed with the goal of conducting a rigorous and valid study that adhered to the qualitative notions of credibility (internal validity) and transferability (external validity) (see Guba, 1981; Miles et al., 2014; Ravitch & Carl, 2021). By triangulating between different methods and participants, checking in with participants to determine their perceptions of my findings, looking for alternative explanations and data that supported different interpretations, and seeking counsel throughout design, fieldwork, and analysis from mentors and peers, I enhanced the study's credibility and transferability.

Furthermore, consistent with the ethnographic tradition, I described the setting and context with enough thick description so that readers of my research can fully understand the research context and determine how the findings do and do not compare to other settings, contexts, situations, and individuals. This will foster the study's transferability so that the findings can be applicable to broader contexts without losing context-specific richness (see Lincoln & Guba,

1985; Ravitch & Carl, 2021; Toma, 2011). Ethnography can help to humanize individuals and resist deficit orientations (Bourgois & Schonberg, 2009; Paulle, 2013). Students' perspectives and experiences of these socializing processes in underserved schools are not often included in empirical research, and this ethnographic study has the potential to generate a new line of inquiry and shed important light on students' schooling experiences.

Notes

Chapter 1: Hidden Curricula and the Myth of Opportunity

1. The dominant group refers to "the group that controls the economic, social and political resources" (Mills & Gale, 2007, p. 435).
2. Scholars refer to this difference between low-income students' schooling outcomes and their peers as the socioeconomic achievement gap. See Bradley (2022) for more information.

Chapter 2: The Curriculum of Control

1. At a later date, I asked Haliegh what this means and where she learned the phrase. She said it is a common phrase in social media like Instagram and that it means being stingy or mean.

Chapter 3: Relational Dynamics, Power Struggles, and Resistance

1. While some interpretations of Bourdieu's concept of habitus consider it to be fixed, I, along with others (e.g., Aries & Seider, 2005; Bourdieu, 1990; Horvat & Davis, 2011; King, 2000), consider habitus to be fluid, especially as a result of pedagogic work.

Chapter 4: Parentification and Infantilization of Students

1. For additional context, students at the public school my children attend are allowed to walk to and from school starting in the fourth grade. There are families I know who allow their children to walk home as early as third grade.

2. The phrase *control your class* was common at Baker School. It was also very common at the school where I taught. Teachers were discussed by the principal, staff members, and other teachers about whether they could control their class. Parents and students also used this type of language to describe teachers.

Chapter 5: Implications of Internalizing the "Deficit Default"

1. At Baker School and many other Philadelphia schools, including the one I taught at, eighth-grade graduation was a very important event for students and families. Because of the high school graduation rate and students who drop out of school after eighth grade, many students think of this as potentially their only graduation, which coincides with comments that students make, such as "tomorrow isn't promised."

Chapter 6: The Realities of Systemic Failure

1. When I was a teacher at a public school in Philadelphia, each teacher received approximately two reams of copy paper a month, and as a middle school teacher with over 90 students, copy paper was always in short supply. Thus, I asked for boxes of copy paper as Christmas presents from my family.
2. The intense feelings of stress that Mr. Barnes described were ones I could relate to. As I mentioned, I taught at a school quite like Baker, in which teachers were frequently absent. In a teaching staff of about the same size as Baker, during my first year teaching, there were a total of nine first-year teachers at my school. I remember coming early to school every day, around 6:30 a.m., and sitting in the parking lot with a knot in the pit of my stomach before walking into the school building on multiple occasions. The second year was easier, but the feelings of exhaustion and burnout are ones I, and many teachers, can relate to.
3. Baker's eighth-grade graduation ceremony was very nice. I used to run the ceremony when I was a teacher, and these events are complicated productions with choreographed songs, dances, and recitations. I also accompanied Baker's eighth-grade students to their dance, which Ms. Johnson planned, and their trip, which was a river cruise and lunch. Ms. Johnson worked hard to make sure that the eighth-grade students felt celebrated and supported.
4. The daily affirmation, which was displayed on computer paper throughout the school, included the following text written in stanza form: "If it is to be / It is up to me / I can be anything / I want to be / I can decide to do / I can do

anything I want to / As long as I listen to the people who care / about me / If I am weak / I am beat / If I am wise / I will survive / I will prepare myself / So that when the doors of opportunity open / I can just walk right in / I can, I will, I believe / It is done."

Chapter 7: Struggling for Humanity

1. This term was developed by Yosso (2005) and refers to students' skills to navigate institutional spaces, such as schools.
2. Theoharis (2009) states, "Part of the appeal of believing that urban students do not care about education is that the responsibility for change lies with them and not the rest of the nation" (p. 110).
3. As discussed in previous chapters, the *culture of power* (Delpit, 1995) refers to the set of values and beliefs (or rules) that those in the culture of power know and that others do not.
4. *Social capital* (Yosso, 2005) refers to the networks and relationships that people are able to utilize to gain access to resources.
5. I am now also a parent of school-aged children, around the same age as Nyeisha, and getting them ready for school is a challenge every morning, so I can empathize with Ms. Crawford.

Conclusion

1. One way that some schools have attempted to more authentically include more student voices is by incorporating youth participatory action research (YPAR) to have students research student-determined issues with the goal of improving their school. Students and teachers who participate in YPAR note how the research processes transformed student and teacher relationships from hierarchical to collaborative and in turn has positive impacts on students' sense of self-efficacy (Carl et al., 2015). Engaging in school-based YPAR or ethnographic research approaches that centralize students' experiences are just two ways that schools could begin more democratic practices.

References

Agopian, T. (2022). Reforms in teacher education programs to enhance the professionalization of the teaching profession. *E-Pedagogium, 22*(2), 7–19.

Alim, S. H. (2004). Preface: Real talk. *American Dialect Society, 89*(1), xiii–xxvi.

Allen, Q., & White-Smith, K. (2018). "That's why I say stay in school": Black mothers' parental involvement, cultural wealth, and exclusion in their son's schooling. *Urban Education, 53*(3), 409–435.

American Psychological Association (2016). *A silent national crisis: Violence against teachers*. American Psychological Association. Retrieved from: http://www.apa.org/education/k12/teacher-victimization.pdf

Anderson, E. (1999). *Code of the street: Decency, violence, and the moral life of the inner city*. Norton.

Ansari, A., Hofkens, T. L., & Pianta, R. C. (2020). Teacher-student relationships across the first seven years of education and adolescent outcomes. *Journal of Applied Developmental Psychology, 71*, 101200.

Anyon, J. (1980). Social class and the hidden curriculum of work. *Journal of Education, 162*(1), 67–92.

Anyon, J. (1997). *Ghetto schooling: A political economy of urban educational reform*. Teachers College Press.

Anyon, J. (2005). *Radical possibilities: Public policy, urban education, and a new social movement*. Routledge.

Anyon, J. (2013). Social class, school knowledge, and the hidden curriculum: Retheorizing reproduction. In *Ideology, curriculum, and the new sociology of education* (pp. 37–45). Routledge.

Apple, M. W. (2018). The hidden curriculum and the nature of conflict. In *Ideology and curriculum* (pp. 85–108). Routledge.

Aries, E., & Seider, M. (2005). The interactive relationship between class identity and the college experience: The case of low-income students. *Qualitative Sociology, 28*, 419–443.

Au, W. (2016). Meritocracy 2.0: High-stakes, standardized testing as a racial project of neoliberal multiculturalism. *Educational Policy, 30*(1), 39–62.

Auerbach, S. (2002). "Why do they give the good classes to some and not to others?" Latino parent narratives of struggle in a college access program. *Teachers College Record, 104*(7), 1369–1392.

Auerbach, S. (2007). From moral supporters to struggling advocates: Reconceptualizing parent roles in education through the experience of working-class families of color. *Urban Education, 42*(3), 250–283.

Auerbach, S. (2012). Conceptualizing leadership for authentic partnerships: A continuum to inspire practice. In *School leadership for authentic family and community partnerships* (pp. 29–51). Routledge.

Backer, D. I., & Cairns, K. (2021). Social reproduction theory revisited. *British Journal of Sociology of Education, 42*(7), 1086–1104.

Barshay, J. (2020). A decade of research in the rich-poor divide in education. *Hechinger Report*.

Barton, A. C., & Yang, K. (2000). The culture of power and science education: Learning from Miguel. *Journal of Research in Science Teaching, 37*(8), 871–889.

Bautista, M. A., Bertrand, M., Morrell, E., Scorza, D., & Matthews, C. (2013). Participatory action research and city youth: Methodological insights from the council of youth research. *Teachers College Record, 115*(2), 1–23.

Bernhardt, P. E. (2022). *Hidden curriculum: Definitions and examples*. Routledge.

Bertrand, S. K. (2017). Class dismissed: An examination of how teacher candidates are prepared for Title I schools. *ProQuest LLC*. https://search.ebscohost.com/login. aspx?direct=true&db=eric&AN=ED579551&site=ehst-live&scope=site

Boen, C. E., Kozlowski, K., & Tyson, K. D. (2020). "Toxic" schools? How school exposures during adolescence influence trajectories of health through young adulthood. *SSM-Population Health, 11*, 100623.

Bogdan, R. C., & Biklen, S. K. (2006). *Qualitative research for education: An introduction to theories and methods* (5th ed.). Pearson.

Borchet, J., Lewandowska-Walter, A., & Rostowska, T. (2018). Performing developmental tasks in emerging adults with childhood parentification — insights from literature. *Current Issues in Personality Psychology, 6*(3), 242–251.

Borrero, N. E., Yeh, C. J., Cruz, C. I., & Suda, J. F. (2012). School as a context for "othering" youth and promoting cultural assets. *Teachers College Record, 114*(2), 1–37.

Bottiani, J. H., Duran, C. A. K., Pas, E. T., & Bradshaw, C. P. (2019). Teacher stress and burnout in urban middle schools: Associations with job demands, resources, and effective classroom practices. *Journal of School Psychology, 77*, 36–51.

Bounous, R. (2001). Teaching as political practice. In V. Sheared & P. A. Sissel (Eds.), *Making space: Merging theory and practice in adult education* (pp. 195–207). Bergin & Garvey.

Bourdieu, P. (1977). *Outline of a theory of practice*. (R. Nice, Trans.). Cambridge University Press. (Original work published 1972.)

Bourdieu, P. (1984). *Distinction: A social critique of the judgement of taste*. (R. Nice, Trans.). Harvard University Press. (Original work published 1979.)

Bourdieu, P. (1986). The forms of capital. In J. Richardson (Ed.), *Handbook of theory and research for the sociology of education* (pp. 241–258). Greenwood Press.

Bourdieu, P. (1989). Social space and symbolic power. *Sociological Theory, 7*(1), 14–25.

Bourdieu, P. (1990). *The logic of practice*. Stanford University Press.

Bourdieu, P. (1991). *Language and symbolic power: The economy of linguistic exchanges*. (G. Raymond & M. Adamson, Trans.). Harvard University Press.

Bourdieu, P. (1998). *Acts of resistance: Against the new myths of our time*. (R. Nice, Trans.). Polity Press.

Bourdieu, P. (2000). *Pascalian meditations*. Stanford University Press. (Original work published 1997.)

Bourdieu, P. (2001). *Masculine domination.* (R. Nice, Trans.). Stanford University Press. (Original work published 1998.)

Bourdieu, P. (2017). Habitus. In *Habitus: A sense of place* (pp. 59–66). Routledge.

Bourdieu, P., & Passeron, J. (1977). *Reproduction in education, culture, and society.* Sage.

Bourdieu, P., & Wacquant, L. (1992) *An invitation to reflexive sociology.* University of Chicago Press.

Bourdieu, P., & Wacquant, L. (2013). Symbolic capital and social classes. *Journal of Classical Sociology, 13*(2), 292–302.

Bourgois, P. (2003). *In search of respect: Selling crack in El Barrio* (2nd ed.). Cambridge University Press.

Bourgois, P., & Schonberg, J. (2007). Intimate apartheid: Ethnic dimensions of habitus among homeless heroin injectors. *Ethnography, 8*(1), 7–31.

Bourgois, P., & Schonberg, J. (2009) *Righteous dopefiend.* University of California Press.

Bowles, S., & Gintis, H. (1976) *Schooling in capitalist America: Education reform and the contradictions of economic life.* Basic Books.

Bradley, Kate. *The socioeconomic achievement gap in the US public schools.* Ballard Brief. December 2022. www.ballardbrief.byu.edu

Brathwaite, J. (2017). Neoliberal education reform and the perpetuation of inequality. *Critical Sociology, 43*(3), 429–448.

Brotherton, D. C., & Barrios, L. (2004). *The almighty Latin king and queen nation: Street politics and the transformation of a New York City gang.* Columbia University Press.

Burton, L. (2007). Childhood adultification in economically disadvantaged families: A conceptual model. *Family Relations, 56*(4), 329–345.

Calarco, J. M. (2011). "I need help!": Social class and children's help-seeking in elementary school. *American Sociological Review, 76*(6), 862–882.

Calarco, J. M. (2018). *Negotiating opportunities: How the middle class secures advantages in school.* Oxford University Press.

Camacho, D. A., Hoover, S. A., & Rosete, H. S. (2021). Burnout in urban teachers: The predictive role of supports and situational responses. *Psychology in the Schools, 58*(9), 1816–1831.

Camacho, D. A., & Parham, B. (2019). Urban teacher challenges: What they are and what we can learn from them. *Teaching and Teacher Education, 85,* 160–174.

Carl, N. M. (2014). Reacting to the script: Teach for America teachers' experiences with scripted curricula. *Teacher Education Quarterly, 41*(2), 29–50.

Carl, N. M., Ravitch, S. M., & Reichert, M. (2015). *Understanding impact in youth participatory action research: Individual, group, and school experiences.* Evaluation White Paper. Center for the Study of Boys' and Girls' Lives, University of Pennsylvania.

Carter, P. L. (2005). *Keepin' it real: School success beyond Black and White.* Oxford University Press.

Carter, P. L. (2013). Student and school cultures and the opportunity gap: Paying attention to academic engagement and achievement. In P. L. Carter & K. G.

Welner (Eds.), *Closing the opportunity gap: What America must do to give every child an even chance* (pp. 143–155). Oxford University Press.

Carter, P. L., & Welner, K. G. (2013). *Closing the opportunity gap: What America must do to give every child a chance*. Oxford University Press.

Carver-Thomas, D., & Darling-Hammond, L. (2019). The trouble with teacher turnover: How teacher attrition affects students and schools. *Education Policy Analysis Archives, 27*(36), 1–32.

Chase, N. (1999). *Burdened children: Theory, research, and treatment of parentification*. Sage.

Chasin, B. H. (2022). *Inequality & violence in the United States: Casualties of capitalism*. Rowman & Littlefield.

Cho, J., & Trent, A. (2006). Validity in qualitative research revisited. *Qualitative Research, 6*(3), 319–340.

Coates, T.-N. (2015). *Between the world and me*. Spiegel & Grau.

Cochran-Smith, M., & Lytle, S. L. (2009). *Inquiry as stance: Practitioner research for the next generation*. Teachers College Press.

Collins, J. (2009). Social reproduction in classrooms and schools. *Annual Review of Anthropology, 38*, 33–48.

Contreras, R. (2012). *The stickup kids: Race, drugs, violence, and the American dream*. University of California Press.

Cook-Sather, A. (2020). Student voice across contexts: Fostering student agency in today's schools. *Theory into Practice, 59*(2), 182–191.

Cortina, R., & Winter, M. (2021). Paulo Freire's pedagogy of liberation. *Current Issues in Comparative Education, 23*(2), 8–19.

Cruz, R. A., Manchanda, S., Firestone, A. R., & Rodl, J. E. (2020). An examination of teachers' culturally responsive teaching self-efficacy. *Teacher Education and Special Education, 43*(3), 197–214.

Cummins, J. (2009). Pedagogies of choice: Challenging coercive relations of power in classrooms and communities. *International Journal of Bilingual Education and Bilingualism, 12*(3), 261–271.

Darder, A., Hernandez, K., Lam, K. D., & Baltodano, M. (Eds.). (2023). *The critical pedagogy reader*. Taylor & Francis.

David, E. J. R., Schroeder, T. M., & Fernandez, J. (2019). Internalized racism: A systematic review of the psychological literature on racism's most insidious consequence. *Journal of Social Issues, 75*(4), 1057–1086.

Dee, T. S. (2004). Teachers, race, and student achievement in a randomized experiment. *Review of Economics and Statistics, 86*(1), 195–210.

Delpit, L. D. (1995). *Other people's children: Cultural conflict in the classroom*. New Press.

Delpit, L. D. (2018). The silenced dialogue: Power and pedagogy in educating other people's children. In *Thinking about schools* (pp. 157–175). Routledge.

Denzin, N. K. (2009). *The research act: A theoretical orientation to sociological methods*. Transaction. (Original work published in 1970.)

Devine, J. (1996). *Maximum security: The culture of violence in inner-city schools*. University of Chicago Press.

DiPrete, T. A., & Eirich, G. M. (2006). Cumulative advantage as a mechanism for inequality: A review of theoretical and empirical developments. *Annual Review of Sociology, 32*, 271–297.

D'Onofrio, M., & Contreras, R. (2024, May 17). *Segregation in Philadelphia schools remains "stubbornly high."* Axios. https://www.axios.com/local/philadelphia/2024/05/17/brown-vs-board-of-education-school-segregation

Duncan-Andrade, J. M. R., & Morrell, E. (2008). *The art of critical pedagogy: Possibilities for moving from theory to practice in urban schools*. Peter Lang.

Edelman, M. W. (2012). *Ending the cradle to prison pipeline and mass incarceration*. Common Dreams. Retrieved from: http://www.commondreams.org/views/2012/07/08/ending-cradle-prison-pipeline-and-mass-incarceration

Emerson, R. M., Fretz, R. I., & Shaw, L. L. (2011). *Writing ethnographic fieldnotes* (2nd ed.). University of Chicago Press.

Farkas, G. (2003). Cognitive skills and noncognitive traits and behaviors in stratification processes. *Annual Review of Sociology, 29*, 541–562.

Farkas, G. (2018). Family, schooling, and cultural capital. In B. Schneider (Ed.), *Handbook of the sociology of education in the 21st century* (chap. 1, pp. 3–38). Springer.

Ferguson, A. A. (2000). *Bad boys: Public schools in the making of Black masculinity*. University of Michigan Press.

Ferreira, M., Martinsone, B., & Talić, S. (2020). Promoting sustainable social emotional learning at school through relationship-centered learning environment, teaching methods and formative assessment. *Journal of Teacher Education for Sustainability, 22*(1), 21–36.

Fitzpatrick, A. (2023). Pa. schools say landmark funding trial decision is final. That means the Legislature needs to increase funding. WHYY. https://whyy.org/articles/pennsylvania-school-funding-lawsuit-final-appeal/#:~:text=The%20case%20began%20in%202014,Pennsylvania%20school%20funding%20system%20unconstitutional

Freire, P. (1998). *Pedagogy of freedom: Ethics, democracy and civic courage*. Rowman & Littlefield.

Freire, P. (2000). *Pedagogy of the oppressed*. (M. B. Ramos, Trans.). Continuum. (Original work published 1970.)

Fuhrer, J. (2023). *The myth that made us: How false beliefs about racism and meritocracy broke our economy (and how to fix it)*. MIT Press.

Fuller, E. (2023). *Exacerbating the shortage of teachers: Rising teacher attrition in Pennsylvania from 2014 to 2023*. Penn State Center for Education Evaluation & Policy Analysis. https://ed.psu.edu/sites/default/files/inline-files/ceepa-research-brief-2023-6-_-exacerbating-the-shortage-of-teachers-ed-fuller-1.pdf

García, E., & Weiss, E. (2017). *Education inequalities at the school starting gate: Gaps, trends, and strategies to address them*. Economic Policy Institute.

Gershenson, S., Hart, C. M., Hyman, J., Lindsay, C. A., & Papageorge, N. W. (2022). The long-run impacts of same-race teachers. *American Economic Journal: Economic Policy, 14*(4), 300–342.

Gertler, P., Heckman, J. J., Pinto, R., Chang, S. M., Grantham-McGregor, S., Vermeersch, C., . . . & Wright, A. (2021). *Effect of the Jamaica early childhood stimulation intervention on labor market outcomes at age 31*. National Bureau of Economic Research.

Gibson, W., & Brown, A. (2009). *Working with qualitative data*. Sage.

Giroux, H. A. (1981). Schooling and the myth of objectivity: Stalking the hidden curriculum. *McGill Journal of Education, 17*, 282–304.

Giroux, H. A. (1983). *Theory and resistance in education: A pedagogy for the opposition*. Bergin & Garvey.

Giroux, H. A. (1985). Critical pedagogy, cultural politics and the discourse of experience. *Journal of Education, 167*(2), 22–41.

Giroux, H. A. (2001). *Theory and resistance in education: A pedagogy for the opposition* (rev. & expanded ed.). Bergin & Garvey.

Golann, J. W. (2018). Conformers, adaptors, imitators, and rejecters: How no-excuses teachers' cultural toolkits shape their responses to control. *Sociology of Education, 91*(1), 28–45.

Goldhaber, D., Theobald, R., & Tien, C. (2019). Why we need a diverse teacher workforce. *Phi Delta Kappan, 100*(5), 25–30. https://doi.org/10.1177/0031721719827540

González, N., Moll, L., & Amanti, C. (Eds.). (2005). *Funds of knowledge: Theorizing practices in households, communities, and classrooms*. Routledge.

Gorski, P. (2011). Unlearning deficit ideology and the scornful gaze: Thoughts on authenticating the class discourse in education. In R. Ahlquist, P. Gorski, & T. Montaño (Eds.), *Assault on kids: How hyper-accountability, corporatization, deficit ideology, and Ruby Payne are destroying our schools* (pp. 152–173). Peter Lang.

Gorski, P. (2018). *Reaching and teaching students in poverty: Strategies for erasing the opportunity gap* (2nd ed.). Teachers College Press.

Gorski, P. (2023). The unintentional undermining of multicultural education: Educators at the equity crossroads. In *White teachers/diverse classrooms* (pp. 75–92). Routledge.

Graham, K. A. (2016). Philly teachers offered contract deal worth $100M. *Philadelphia Inquirer*. Retrieved from: http://www.philly.com/philly/education/20161128_Philly_teachers_offered_contract_deal_worth__100M.html

Graham, K. A. (2022). In Philly schools, decisions must often be 'revenue-driven . . . as opposed to needs-driven,' CFO testifies in funding trial. *Philadelphia Inquirer*. Retrieved from: https://www.inquirer.com/news/pa-school-funding-trial-philadelphia-school-district-monson-20220124.html

Green, D. (2020). Exploring the implications of culturally relevant teaching: Toward a pedagogy of liberation. *Journal of Contemporary Ethnography, 49*(3), 371–389.

Guba, E. G. (1981). Criteria for assessing the trustworthiness of naturalistic inquiries. *Educational Resources Information Center Annual Review Paper, 29*, 75–91.

Guerriero, S., & Deligiannidi, K. (2017). "The teaching profession and its knowledge base." In S. Guerriero (Ed.), *Pedagogical knowledge and the changing nature of the teaching profession*. Educational Research and Innovation, OECD, Paris. https://doi.org/10.1787/ 9789264270695-en

Hammersley, M., & Atkinson, P. (2007). *Ethnography: Principles in practice* (3rd ed.). Taylor & Francis.

Hammond, Z. (2015). *Culturally responsive teaching and the brain: Promoting authentic engagement and rigor among culturally and linguistically diverse students*. Corwin Press.

Hanushek, E. A., & Lindseth, A. A. (2009). *Schoolhouses, courthouses, and statehouses: Solving the funding-achievement puzzle in America's public schools*. Princeton University Press.

Hanushek, E. A., Peterson, P. E., Talpey, L. M., & Woessman, L. (2020). *Long-run trends in the US SES-achievement gap*. Program on Education Policy and Governance Working Papers Series. PEPG 20-01. Program on Education Policy and Governance.

Heitzeg, N. A. (2023). The school-to-prison pipeline. In C. Cunneen, A. Deckert, A. Porter, J. Tauri, & R. Webb (Eds.), *The Routledge International Handbook on Decolonizing Justice*. Routledge.

Hewko, C. (2024). Teachers' perspectives of their development of culturally sustaining pedagogical practices: Lessons for teacher learning. *Pedagogies: An International Journal*, 1–21. https://doi.org/10.1080/15544 80X.2023.2299804

Hinton, H., & Cook, D. (2021) The mass criminalization of Black Americans: A historical overview. *Annual Review of Criminology, 4*, 261–286.

Hoffmann, F., Lee, D. S., & Lemieux, T. (2020). Growing income inequality in the United States and other advanced economies. *Journal of Economic Perspectives, 34*(4), 52–78.

Hooper, L. M., Tomek, S., Bond, J. M., & Reif, M. S. (2015). Race/ethnicity, gender, parentification, and psychological functioning: Comparisons among a nationwide university sample. *The Family Journal: Counseling and Therapy for Couples and Families, 23*(1), 33–48.

Horvat, E. M., & Antonio, A. L. (1999). "Hey, those shoes are out of uniform": African American girls in an elite high school and the importance of habitus. *Anthropology & Education Quarterly, 30*(3), 317–342.

Horvat, E. M., & Davis, J. E. (2011). Schools as sites for transformation: Exploring the contribution of habitus. *Youth & Society, 43*(1), 142–170.

Howard, T. C. (2003). Culturally relevant pedagogy: Ingredients for critical teacher reflection. *Theory into Practice, 42*(3), 195–202.

Hyde, B. (2023). Discourses of "deficit" and practices of "othering": The problematic relationship between the neoliberal school reform agenda and social justice education. In J. Zajda, P. Hallam, & J. Whitehouse (Eds.), *Globalisation, Values Education and Teaching Democracy* (pp. 31–42). Springer International.

Ingersoll, R. M. (1999). The problem of underqualified teachers in American secondary schools. *Educational Researcher, 28*(2), 26–37.

Ingersoll, R. M., & Collins, G. J. (2018). The status of teaching as a profession. In J. Ballantine, J. Spade, & J. Stuber (Eds.). *Schools and society: A sociological approach to education,* 6th ed. Pine Forge Press/Sage.

Jackson, C. K. (2020). Does school spending matter? The new literature on an old question. In L. Tach, R. Dunifon, & D. L. Miller (Eds.), *Confronting inequality: How policies and practices shape children's opportunities* (pp. 165–186). American Psychological Association.

Jackson, C. K., Johnson, R. C., & Persico, C. (2016). The effects of school spending on educational and economic outcomes: Evidence from school finance reforms. *Quarterly Journal of Economics, 131*(1), 157–218.

Jackson, C. K., & Mackevicius, C. L. (2024). What impacts can we expect from school spending policy? Evidence from evaluations in the United States. *American Economic Journal: Applied Economics, 16*(1), 412–446.

Jackson, P. W. (1968). *Life in classrooms.* Rinehart & Winston.

Jardina, A., & Piston, S. (2021). Hidden in plain sight: Dehumanization as a foundation of White racial prejudice. *Sociology Compass, 15*(9), 1–15.

Jean, J. Y. (2022). Why school nurses are leaving the career. *Nurse Journal.* https://nursejournal.org/articles/why-school-nurses-are-leaving/

Johnson, J. A. (1995). Life after death: Critical pedagogy in an urban classroom. *Harvard Educational Review, 65*(2), 213–230.

Khalifa, M. (2018). *Culturally responsive school leadership.* Harvard Education Press.

Keibler, D. M. (2019). Changing teachers' perspective of students from lower socioeconomic families. *ProQuest LLC.* https://search-ebscohost-com.byu.idm.oclc.org/login.aspx?direct=true&db=eric&AN=E608617&site=ehost-live&scope=site

Kennedy, B. L., & Soutullo, O. (2018). "We can't fix that": Deficit thinking and the exoneration of educator responsibility for teaching students placed at a disciplinary alternative school. *Journal of At-Risk Issues, 21*(1), 11–23.

Kennedy, N. A., & Marsano, E. O. C. (2024). Targeted solutions to improve the school-to-prison pipeline. In P. S. De Walt & D. N. Nix-Stevenson (Eds.), *PK-12 professionals' narratives of working as advocates impacting today's schools* (pp. 29–49). IGI Global.

Kincheloe, J. (2008). *Critical pedagogy primer* (2nd ed.). Peter Lang.

King, A. (2000). Thinking with Bourdieu against Bourdieu: A "practical" critique of the habitus. *Sociological Theory, 18,* 417–433.

Koretz, D. (2017). *The testing charade: Pretending to make schools better.* University of Chicago Press.

Kumashiro, K. K. (2015). Against common sense: Teaching and learning toward social justice (3rd ed.). Routledge. https://doi.org/10.4324/9781315765525

Kuriloff, P., Andrus, S., & Jacobs, C. (2017). *Teaching girls: How teachers and parents can reach their brains and hearts.* Rowman & Littlefield.

Kuriloff, P., & Carl, N. M. (2015, July 28–30). Studying with, not on: Addressing the challenges and possibilities of excavating the hidden curricula of power in elite schools [Conference presentation]. Researching Elite Education Conference: Addressing the Conceptual, Methodological, and Ethical Challenges, Toronto, Ontario.

Ladson-Billings, G. (1994). *The dreamkeepers*. Jossey-Bass.

Ladson-Billings, G. (2006). From the achievement gap to the education debt: Understanding achievement in US schools. *Educational Researcher, 35*(7), 3–12.

Ladson-Billings, G. (2017). "Makes me wanna holler": Refuting the "culture of poverty" discourse in urban schooling. *Annals of the American Academy of Political and Social Science, 673*, 80–90.

Lareau, A. (2011). *Unequal childhoods: Class, race, and family life* (2nd ed.). University of California Press.

Lareau, A., & Horvat, E. M. (1999). Moments of social inclusion and exclusion: Race, class, and cultural capital in family-school relationships. *Sociology of Education, 71*(1), 37–53.

Lareau, A., & Shumar, W. (1996). The problem of individualism in family-school policies. *Sociology of Education, 69*, 24–39.

Lareau, A. (2019). Parent involvement in schooling: A dissenting view. In C. L. Fagnano & B. Werber (Eds.), *School, family, and community interaction* (pp. 61–73). Routledge.

Lavy, S., & Naama-Ghanayim, E. (2020). Why care about caring? Linking teachers' caring and sense of meaning at work with students' self-esteem, well-being, and school engagement. *Teaching and Teacher Education, 91*, 103046.

Lincoln, Y. S., & Guba, E. G. (1985). *Naturalistic inquiry*. Sage.

Loeb, P. (2022, September 15). City poverty rate falls again, but not for children and Black Philadelphians. KYW Newsradio.

Lopez Kershen, J., Weiner, J. M., & Torres, C. (2018). Control as care: How teachers in "no excuses" charter schools position their students and themselves. *Equity & Excellence in Education, 51*(3–4), 265–283.

MacLeod, J. (2018). *Ain't no makin' it: Aspirations and attainment in a low-income neighborhood*. Routledge.

Madigan, D. J., & Kim, L. E. (2021). Does teacher burnout affect students? A systematic review of its association with academic achievement and student-reported outcomes. *International Journal of Educational Research, 105*, 1–12.

Mandviwala, T. M., Hall, J., & Beale Spencer, M. (2022). The invisibility of power: A cultural ecology of development in the contemporary United States. *Annual Review of Clinical Psychology, 18*, 179–199.

Marsh, L. T. S., & Walker, L. J. (2022). Deficit-oriented beliefs, anti-Black policies, punitive practices, and labeling: Exploring the mechanisms of disproportionality and its impact on Black boys in one urban "no-excuses" charter school. *Teachers College Record, 124*(2), 85–116.

Martin, J. L., Hill Magoulias, C. M., Akbar, N. J. (2022) Evidence based funding in Illinois: A discussion of equity in urban education. *Journal of Urban Learning, Teaching, and Research, 16*(2), 1–28.

Maslach, C., & Jackson, S. E. (1981). *Maslach burnout inventory manual.* CPP.

Maslach, C., Jackson, S. E., & Leiter, M. P. (1996). *Maslach burnout inventory manual* (3rd ed.). CPP.

Mathis, W. J., & Welner, K. G (2015). *Reversing the deprofessionalization of teaching.* National Education Policy Center. Retrieved from http://nepc.colorado.edu/publication/research-based-options

Maxwell, J. A. (2013). *Qualitative research design: An interactive approach* (3rd ed.). Sage.

Maxwell, J. A., & Chmiel, M. (2014). Notes toward a theory of qualitative data analysis. In U. Flick (Ed.), *The Sage handbook of qualitative data analysis* (pp. 21–34). Sage.

Maxwell, J. A., & Miller, B. A. (2008). Categorizing and connecting strategies in qualitative data analysis. In S. N. Hesse-Biber, S. Nagy, & P. Levy (Eds.), *Handbook of emergent methods* (pp. 461–477). Guilford.

McCorry, K. (2016). School by school breakdown of Philadelphia's substitute teacher crisis. Newsworks, WHYY. Retrieved from http://www.newsworks.org/index.php/local/education/91161-school-by-school-breakdown-of-philadelphias-substitute-teacher-crisis

McCrory Calarco, J., Horn, I. S., & Chen, G. A. (2022). "You need to be more responsible": The myth of meritocracy and teachers' accounts of homework inequalities. *Educational Researcher, 51*(8), 515–523.

McFadden, K. (2023). Infrastructures of social reproduction: Schools, everyday urban life, and the built environment of education. *Dialogues in Human Geography, 15*(1). https://journals.sagepub.com/doi/10.1177/20438206231178827

McLaren, P. (2003). *Life in schools: An introduction to critical pedagogy in the foundations of education* (2nd ed.). Allyn & Bacon.

McLaren, P. (2015). *Life in schools: An introduction to critical pedagogy in the foundations of education* (6th ed.). Routledge.

McMahon, S. D., Anderman, E. M., Astor, R. A., Espelage, D. L., Martinez, A., Reddy, L. A., & Worrell, F. C. (2022). *Violence against educators and school personnel: Crisis during COVID.* Technical Report. American Psychological Association.

Mezzacappa, D. (2015). *Regressive funding formula.* The Notebook.

Mezzacappa, D. (2022, May 23). Philadelphia area schools among most segregated in country. Chalkbeat. https://www.chalkbeat.org/philadelphia/2022/5/23/23137855/philadelphia-area-schools-among-most-segregated-country/

Miles, M. B., Huberman, A. M., & Saldaña, J. (2014). *Qualitative data analysis: A methods sourcebook.* Sage.

Miller, C. L. (2018, January). The effect of education spending on student achievement. In *Proceedings. Annual Conference on Taxation and minutes of the annual meeting of the National Tax Association* (vol. 111, pp. 1–121). National Tax Association.

Mills, C. (2008). Reproduction and transformation of inequalities in schooling. *British Journal of Sociology of Education, 29*(1), 79–89.

Mills, C. (2021). Implications of the My School website for disadvantaged communities: A Bourdieuian analysis. In L. Jackson & M. A. Peters (Eds.), *Marxism, neoliberalism, and intelligent capitalism* (pp. 124–137). Routledge.

Mills, C., & Gale, T. (2007). Researching social inequalities in education: Towards a Bourdieuian methodology. *International Journal of Qualitative Studies in Education, 20*(4), 433–47.

Milner, H. R.(2008). Disrupting deficit notions of difference: Counter-narratives of teachers and community in urban education. *Teaching and Teacher Education, 24*(6), 1573–1598.

Milner, H. R. (2012). Beyond a test score: Explaining opportunity gaps in educational practice. *Journal of Black Studies, 43*(6), 693–718.

Milner, H. R. (2013). *Policy reforms and the de-professionalization of teaching.* National Education Policy Center. Retrieved from http://nepc.colorado.edu/publication/policy-reforms-deprofessionalization

Milner, H. R. (2021). *Start where you are, but don't stay there: Understanding diversity, opportunity gaps, and teaching in today's classrooms.* Harvard Education Press.

Moll, L. C. (2000). Inspired by Vygotsky: Ethnographic experiments in education. In C. D. Lee and P. Smagorinsky (Eds.), *Vygotskian perspectives on literacy research: Constructing meaning through collaborative inquiry* (pp. 256–268). Cambridge University Press.

Moon, B., Morash, M., & McCluskey, J. (2021). Student violence directed against teachers: Victimized teachers' reports to school officials and satisfaction with school responses. *Journal of Interpersonal Violence, 36*(13–14), NP7264–NP7283. https://doi.org/10.1177/0886260519825883

Morris, M. W. (2016). *Pushout: The criminalization of Black girls in schools.* New Press.

Nakkula, M. J., & Toshalis, E. (2020). *Understanding youth: Adolescent development for educators.* Harvard Education Press.

National Center for Education Statistics (NCES). (2021). *Characteristics of public school teachers.* https://nces.ed.gov/programs/coe/indicator/clr

Nieto, S. (2008). Chapter 9: Culture and education. *Yearbook of the National Society for the Study of Education, 107*(1), 127–142.

Noguera, P. A. (2009). *The trouble with Black boys: . . . And other reflections on race, equity, and the future of public education.* John Wiley & Sons.

Noguera, P. (2019). Equity isn't just a slogan: It should transform the way we educate kids. *Insight.* The Holdsworth Center. Retrieved June 16, 2020, from: https://holdsworthcenter.org/blog/equity-isnt-just-a- slogan/

Noguera, P. A., & Syeed, E. (2020). *City schools and the American dream 2: The enduring promise of public education.* Multicultural Education.

Nolan, K. M. (2011). *Police in the hallways: Discipline in an urban high school.* University of Minnesota Press.

Nuttall, A. K., Zhang, Q., Valentino, K., & Borkowski, J. G. (2019). Intergenerational risk of parentification and infantilization to externalizing moderated by child temperament. *Journal of Marriage and Family, 81*(3), 648–661.

Nygreen, K. (2013). *These kids: Identity, agency, and social justice at a last chance high school.* University of Chicago Press.

Ogbu, J. U. (1978). *Minority education and caste: The American system in cross-cultural perspective.* Academic Press.

Ogbu, J. U. (2003). *Black American students in an affluent suburb: A study of academic disengagement.* Routledge.

Owens, A., & Candipan, J. (2019). Social and spatial inequalities of educational opportunity: A portrait of schools serving high- and low-income neighbourhoods in US metropolitan areas. *Urban Studies Journal, 56*(15), 3178–3197.

Paulle, B. (2013). *Toxic schools: High-poverty education in New York and Amsterdam.* University of Chicago Press.

Pendakur, V. (Ed.). (2023). *Closing the opportunity gap: Identity-conscious strategies for retention and student success.* Taylor & Francis.

PEW Charitable Trusts (2015). *A school funding formula for Philadelphia: Lessons from urban districts across the United States.* Retrieved from: http://www.pewtrusts.org/en/research-and-analysis/reports/2015/01/a-school-funding-formula-for-philadelphia [[AU: I didn't find a citation for this source.]]

Pew Charitable Trusts (2017). *Philadelphia's poor: Who they are, where they live, and how that has changed.* https://www.pewtrusts.org/-/media/assets/2017/11/pri_philadelphias_poor.pdf

Phelan, P., Davidson, A. L., & Yu, H. C. (1993). Students' multiple worlds: Navigating the borders of family, peer, and school cultures. In P. Phelan & A. L. Davidson (Eds.), *Renegotiating cultural diversity in American schools* (pp. 52–88). Teachers College Press.

Phelan, P., Yu, H. C., & Davidson, A. L. (1994). Navigating the psychosocial pressures of adolescence: The voices and experiences of high school youth. *American Educational Research Journal, 31*(2), 415–447.

Philadelphia City Council. (2019). *Analysis of 2018 American Community Survey (ACS) data relevant to Philadelphia and update on 2017 data.* https://phlcouncil.com/wp-content/uploads/2019/10/Analysis-of-2018-American-Community-Survey-ACS-Data-Relevant-to-Philadelphia-and-Update-on-2017-Data-Final.pdf

Ponterotto, J. G. (2006). Brief note on the origins, evolution, and meaning of the qualitative research concept "thick description." *Qualitative Report, 11*(3), 538–549.

Posey-Maddox, L., & Haley-Lock, A. (2020). One size does not fit all: Understanding parent engagement in the contexts of work, family, and public schooling. *Urban Education, 55*(5), 671–698.

Quaglia, R. J., Fox, K. M., & Corso, M. J. (2010). Got opportunity? *Educational Leadership, 68*(3), 22–26.

Quinn, R., & Carl, N. M. (2015). Teacher activist organizations and professional agency. *Teachers and Teaching: Theory and Practice, 21*(6), 745–758.

Raider-Roth, M. (2005). *Trusting what you know: The high stakes of classroom relationships*. Jossey-Bass.

Ravitch, D. (2011). *The death and life of the great American school system: How testing and choice are undermining education* [Kindle iPad version]. Retrieved from: http://www.amazon.com/

Ravitch, S. M., & Carl, N. M. (2021). *Qualitative research: Bridging the conceptual, theoretical, and methodological*. Sage.

Reardon, S. F. (2011). *The widening academic achievement gap between the rich and poor: New evidence and possible explanations*. Retrieved from: http://cepa.stanford.edu/sites/default/files/reardon%20whither%20opportunity%20-%20chapter%205.pdf

Reardon, S. F. (2018). The widening academic achievement gap between the rich and the poor. In D. B. Grusky (Ed.), *Social stratification* (pp. 536–550). Routledge.

Reardon, S. F., & Kalogrides, D. (2019). The geography of racial/ethnic test score gaps. *American Journal of Sociology, 124*(4), 1164–1221.

Reay, D. (1998). Cultural reproduction: Mothers' involvement in their children's primary school. In M. Grenfell & D. James (Eds.), *Bourdieu and education: Acts of practical theory* (pp. 55–71). Falmer Press.

Reay, D. (2017). *Miseducation: Inequality, education and the working classes* (1st ed.). Bristol University Press.

Reay, D. (2020). The perils and penalties of meritocracy: Sanctioning inequalities and legitimating prejudice. *Political Quarterly, 91*(2), 405–412.

Reay, D. (2022). 'The more things change the more they stay the same': The continuing relevance of Bourdieu and Passeron's reproduction in education, society and culture. *RES: Revista Española de Sociología, 31*(3), 2.

Redding, C. (2019). A teacher like me: A review of the effect of student–teacher racial/ethnic matching on teacher perceptions of students and student academic and behavioral outcomes. *Review of Educational Research, 89*(4), 499–535. https://doi.org/10.3102/0034654319853545

Rist, R. C. (2017). On understanding the processes of schooling: The contributions of labeling theory. In A. R. Sadovnik, P. Cookson Jr., S. Semel, & R. Coughlan (Eds.), *Exploring education* (pp. 165–176). Routledge.

Roach, J. C. (2023). Substitute teachers needed: Closing the gap on supply versus demand. *Monthly Labor Review*. https://www.bls.gov/opub/mlr/2023/beyond-bls/substitute-teachers-needed-closing-the-gap-on-supply-versus-demand.htm

Royal, C., & Cothorne, A. (2021). School closures and urban education. In H. R. Milner IV & K. Lomotey (Eds.), *Handbook of urban education* (pp. 483–493). Routledge.

Schaufeli, W. B., & Salanova, M. (2007). Efficacy or inefficacy, that's the question: Burnout and work engagement, and their relationships with efficacy beliefs. *Anxiety, Stress, & Coping: An International Journal, 20,* 177–196.

Scheper-Hughes, N. (1992). *Death without weeping: The violence of everyday life in Brazil.* University of California Press.

School Funding in PA: We must do better. Level Up Initiative. https://leveluppa.org/

Schultz, B. D. (2018). *Spectacular things happen along the way: Lessons from an urban classroom.* Teachers College Press.

Sethi, J., & Scales, P. C. (2020). Developmental relationships and school success: How teachers, parents, and friends affect educational outcomes and what actions students say matter most. *Contemporary Educational Psychology, 63,* 101904.

Sharma, A. (2022). Neoliberal etiology and educational failure: A critical exploration. *Curriculum Inquiry, 51*(5), 542–561.

Shulman, L. S. (1987). The wisdom of practice: Managing complexity in medicine and teaching. In D. C. Berliner & B. V. Rosenshire (Eds.), *Talks to teachers: A festschrift for N. L. Gage* (pp. 369–386). Random House.

Silva-Laya, M., D'Angelo, N., García, E., Zúñiga, L., & Fernández, T. (2020). Urban poverty and education: A systematic literature review. *Educational Research Review, 29,* 1–20.

Simon, C. (2021). How COVID taught America about inequity in education. *Harvard Gazette.*

Skaalvik, E. M., & Skaalvik, S. (2010). Teacher self-efficacy and teacher burnout: A study of relations. *Teaching and Teacher Education, 26,* 1059–1069.

Skaalvik, E. M., Skaalvik, S. (2017). Dimensions of teacher burnout: Relations with potential stressors at school. *Social Psychology of Education, 20,* 775–790.

Snyder, A. (2020). *Location and inequitable education* [White paper]. University of Rhode Island.

Sojoyner, D. M. (2018). Changing the lens: Moving away from the school to prison pipeline. In A. J. Nocella II, P. Parmar, & D. Stovall (Eds.), *From education to incarceration: Dismantling the school-to-prison pipeline* (2nd ed., pp. 61–76). Peter Lang.

Stahl, G. (2018). Critiquing the corporeal curriculum: Body pedagogies in 'no excuses' charter schools. *Journal of Youth Studies, 23*(10), 1330–1346.

Steiner, E. D., Woo, A., & Doan, S. (2023). *All work and no pay: Teachers' perceptions of their pay and hours worked.* Rand Corporation.

Stevenson, H. C. (2014). *Promoting racial literacy in schools: Differences that make a difference.* Teachers College Press.

Strum, L. C. (2015). Education: Sick at school? No nurse on duty. *Philadelphia Neighborhoods.* A Publication of Temple University's Multimedia Urban Reporting Lab. Retrieved from https://philadelphianeighborhoods.com/2015/12/03/education-sick-at-school-no-nurse-on-duty/

Szabó, L., Zsolnai, A., & Fehérvári, A. (2024). The relationship between student engagement and dropout risk in early adolescence. *International Journal of Educational Research Open, 6*, 100328.

Theoharis, J. (2009). "I hate it when people treat me like a fxxx-up": Phony theories, segregated schools, and the culture of aspiration among African American and Latino teenagers. In G. Alonso, N. S. Anderson, C. Su, & J. Theoharis (Eds.), *Our schools suck: Students talk back to a segregated nation on the failures of urban education* (pp. 69–111). New York University Press.

Theoharis, G. (2020). Adults failed our young people: Now we are preparing to blame them for it. *Post Standard, Syracuse, NY.* https://www.syracuse.com/opinion/2020/08/adults-failed-our-young-people-and-now-were-going-to-blame-them-for-it-commentary.html

Thompson, C. L., & Maris, M. (2014). Attachment disorders in inner-city adolescent males. In K. Vaughans & W. Spielberg (Eds.), *The psychology of Black boys and adolescents* (2nd ed., pp. 75–86). Praeger.

Toma, J. D. (2011). Approaching rigor in applied qualitative research. In C. F. Conrad & R. C. Serlin (Eds.), *The Sage handbook for research in education: Pursuing ideas as the keystone of exemplary inquiry* (2nd ed., pp. 263–280). Sage.

Torrance, H. (2017). Blaming the victim: Assessment, examinations, and the responsibilisation of students and teachers in neo-liberal governance. *Discourse: Studies in the Cultural politics of Education, 38*(1), 83–96.

Toshalis, E. (2015). *Make me! Understanding and engaging student resistance in school.* Harvard Education Press.

Tosolt, B. (2020). Dear White teacher: This Black history month, take a knee. *International Journal of Qualitative Studies in Education, 33*(7), 773–789.

Tyson, K. (2013). Tracking segregation, and the opportunity gap. In P. L. Carter & K. G. Welner (Eds.), *Closing the opportunity gap: What America must do to give every child an even chance* (pp. 169–180). Oxford University Press.

Tyson, K., Darity, W., & Castellino, D. (2005). It's not "a Black thing": Understanding the burden of acting White and other dilemmas of high achievement. *American Sociological Review, 70*(4), 582–605.

Tyson, K., & Lewis, A. E. (2021). The "burden" of oppositional culture among Black youth in America. *Annual Review of Sociology, 47*(1), 459–477. https://doi.org/10.1146/annurev-soc-090420-092123

Valencia, R. R. (2010). *Dismantling contemporary deficit thinking: Educational thought and practice.* Routledge.

Valencia, R. R. (2019). *International deficit thinking: Educational thought and practice.* Routledge.

Voight, A., & Velez, V. (2018). Youth participatory action research in the high school curriculum: Education outcomes for student participants in a district-wide initiative. *Journal of Research on Educational Effectiveness, 11*(3), 433–451.

Wacquant, L. (1998). Inside the zone: The social art of the hustler in the Black American ghetto. *Theory, Culture & Society, 15*(2), 1–36.

Wacquant, L. (2008). Pierre Bourdieu. In R. Stones (Ed.), *Key sociological thinkers* (pp. 261–277). Palgrave Macmillan.

Walker, S., & Graham, L. (2021). At risk students and teacher-student relationships: student characteristics, attitudes to school and classroom climate. *International Journal of Inclusive Education, 25*(8), 896–913.

Walker, T. (2022). Violence, threats against teachers, school staff could hasten exodus from profession. *NEA Today*. https://www.nea.org/advocating-for-change/new-fromnea/violence-threats-against-teachers-school-staff-could-hasten

Waller, W. (1932). *The sociology of teaching*. John Wiley and Sons.

Whitman, D. (2008). Sweating the small stuff: Inner-city schools and the new paternalism. Thomas B. Fordham Institute.

Williams, K. L., Coles, J. A., & Reynolds, P. (2020). (Re) creating the script: A framework of agency, accountability, and resisting deficit depictions of Black students in P-20 education. *Journal of Negro Education, 89*(3), 249–266.

Willis, P. (1977). *Learning to labor: How working class kids get working class jobs*. Columbia University Press.

Wright, B. L., Ford, D. Y., & Young, J. L. (2017). Ignorance or indifference? Seeking excellence and equity for under-represented students of color in gifted education. *Global Education Review, 4*(1), 45–60.

Wolfman-Arent, A., & Mezzacappa, D. (2017). SRC will be out by June, replaced by Philadelphia school board. WHYY. https://whyy.org/articles/src-will-june-replaced-philadelphia-school-board/

Wronowski, M. L. (2021). De-professionalized and demoralized: A framework for understanding teacher turnover in the accountability policy era. *Leadership and Policy in Schools, 20*(4), 599–629.

Yosso, T. J. (2005). Whose culture has capital? *Race, Ethnicity and Education, 8*(1), 69–91.

Zevenbergen, R. (2006). Teacher identity from a Bourdieuian perspective. In P. Grootenboer, R. Zevenbergen, & M. Chinnapan (Eds.), *Proceedings of the 29th annual conference of the Mathematics Education Research Group of Australasia*. MERGA.

Zion, S., Kirshner, B., Sung, K., & Ventura, J. (2021). *Urban schooling and the transformative possibilities of participatory action research: The role of youth in struggles for urban education justice*. Routledge.

Index

About the Author

Dr. Nicole Mittenfelner Carl is an experienced qualitative researcher and scholar of urban education. Perhaps more importantly for this book, she is a former teacher in a K–8 school very similar to Baker School in Philadelphia. Carl also served as a teacher mentor and coach to teachers throughout Philadelphia's district and charter schools. Carl is now a teacher educator and is the director of a teacher education program, the Urban Teaching Residency program at the University of Pennsylvania Graduate School of Education (Penn GSE) and the Urban Education online master's program. Teachers in Carl's programs work in Philadelphia or in other large, urban school districts while they are earning their teaching certification and/or master's degree. Carl teaches courses about urban education and qualitative research at Penn GSE. This book combines Carl's knowledge of social theory, her in-depth ethnographic research skills, and her firsthand knowledge of education in large urban districts such as Philadelphia. These experiences allowed her to build relationships with research participants and to humanize, theorize, and contextualize what she observed in her research at Baker with other experiences in similar public urban schools. Carl has taught, mentored, and researched in urban public schools since 2006, and while changes have occurred in terms of education governance and curricula, little has changed in the daily lives of students in urban public schools. Carl believes that if students' experiences are shared and taken seriously they can shape how people think about urban schooling and ultimately contribute to positive changes for students' future opportunities.